Joyriding in Riyadh

Why do young Saudis, night after night, joyride and skid cars on Riyadh's avenues? Who are these "drifters" who defy public order and private property? What drives their revolt? Based on four years of fieldwork in Riyadh, Pascal Menoret's *Joyriding in Riyadh* explores the social fabric of the city and connects it to Saudi Arabia's recent history. Car drifting emerged after Riyadh was planned and oil became the main driver of the economy. For young rural migrants, it was a way to reclaim alienating and threatening urban spaces. For the Saudi state, it jeopardized its most basic operations: managing public spaces and enforcing law and order. A police crackdown soon targeted car drifting, feeding a nationwide moral panic led by religious activists who framed youth culture as a public issue. The book retraces the politicization of Riyadh youth and shows that, far from being a marginal event, car drifting is embedded in the country's social violence and economic inequality.

Pascal Menoret is Assistant Professor of Middle Eastern Studies at New York University Abu Dhabi. His research combines urban history and social anthropology. His publications include *The Saudi Enigma: A History* (2005) and *L'Arabie, des routes de l'encens à l'ère du pétrole* (2010).

Joyriding in Riyadh

Oil, Urbanism, and Road Revolt

PASCAL MENORET
New York University Abu Dhabi

CAMBRIDGE
UNIVERSITY PRESS

CAMBRIDGE
UNIVERSITY PRESS

32 Avenue of the Americas, New York, NY 10013-2473, USA

Cambridge University Press is part of the University of Cambridge.

It furthers the University's mission by disseminating knowledge in the pursuit of
education, learning, and research at the highest international levels of excellence.

www.cambridge.org
Information on this title: www.cambridge.org/9781107641952

First published 2014

Printed in the United States of America

A catalog record for this publication is available from the British Library.

Library of Congress Cataloging in Publication Data
Ménoret, Pascal, 1976–
Joyriding in Riyadh : oil, urbanism, and road revolt / Pascal Menoret, New York
University Abu Dhabi.
    pages   cm. – (Cambridge Middle East studies)
Includes bibliographical references and index.
ISBN 978-1-107-03548-5 (hardback) – ISBN 978-1-107-64195-2 (pbk.)
    1. Petroleum industry and trade – Saudi Arabia.   2. Cities and towns – Growth.   I. Title.
HD9576.S33M46   2014
953.8–dc23   2013040959

ISBN 978-1-107-03548-5 Hardback
ISBN 978-1-107-64195-2 Paperback

To Bazil, and to A., M., and T.

I climb into my GMC truck when my heart feels heavy
And relax when I hold its steering wheel in my hands.
Then I do as I like, driving to Kuwait or the Iraqi border,
And if I'm done there I travel throughout Saudi Arabia,
Plunging into the waves of adventure, God being my protector,
For no longer do I feel any desire for a life of ease and comfort.

Bkhetan[1]

---

[1] Quoted by Marcel Kurpershoek, *Oral Poetry and Narratives from Central Arabia*, vol. III: *Bedouin Poets of the Dawasir Tribe: Between Nomadism and Settlement in Southern Najd* (Brill 1999), p. 110.

Contents

Figures

Maps

A Night with 'Ajib

My research almost came to a crashing end during a freezing night in February, while I was following a drifting (*tafhit*) procession in Riyadh. Drifting is the practice of using stolen cars to skid at full speed on urban highways – a high-octane gymnastics that is for cars what dressage is for prize horses. I was driving my car, a worn-out Jeep Cherokee, behind the red lights of a Toyota pickup that was careering from one side of the street to the other. Its driver, 'Ajib,[1] was skillfully playing with the steering wheel and the handbrake. My informant Rakan was pestering me to salute each skid with a flash of my headlights in a gesture of appreciation. I complied, also using my blinkers to convey what I was told were messages of enthusiasm. A zigzagging pickup followed at full speed by a flashing Jeep was not an uncommon scene in suburban Riyadh.

Soon 'Ajib turned off the main street onto one side road, and then a second. He swerved into the wrong lane and I followed, alarmed by his carelessness but determined not to lose him. "He is testing you," declared Rakan. We were headed to what some local youth call Tariq al-Ba'arin ("Dromedary Drive"), a six-lane thoroughfare in the east of Riyadh. The road's nickname came from the corrals on both sides of the street, where families kept herds of dromedaries for their enjoyment or profit. Located on the outskirts of the city, the wide thoroughfare was an ideal spot for joyriding and car drifting. 'Ajib was driving expertly through a maze of side roads so as to avoid the police patrols. I was in a mixed state of excitement and fear; this was my first night of joyriding.

1.1. Joyriding in Riyadh

At around 2 AM we pulled into a gas station on al-Ba'arin. Several police cars were cruising the road, and 'Ajib's ear was glued to his cell phone: he was collecting information and trying to catch up with the joyriders. His two friends, a heavyset, shy guy and a skinny younger boy, remained inside the pickup, staring at us with blank expressions. "*Zlayeb* (morons)," Rakan said in a shiver. "They should go out and say hello at least." The temperature had dropped and I was shivering too. "You both afraid?" asked 'Ajib. "No, we're cold." "*Ayy wallah*, this is what joyriding is all about: cold nights, wind and darkness."

'Ajib was twenty-three. Short, slim, and sturdy, he adorned his musical colloquial Arabic with masculine gesticulations. Rakan was more vocal than I and was trying to bend his standard Riyadh Arabic to the brisk pace of 'Ajib's Bedouin dialect. In spite of my efforts to speak clearly, 'Ajib's eyes widened whenever I opened my mouth, and he had me repeat every single sentence. I understood him well, but he seemed not to grasp what I was saying. Rakan later told me: "Don't forget that you are European; people aren't used to talking to you folks, and they always assume you won't understand them." The police patrols, now more frequent, reminded 'Ajib of a scene he had witnessed a few months ago. One night, a drifter had stopped next to a police car, opened his window and shouted: "Come here, *ia wir'*, you sissy, I'll give you a ride!" The boy had sped away immediately, chased maladroitly by the patrol, and managed to dodge out of sight. According to 'Ajib, joyriding was distilled in this vignette; it was about being a real man, having a good laugh and jeering at the powers that be.

'Ajib was still on his cell phone. "*Hanuti* ('undertaker') will drift a GMC Suburban in al-Quds," a residential neighborhood in the east of Riyadh. We barely had enough time to rejoice before a second phone call changed the plans: the police presence on al-Ba'arin had forced the drifters to move to another part of the city. We jumped in our cars and drove away, slowing down when crossing paths with police cars before we accelerated again, zigzagging in and out of our lane. After a twenty-minute drive along various thoroughfares, we found ourselves in a calm residential neighborhood, in the middle of an unexpected traffic jam. Still following 'Ajib, we drove around and parked on the sidewalk of Turki bin Ahmad al-Sudairi Street, an avenue six lanes wide surrounded by the high walls of luxurious villas. The drifting was about to begin.

FIGURE 1.1. The drifting spot on Turki b. Ahmad al-Sudairi Street. Copyright ©
Pascal Menoret.

We stood in the middle of the gathering of seventy to eighty cars
packed with young people who, restless but strikingly silent, poured out
of their vehicles, walking in all directions and climbing on car roofs and
streetlamps. (See Figure 1.1.) I had just started to take pictures when
everybody suddenly moved to the other side of the street and massed on
the traffic median. The drifters were coming. A Toyota Camry, closely
followed by a Hyundai Sonata, shot out in front of us at an outrageous
140 to 150 mph. Both cars spun four or five times, their tires shrieking on
the asphalt. (See Figure 1.2.) Inside each vehicle, besides the driver, three
youngsters were raising their arms through the open windows toward
the sky and shouting, their faces hidden by their checkered headdresses.
I was astounded but tried to keep my composure in line with the blasé
audience. After the two cars vanished, everybody ran to his vehicle and
drove swiftly away. Our massive procession swarmed in the direction of
the ring road. The police were suddenly ahead of us, stopping cars at an
improvised checkpoint. We managed to escape and drove in a wide loop
to catch up with the joyriding party.

FIGURE I.2. A Honda Accord swerves in front of a crowd of admirers on the outskirts of Riyadh. Copyright © THE BEST.

As more and more cars joined in, the procession snaked its way through the sprawling city like a massive hydra, adrenaline-filled shouting peppering the blasting music and the roaring engines. I was driving inside a parade of about a hundred cars, streaming down all four lanes of the ring road at 110 mph, close enough to other vehicles to follow every emotion on their passengers' faces. Something odd happened. Carried away by the scene, I burst into laughter and shouted in Rakan's direction, "This is awesome! This is what I should have been doing all my life!" I was excited to drive fast, to break the law, to belong, even for a night, to a community of agitated young men who were defying the police in a country reputed for its harsh handling of the slightest incivility. Speed had given me a sense of invulnerability I had never experienced before.

We were speeding to catch up with the procession after another drifting show when catastrophe struck. A driver started to spin his Camry ahead of us, in the middle of a group of twenty cars moving at about 100 mph. His car began to waltz on the asphalt, sliding with a shriek while presenting its flank to us. It hit another car, hurling it onto a security rail on the left side of the freeway. The entanglement of cars, skidding fast in front of us, was so terrifying that I stepped on my brakes. Finding a way out on the right side of the road, I accelerated again to avoid triggering a pile-up.

It was too late: a powerful shock projected us toward the dashboard and then back into our seats. Still accelerating, and with my car making an alarming noise, I looked for a safe spot and pulled over away from the gigantic accident that I imagined was unfolding. The driver of the other car stopped behind me. I gazed at the highway, expecting to find a heap of cars and wounded drivers. To my bewilderment, the asphalt was empty. All the cars had sped up and avoided the accident my clumsiness should have caused.

A police patrol car soon reached us. Before he opened his window, the policeman popped a captagon (amphetamine) pellet into his Power Horse energy drink and swallowed it with a gulp. Seeing that nobody was hurt, stumbling and stuttering, obviously unable to articulate his thoughts, he unexpectedly drove away, soon followed by the other driver. Calling from his car, 'Ajib told us to fix our car and join them, but I needed the help of more than just a mechanic, and Rakan and I spent the next few hours at the hospital for a checkup.

The accident happened a year after I arrived in Riyadh. I had started my study of drifting in the preceding months, collecting articles, interviewing drifters and their fans, and trying to secure access to a group I would follow and observe. My hopes thinned out after that night, as 'Ajib became more and more elusive. Like most drifters we approached, he was on his guard, wary of the improbable duo: a French PhD student and the young Saudi professional who claimed to be researching the dynamics of joyriding. In the eyes of many, Rakan and I were spies sent by the local police to infiltrate the drifters. To 'Ajib, my gaucherie and our retreat after such a minor incident were evidence of our suspiciousness: how could he trust such a poor driver and his unfathomable friend?

1.2. Cars and Road Violence

Joyriding in Riyadh doesn't look at joyriding as an extreme manifestation of Saudi youth criminality. Rather, it looks at both drifting and its criminalization as embedded in global networks of power and knowledge. The surprising behavior of the police and Ajib's conduct pointed to an unspoken alliance between law enforcement and law breakers that could only be understood by stepping back and looking at Saudi roads, cars, and male youth in the light of the global importance of Saudi Arabia, since World War II, as a major oil exporter, commodity market, and inventor of traditions. The book explores an idea that will sound both simple and obscure: in Saudi Arabia today, road violence is a form of political violence. And by road violence I mean not only the most visible forms of violence that are road rage or joyriding, but also the structural violence that roads, infrastructure, and the automobile system in general inflict on individuals.

Violence must have been consubstantial to the idea of road making, for Arabian Peninsula rulers have long eyed roads with suspicion. Both imam Yahya Hamid al-Din of Yemen (1869–1948) and 'Abd al-'Aziz Al Sa'ud (1876–1953), the first Saudi king, convinced that highways were primarily used by invaders, were reluctant to have their roads asphalted.[2] In the 1940s, 'Abd al-'Aziz reportedly considered trucks "as enemies, like the Germans and Russians," and thought that "highways provided advantages to enemies close by, leaving his capital vulnerable to invasion."[3] The Al Sa'ud didn't opt for automobile development right away. Instead, they favored railroads, which linked their rule to other train-loving states: Khedival Egypt and the Ottoman Empire. Besides, trains were less likely than trucks and cars to be the prey of the highwaymen (*quta' turuq*) who, like the infamous Rashshash al-Shaybani, terrified Najd, the central region of Arabia, until the late 1980s.

While the Al Sa'ud pursued their dream of railways, the American oil company Aramco and Californian construction giant Bechtel built the first asphalt roads. Often presented as a goodwill measure demonstrating U.S. companies' care for local society, the layout of roads in Saudi Arabia was of strategic importance not only to Aramco and Bechtel but also to the U.S. federal state. Yahya Hamid al-Din and 'Abd al-'Aziz were right to be cautious, as both companies were "loaded with CIA" agents who gathered vital information on the Saudi territory and its populations.[4] Thanks to roads, both state power and imperial sway crept into the heart of the Arabian Peninsula.

Road building in Arabia was an ambiguous venture. In the late 1920s, when Sayyid Abu Bakr, the Singapore-born scion of an opulent South Yemeni family, "felt stuck" in his inland province of Hadhramaut, "he built himself a road, all the way from Tarim to the coastal port of al-Shihr, a hundred miles away." This new mobility was threatening as well as empowering. Was the road a way to invite the British Empire onto shore? Or an attempt by a landlocked yet wealthy polity "to break out of an impasse" and reach the ocean? Whether the outcome was the reinforcement of Sayyid Abu Bakr's political ascendance or the British colonization of the region a few years later, "it all had to do with the roads."[5] Just like South Yemeni diasporic and imperial routes, Saudi highways were taken, from their very origin, by political ambitions, imperial greed, and global networks of expertise, capital, and power.

After World War II, the Saudi state launched ambitious transportation policies, and roads became a central site of identity making. As motoring progressed, young and old, men and women were increasingly mobile, leaving villages, small towns, and steppes for the opportunities of the big cities. With the rapid expansion of the cities of Riyadh, Jeddah, and Dammam, thoroughfares and roundabouts were made to embody the spatial politics of the Saudi state. Like road building, the import of cars was a political and imperial business. Harry St. John Bridger Philby, the British colonial agent who became one of 'Abd al-'Aziz's advisers in 1924, made a fortune as the first Ford dealer in the country. Others followed suit. Cars, previously American and increasingly Japanese, signaled their owner's ambitions and success and were a symbol of individual freedom, technical mastery, and masculinity. The Saudis became a driving nation. Inside the cities, Egyptian, Greek, and French urban planners designed regular grids of perpendicular highways on behalf of the Al Sa'ud elite. Everything happened as though the princes wished urban development would exorcise Lord Cromer's racist remark about the Egyptians: "The European is a close reasoner . . . his trained intelligence works like a piece of mechanism. The mind of the Oriental on the other hand, like his pic- turesque streets, is eminently wanting in symmetry."[6] With its south Cali- fornian regularity, overpasses, and tunnels, the new Riyadh that emerged after the 1973 oil boom was picturesque only to its Saudi users.

Urban symmetry was not just pleasing to the ruler's mind, nor was it only a gentle rebuttal of European spatial metaphors and racial assump- tions. It was also a tool to organize the real estate market, which became one of the primary means of private enrichment. More and more oil money was invested in land development; royal privileges, state loans, and middle-class wages fueled real estate speculation, of which a few actors were profiteering. The straight and wide urban highways of Riyadh and Jeddah became the Saudi equivalent of Wall Street, the spatial symbol of the new landed bourgeoisie and a manifestation of heightened class warfare.

Road construction drew a geometrical grid. This abstract space unfolded its perpendicular highways on the plateau surrounding Riyadh, erasing the landscape north of the city, where hill after hill was dynamited to leave space for new subdivisions. Nature and history were pushed aside. As more and more Saudis were motoring, the use of the body receded to the effortless operation of switches and wheels. Urban growth came with the imposition of the national costume on all Saudis, in the form of a white *thawb* and a *shmagh* (headdress) for men, a black *'abaya* and a veil for women. It also came with the general adoption of the single-family detached house, which gradually replaced the multifamily dwellings of yore. Standardization of landscape, memory, dress, dwelling, and mobility was now the norm. Forced to use cars, banned in practice from walking, their dress standardized, Saudis were intimately transformed by urbanization.

Several Saudi novelists explored in often-poignant words the abandonment of the old Riyadh after the 1973 oil boom, and the shock of moving to the new, perpendicular city.[7] Presented by the state as modernization and development, this internal exile created a space where nature and memory had receded, desolated places were ubiquitous and threatening, roads had taken over most of the city's surface, and commercial centers had become the main attraction. Space itself had "become a commodity to be sold wholesale,"[8] and roads were but the aisles of this humongous open-air market.

After the 1973 oil boom, Riyadh presented a particularly crude image of capitalist accumulation and authoritarian closure. The city had become a disciplinary space, where social and economic pressures enclosed individuals in tiny, dehumanizing routines, and where all shades of public debate were banned. During a conversation at his home – a typical concrete villa surrounded by high walls – a Saudi novelist dwelled on the pointless daily life of most Saudi males. Waking up, driving children to school, driving to and from work, driving female relatives to the supermarket, driving everybody back home, driving to friends', driving to restaurants and cafes, driving back home, going to bed: that constant mobility rarely led to a space where you could assemble with others and enter a public conversation. Roads and cars turned individuals into mere cogs in a disciplinary mechanism. The infrastructure state aimed at abolishing agency and protest, and establishing what Henri Lefebvre dubbed "the silence of the 'users':"[9] a general state of apathy and depoliticization.

The rapid movement of capital had created Riyadh's geometric street grid, gigantic suburbs and massive road system, which in turn influenced individual and collective behavior. Just like other car-based spaces, from southern France to southern California, the city was an oil-based city, an environment produced, operated, and navigated, thanks to oil. The development of Riyadh, far from being exceptional or marginal, followed the evolution of the global energy market toward the domination of oil.

Since the 1973 oil boom, it is not only petro-monarchies that derive their economies and power structure from petroleum: thanks to their dependence on the black gold, "the leading industrialized countries are also oil states."[10] The extreme road revolt of Saudi youths was thus neither exceptional nor peripheral. It was a spectacular response to the global emergence of oil-based spaces.

In the late 1960s, Western experts still looked at Saudi Arabia as an exotic, far-flung locale they had to accompany on the path of development and "modernization." This view was already anachronistic. After 1945, the country proved crucial to the creation of the global oil trade, and to the functioning of U.S. hegemony. Post–World War II globalization didn't result from the gradual integration of bilateral markets, but followed the postwar shift from coal to oil as the fuel for the reconstruction of Western Europe and Japan, and the prosperity of the region that came to be called "the West." With their American- and European-owned oil companies, Saudi Arabia and the other Gulf oil producers were an important node in a "neo-triangular trade": U.S. and European capital and security were invested in oil exploration and production, while cheap Gulf crude fueled European and Japanese growth and kept world oil prices low, which in turn contributed to U.S. hegemony.[11] After the 1973 oil boom and the gradual nationalization of Aramco, there was no longer any metropolitan center from the vantage point of which Saudi Arabia could be considered as a periphery. Riyadh had become an important node of the global trade in energy and one of the world's main crossroads of cash and human flows.

How do the inhabitants of Riyadh cope with the pressures of these global networks of power, trade, and expertise? Are they prisoners of disciplining routines? Do they let state and market actors silence them without revolting? Because political parties, trade unions, and independent organizations are prohibited, is the political public sphere restricted to the princes and their clients? Is there no place in Saudi Arabia for popular forms of protest and expression? If "class struggle is inscribed in space"[12] but demonstrations, sit-ins, and strikes are banned, what spatial form can that struggle take?

1.3. The Emergence of a Plebeian Public Sphere

The idea that road violence was a public policy came back full force when the state decided that only men were allowed to drive. When in 1990 the Interior Ministry banned women from driving, it was not only to protect the fairer sex from the vision of such eloquent bumper stickers as "Your Sister Rides With Me" (*ukhtek rakba ma'i*). Nor was it just to uphold the controversial religious principle of the "impediment of the pretexts" (*sidd al-zhara'i'*), which prevented believers from engaging in any behavior that, although not sinful in itself, could lead to sin. In other words, it was not only to prevent women from undermining the conservative fabric of society by selecting "their own mates," which state officials thought would happen if they were "free to drive."[13]

The Interior Ministry banned female driving in reaction to a demonstration of forty-seven women who drove down Riyadh's 'Ulayya Avenue on November 6, 1990 – in the midst of the U.S.-led Operation Desert Storm. They demanded more rights for women, including the right to drive: although not yet banned by law, female driving, deemed socially unacceptable, was common only in rural areas. The forty-seven protestors contributed to politicizing urban spaces. If "social order" was established through "the control of traffic," it was possible to wage a revolt by ways of "traffic jams, illegal parking, multiple crashes, collisions" – or women taking the wheel.[14] Gender struggle, just like class struggle, was inscribed in the car-based spaces of the city. If roads and cars were tools of policing and market discipline, could they also lead to the emergence of an alternative public sphere? Could car traffic be politicized?

Joyriding in Riyadh develops Jürgen Habermas's notion of a "*plebeian* public sphere,"[15] which he leaves aside in his study of the public sphere, to focus instead on the "bourgeois," "educated classes," and the "public use of their reason." Working on eighteenth-century France, Arlette Farge showed that the elites did not have a monopoly on political expression, and that everyday Parisians were just as vocal and opinionated as the bourgeois. On the streets of the capital, average people couched their concerns and their revolt in "subversive words" that were spied on and reported by the state police. Their opinions "were denied by a government which, at the same time, was observing them continually," thus creating the very police archives that now testify to their relevance. This "chaotic anthill of disconnected information," gossip, and rumors gradually gave birth, in the second half of the eighteenth century, to "something firm and solid: quite simply, the right to know and to judge, the right to expect the king to divulge his secrets," and a dominant "feeling that [popular] political knowledge was legitimate."[16] Slowly burrowing through absolutism, everyday attitudes prepared the way for the landslide of 1789.

In this book, I analyze joyriding as an emerging plebeian public sphere. I examine the everyday attitudes of those Saudis who are not part of a

political, economic, or intellectual elite. In the two last chapters, I explore
how fleeting words, vernacular poems, homemade videos, and road delinquency convey a widespread disaffection from the Saudi political, economic, and social model. The joyriding scene displays various genres of
opposition: the violation of road regulations, the organization of nightly
parades, and the production of songs, poems, videos, and photographs.
Joyriding is not only a thriving subculture, but also a way of confronting
the state in its most basic operations: managing public spaces, protecting
private property, and enforcing the law.

"Originating in the United States, the term 'joyriding' arrived in the
United Kingdom in 1912 and was defined simply as a 'ride at high speed.
Esp. in a motorcar.'" Belfast is one of the best-studied theaters of what
British law criminalized in 1930, "when it was made an offense to take
and drive away a vehicle without its owner's consent." "Belfast joyriders have resisted 'adult, police or paramilitary authority' and neither
custodial sentences, punishment beatings nor several fatal shootings by
British soldiers served to quench" the phenomenon.[17] Joyriding emerged
in Saudi Arabia after 1973, when an expansion of single-family housing
and state-guaranteed household debt allowed a handful of players to
reengineer the space of Riyadh around car transportation. Either in 1930s
Belfast or 2000s Riyadh, the study of joyriding is crucial to the story of
the relations between infrastructure and mobility in environments characterized by technological sophistication and political repression. Since
its creation in the 1930s, the Saudi state asserted its authority by stopping
the movements of the Bedouin tribes and by funneling mobility through
roads and other official means of transportation, thus opening massive
markets to private and public investment. Could joyriding's exuberant
and aggressive mobility be a direct response to the state's disciplinary
techniques, a noisy encroachment of the subaltern on the quiet normality
imposed by the state?

The emergence of a Saudi religious public sphere in the 1980s and its
repression in the 1990s has been examined by several scholars.[18] Just as
1973 was a turning point for the Saudi economy, 1990 was a turning point
for Saudi politics: as the country was turned by an international coalition
into a military launch pad against Iraq, political opposition crystallized
around the questions of governance, transparency, the independence of
the judiciary, and the fight against corruption. Marches and petitions
were met with a heavy-handed repression.[19] Joyriding reportedly boomed
during the years of repression, as the state deployed the rhetoric and
police methods of the war on terror. As pedestrians and political activists

were thrown in jail, rebel car drivers unwittingly gained a new prestige. Meanwhile, by rendering female driving sinful, the state paradoxically acknowledged the subversive and liberating nature of car mobility.

Driving became increasingly politicized as the use – or misuse – of cars pointed to a grammar of acquiescence and protest. Could speed be a way to challenge the abstract space of the city? Was joyriding a revolt against the discipline imposed by the real estate market? Could accidents and car crashes, regularly experienced by joyriders and panicking the Saudi public, be an intentional way to denounce the "illusion of safety" that was one of the tenets of the Saudi public order? Could crashes be at the "center of the car culture" joyriders developed against surveillance and repression?[20]

Joyriding in Riyadh examines these questions by analyzing the networks of power and knowledge that created the space of Riyadh, and by exploring joyriding as an extreme practice that continuously "un-builds" the city.[21] It uses an anthropological method to understand Riyadh's disciplinary space, anarchic driving, and geography of power.

1.4. Reflexive Anthropology and the War on Terror

This book is inspired by the anthropological tradition developed by Pierre Bourdieu and his students.[22] With its attention to the social, economic, and political conditions of fieldwork, reflexive anthropology requires that researchers distance themselves from the "scholastic illusion": the misleading belief that academic knowledge stands by itself and is not conditioned by class, race, gender, power, or relations of domination.[23]

Despite its consideration of the context of fieldwork and the position of the researcher, the reflexive anthropology of Arab societies has long failed to locate its imbrication with the colonial or postcolonial order. Edward Said's insights into the entanglement of knowledge and power can hardly be overstated:

if it is true that no production of knowledge in the human sciences can ever ignore or disclaim its author's involvement as a human subject in his own circumstances, then, it must also be true that for a European or American studying the Orient there can be no disclaiming the main circumstances of *his* actuality: that he comes up against the Orient as a European or American first, as an individual second. And to be a European or an American in such a situation is by no means an inert fact. It meant and means being aware, however dimly, that one belongs to a power with definite interests in the Orient, and more important, that one belongs to a part of the earth with a definite history of involvement in the Orient . . .[24]

The first human subject that an anthropologist has to understand is herself in her interactions with her object. "Every interpretive strategy," writes Vincent Crapanzano, "involves choice and falls, thereby, into the domain of ethics and politics."²⁵ In other words, anthropological ethics are not a set of mindless procedures, but find their basis in reflexivity.

Assessing in the early 1970s the incestuous relationship of anthropology to colonial enterprises, Talal Asad regretted that "the general drift of anthropological understanding did not constitute a basic challenge to the unequal world represented by the colonial system."²⁶ More than ten years later, Lila Abu-Lughod argued that anthropology was still oblivious to its imperial ramifications: although dwelling on the "remnants of a dying colonialism" and making snarky comments on the "merely inferior" French expats,²⁷ Paul Rabinow, for example, did not make explicit his own position as an American anthropologist in post-1967 Morocco, and the various distortions that this geopolitical fact impressed upon his work.²⁸

Abu-Lughod writes that Bourdieu neglected to "consider...the particular implications of being a Frenchman in French-occupied Algeria."²⁹ Yet Bourdieu explored early on his own positionality as both a scholar on the payroll of the French state and a pro-Algerian intellectual. Between 1955 and 1960, he conducted invaluable fieldwork on the consequences of colonization, dispossession, displacement, and war on Algerian society. The murder of his friend Mouloud Feraoun by French extremists and the threats directed at Bourdieu by the French army are evidence of the acute challenge reflexive anthropology did represent to the colonial system.³⁰

By reflecting upon the conditions of fieldwork, Bourdieu turned reflexive anthropology into a potent scientific and political weapon. Reflection was not a matter of ethical responsibility, but of political awareness: it was what distinguished anthropology from what he dubbed "colonial science." Bourdieu critiqued anthropological ethics as a naive and self-serving attempt at restoring one's "clear conscience" and "good will" in the face of colonial domination. Instead of trying to selfishly "salvage their responsibility" from the imperial wreck, he expected anthropologists operating in colonial settings "to do [their] best to restore to other men the meaning of their behaviors, a meaning of which, among other things, they have been dispossessed by the colonial system."³¹

Drawing on Bourdieu's methods and concepts, his students have studied the margins of Western societies. Philippe Bourgois and Loïc Wacquant in North American inner cities, Stéphane Beaud and Michel

Pialoux in French banlieues and working-class neighborhoods refined existing fieldwork methods.[32] They reconstituted power relations and were sensible to the multiple spatial and temporal scales of the anthropological inquiry, which could no longer pretend to be the description of a "local culture." Anthropology was no longer the science of "the small, the simple, the elementary, the face-to-face," the instantaneous, the here and now.[33] It was politically situated and, bridging several disciplinary and spatial divides, flirted with social history, political science, and urban geography.

Conducting fieldwork as a Frenchman in Saudi Arabia during the war on terror was no less problematic than doing so as a Frenchman in colonial Algeria, or as an Englishman in colonial Sudan for that matter. Even if I had planned on living off scholastic illusions, friends, interviewees, and informants constantly reminded me of my position. "Don't forget that you are European," Rakan had told me during our night with 'Ajib. This short injunction could have become the motto of my stay in Riyadh. Rakan was not alone in putting me in my place. In a recorded interview, a young middle class Saudi who, challenging the ban on demonstrations, had joined marches for the release of political prisoners could hardly hide his contempt for my privileged status. Mentioning one of Saudi Arabia's most famous prisoners of opinion, he vehemently said, "You think he's at home now, living a comfortable life? Before *you* go to sleep, the secret police (*al-mabahith al-'amma*) explore under your bed before you get in it. Are *you* happy with your life?"

After a long conversation about the Islamic movements, another interviewee told me why he was sharing his experience with me. He suggested that the West couldn't afford to be ignorant of Arab countries and that through his participation in my study he was trying to rectify the global balance of knowledge: "Power and ignorance? I prefer power and knowledge." I could introduce myself as a specific individual, Pascal or Bassel, the latter being the Arabic name I used to spare my interviewees the awkwardness of telling their wife or mother that they had spent the evening with "Pascale," a female name in Arabic. But I couldn't escape the power dynamic that was shaping my daily encounters with Saudis.

I couldn't escape a pervasive sense of vulnerability either. I could think of myself as actively conducting fieldwork, but I was more often an object of suspicion or disbelief than a sovereign subject. Even if their rebuttal was gentle or coated in politeness, most people I approached refused to be interviewed. And my middle class interlocutor made it very clear that *he* was the one actually conducting the interview. After I asked him what, in his view as a demonstrator and activist, could be a solution to political apathy, he burst in excitement and, pointing to my tape recorder, exclaimed,

The solution is this! Part of what I'm telling you, I hope you'll publish it. Part of what I say is part of the solution; it is part of a harassment strategy.... If I talk to you, it is not to fulfill *your* desire. It is something that *I* want, something that *I* decide.

For most of my interlocutors, I was first and foremost a male Western Orientalist whose research could add some day to the information gathered by Western governments, security agencies, and private and public armies. My initial research project, on Saudi Islamic movements and youth politicization, was partly dictated by debates within the French public institutions that granted me access to the field. I was a philosophy teacher and a student of Arabic when I first came to Saudi Arabia in September 2001. I went there to do my national service: I would teach in one of the many neocolonial outposts (or "cultural centers") the French operate across the world. I was unsure about my commitment to writing a PhD on Hegel, whose *Philosophie der Religion* I had packed with me. The rich history of Central Arabia and my students' communicative passion for the place convinced me, instead of writing a philosophy thesis, to enroll in a Middle Eastern Studies program. My decision to study the politicization of youth was compounded by the desire to critique widespread stereotypes on Arab youth and to show that Islamic groups were not the hotbeds of religious radicalization that were regularly demonized by the Western "Islamic study industry."[34]

I wanted to test in Riyadh the fieldwork techniques and social history hypotheses of Bourgois, Beaud, and Pialoux, who deconstructed sensationalist clichés about urban violence and social marginalization in U.S. inner cities and French banlieues.[35] One of my aims was to show that Islamic groups articulated an informed critique of the state policies. That topic was congruent with the preoccupations of the French Foreign Office, which granted me a doctoral scholarship and a rare four-year research visa to Saudi Arabia. With that scope in mind, I started fieldwork in January 2005 in a Saudi context that was loaded with the proximity of the invasions of Afghanistan (2001) and Iraq (2003), and marked by several decades of internal repression backed by European and North American powers. I was there with a French scholarship and on a French research visa (*ta'shira bahth*). No wonder most of my contacts were convinced that the researcher (*al-bahith*) was clocking in at the secret police (*al-mabahith*).

1.5. Saudi Youth and the Politics of Representation

While I continued studying Islamic groups, my work on car drifting moved more and more center stage, and triggered my postdoctoral archival study of the urban planning of Riyadh between 1967 and 1972. Saudi Islamic groups today are confronted with a particularly harsh dilemma: be depoliticized and stay unharmed, or politicize their activities and be threatened with repression and accusations of terrorism. Repression and co-optation have deprived most Islamic groups of their political acumen, and state violence increased after 2001, as the royal family joined the U.S.-led war on terror. Islamic groups progressively turned into elite socialization circles. Instead of looking at the politicization of these socially and culturally endowed youth who participated in Islamic activities, I adopted a more comprehensive view and looked at the broader dynamics of political, economic, and social marginalization. Joyriding and drifting were an ideal object to examine the link between structural violence (exercised by the state through economic laissez-faire policies, social and spatial segregation, and police crackdown) and what was presented by Saudi and western media as gratuitous violence, the mere outcome of individual boredom and of a banal car-oriented youth subculture.[36]

The choice of such loaded objects as youth violence, car drifting, and joyriding deserves an explanation. An ethnography of joyriding runs the risk of being perceived as a piece of sensationalist and voyeuristic scholarship that looks at a marginal population and is therefore unable to say anything substantial about the whole political, social, and economic picture. Furthermore, searching for a political significance in joyriding seems to fall under the "romance of resistance,"[37] and to end up naively interpreting youthful exuberance as subversive rebellion.

Does a study of joyriding youth contribute to the exoticisation of Saudis, to their portrayal as irreducible others and aliens? I don't think so. On the contrary: by bringing Riyadh back into the mainstream of dysfunctional urban societies, it shows the deceptive ordinariness of Saudi Arabia. Whereas most studies emphasize the conservative and reactionary elements of Saudi politics, I draw attention to the way the Saudi state, like most liberal nation-states, forces people into various gender, class, ethnic and religious categories while claiming to promote equality between them (we, the Saudi nation). Yet Riyadh is not only the product of the Saudi state and deserves its place on the world map of urban marginality and revolt. The *dakhl al-mahdud* (low-income) areas of Riyadh match the ghettos, banlieues, *problemområde*, and *favelas* of other cities and testify to the fact that, in liberal societies as in those systems that are described as "authoritarian," political power is equally based on economic violence.[38]

Still, why choose joyriding as a case study of disenfranchisement? In Saudi Arabia, joyriding is commonly associated with various violent practices, including rape and drug dealing, and could reinforce racist stereotypes about Saudi youth as idle pests, culturally unsuited for regular employment, and prone to enrollment in violent activities. Can I, in good faith, wish to critique stereotypes of Arab youth while studying an activity that seems to reinforce this typecasting?

In Saudi Arabia, as in the United States, studies of disenfranchisement and marginality run the risk of being "misread as negative stereotypes . . . , or as a hostile portrait of the poor."[39] In the Saudi case, this common bias is reinforced by geopolitical considerations: since at least September 2001, it has been open season on Saudi youth, who have become fodder in media reports and research papers that link them to political radicalization and militant Islamism. Youth unemployment has been studied through the facile lens of the war on terror, not the demanding perspective of a transnational critique of urban and economic policies. By constructing an ideological straw man, think tanks and security experts have carefully avoided looking into the very mechanisms of social and economic exclusion, and merely rehearse widespread racist and Islamophobic assumptions.

One of the reasons for the eruption of security-oriented discourses is the dearth of reliable sources about Saudi demographics, poverty, and unemployment (the latter is estimated anywhere between 10 percent and 30 percent). In an environment characterized by a scarcity of reliable statistics, the pervasiveness of informal economic activities, and the inaccessibility of public archives, anthropological fieldwork is a way to answer pressing sociological and political questions. No doubt extensive fieldwork on unemployment, for instance, would refine existing hypotheses about the role of state policies (the absence of a minimum wage) and business practices (the exploitation of cheap imported labor in violation of Saudi and international regulations) in the economic marginalization of Saudi youth.

Joyriding in Riyadh is not such a study, and its scope is both narrower and wider. By focusing on joyriding in the urban space of Riyadh, I enlist anthropological fieldwork and archival investigation in the task of deciphering the responsibilities of the Saudi state in the production of marginalization and urban violence. The photographer of U.S. skate culture Warren E. Bolster wrote, "when fun is outlawed, only the outlaws have fun:"[40] I analyze joyriding as a politics of fun and a way to flaunt extreme leisure in the face of state repression.[41] Yet I do not wish to romanticize joyriding or to present it as a fight for freedom. Neither do I wish to sanitize or justify the violence endured by young Saudi males at the hands of the various institutions entrusted with their disciplining (the family, the school, the police, the prisons).

The dangers faced by young Saudis in their dubious battle with the state match the self-destructive riskiness of joyriding. Since its emergence, joyriding has been the target of police campaigns, sociological studies, and reform attempts. Saudi experts and journalists view it as a symptom of a deep-seated malaise within Saudi society. I tend to view it as the outcome of the poorly managed integration of Saudi Arabia within global networks of expertise, business, and power. Far from reading joyriding as an abnormal local production or an exotic carnival, I see it emerging at the meeting point between local and international politics, national and global markets, state and economic violence. As I hope to show in the following chapters, it is not only the Saudi Kingdom that is adrift, but also the networks that crisscross it and weave it firmly into a global fabric that, itself, is moving.

Joyriding in Riyadh is not a hopeless book, however. I wish to present a humanized image of Saudi youth and to celebrate their courage, inventiveness, and humor. Road violence can, in my view, be solved by drastically reducing the number of cars, just like gun violence in the United States can be alleviated by drastically reducing the number of guns in circulation. Abandoning the all-car development scheme followed by the Saudi state since the 1960s will be costly and painful. It will entail a dramatic increase of public transportation alternatives and the generalization of the Riyadh and Mecca subway projects. It will require a densification of urban areas and the reversal of the massive land development policies that have been de rigueur since the 1970s. This will undoubtedly be the most painful change, as real estate is one of the ways the state co-opts and silences economic elites. U.S. anthropologist Laura Nader warned her colleagues in the 1970s, "Don't study the poor and powerless because everything you say about them will be used against them."[42]

I write this book in the hope that everything I say will be used not against young Saudis, but as a critique of those public and private institutions that are complicit of destruction on Saudi roads. If road violence is a form of political violence, then road deaths are also political deaths, and ordinary Saudis have some right to hold the state responsible for them.

1.6. Plan of the Book

Joyriding in Riyadh is a work of urban and historical anthropology. In the continuation of current trends of urban anthropology in the Middle East, it is based on a thorough critique of the idea that Middle Eastern cities are exceptional environments.[43] The book is composed of six chapters, including this introduction. It can be read from cover to cover or in any order the reader wants to follow. Readers who wish to know more about car drifting, and are eager to read 'Ajib and Rakan's stories, may jump directly to Chapters 5 and 6. They may come back later to Chapters 3 and 4 to understand the development of Riyadh since the late 1960s. Chapters 3 and 4 tell the story of Riyadh from the point of view of the state and urban planners. Chapters 5 and 6 tell it from the standpoint of young drifters and their followers. Each chapter can also be read individually.

Chapter 2 traces the contours of the Saudi political realm. It explores the barriers to fieldwork and shows how I reacted to them. Anthropologists live with the people they study and enter in complex relationships of friendship, collaboration, and respect. They themselves become a benchmark and progressively shape their language abilities, their senses, and their analytical capacities. In the Saudi context, marked by a pervasive yet unpredictable repression, the anthropologist is confronted with situations that shape her research in often-unpredictable ways, and the second chapter is an essay in self-reflexivity.

Chapters 3 and 4 track the emergence of Riyadh as an oil-based space, and contribute to both debunking the myth of the "Islamic city" and tracking its origins. Chapter 3 shows how the 1971 Riyadh master plan was designed by Greek urban planner Constantinos A. Doxiadis and his team of experts in conversation with princes, brokers, bureaucrats, investors, and landowners. In the debates surrounding the publication of the plan, the city became a capitalist, high modernist space. Chapter 4 examines the urban dynamics after the 1973 oil boom. It shows how the 1971 master plan was not the "Dictator" envisioned by Le Corbusier, but was disrupted by post–oil boom dynamics of real estate investment and political favoritism. These two chapters show that the city's expansion entailed a demise of the initial high modernist project. In that sense, my analysis is situated within the "critical ethnography of modernism" pursued by James Holston in Brasília.[44]

The last two chapters move from the making of Riyadh to the way young disenfranchised Saudis reclaim the capital's urban space through their use, misuse, and abuse of cars. Car drifting turns the whole commoditization process upside down. In Chapters 3 and 4, the city of Riyadh, constituted by flows of capital, migrants, goods, and ideas, has become a central character of the book. This cast is now joined by the joyriders and their followers, who invent a specific urban landscape through their driving performances, and explore the possibilities for political expression through car figures, poetry, songs, and videos. Chapter 5 describes how joyriding emerged from the oil boom, at the frontier of the expanding city, where marginalized youth tried to appropriate the spaces created by developers and builders. By studying the state's reaction to joyriding and the various moralization and repression campaigns launched by sociologists, religious preachers, and the police, Chapter 6 shows how joyriding became, eventually, political.

2

Repression and Fieldwork

You've been here for more than a year and you still don't get it: some Saudis are dying to meet a Westerner while others would rather die than meet one.

– 'Adil

This is a country where 12,000 to 30,000 political prisoners and prisoners of opinion rot in overcrowded, violent jails;[1] a country where public expression of dissidence, be it on the street, in writing, on the Internet, or in meetings, is closely monitored and punished; a country where repression is organized by security forces that report to a handful of senior princes, out of the reach of an abrupt, arbitrary judicial system; a country where physical punishment, torture, and the threat thereof, in the absence of transparent and fair procedures, are the alpha and omega of the judiciary and the ultima ratio of political acquiescence.

This situation is not new. Torture in Saudi jails is the topic of the third volume of Turki al-Hamad's best-selling fiction *Ghosts in the Deserted Alleys*, in which the hero is taken to Jeddah's political prison and subjected to interrogations and beatings for belonging to the banned Ba'th Socialist Party. The scene is in the early 1970s, but the novel was published in 1998, during the crackdown on the activists who in 1991–1993 had petitioned for political reforms.[2] More recently, international organizations and independent Saudi groups have repeatedly assessed Saudi repression.[3] In 2001, Human Rights Watch reported that in the 1990s, *al-mabahith al-'amma*, the ominous Interior Ministry's secret police, had arbitrarily arrested, detained, and tortured hundreds of political activist.[4]

According to both Human Rights Watch and Amnesty International, the situation grew worse after 9/11, when political crackdown was justified and facilitated by the U.S.-Saudi antiterrorism joint effort: "Since 2001 ... the number of people detained arbitrarily in Saudi Arabia has risen from hundreds to thousands." Most detainees "have been held for years without trial and without access to lawyers," are regularly tortured, and usually have "no idea of what is going to happen to them."[5] Some others were submitted to "rehabilitation" programs, the mixed record of which was packaged for Western audiences as feel-good stories in which bad Muslims were reformed into positive citizens.[6]

Yet recent scholarship on political unrest in Saudi Arabia hasn't taken the full measure of repression and has tended to minimize its effects on the public sphere. According to a recent study of Saudi armed activism and counterterrorism efforts, the 2000s "relatively measured and targeted" security operations – that have still resulted in thousands of extralegal imprisonments – not only "constituted effective counterterrorism," but were also "commendable from a human rights perspective."[7] Its author does mention the regular usage of torture in the 1990s, using Human Rights Watch and Amnesty International's reports to document his claims. But in his view, "the use of torture in Saudi prisons decreased significantly" in the late 1990s. He attributes this evolution to a "limited political opening"[8] and does not contrast his claims to human rights organization's latest findings, which confirm the widespread usage of torture, beatings, and coerced confessions in Saudi jails.[9]

In this chapter I examine the consequences of severe repression on social relations as evidenced by the practice of fieldwork. I argue that repression and torture are not a "discursive theme" used by Saudi activist groups to recruit their members. Torture is not a "frame" either, devised by violent groups to "decrease the risk of defection" by portraying the horrors that "would befall militants if they were captured."[10] Surveillance, repression, and the eventuality of torture are realities that shape everyday life and deeply modify people's interactions with each other – and with the anthropologist or fieldworker. I contend that the anthropologist's (or the political scientist's, or the sociologist's) very access to the field cannot be thought independently from the distortions triggered by political repression, especially when their work touches upon resistance, activism or militancy. While describing my own fieldwork trajectory, in this chapter I also scout the contours of the political realm: describing the barriers to fieldwork, I also explore the question of how Saudis react to surveillance and repression.

2.1. In the Steppes of Upper Najd

It took a long time for the questions of urban space, surveillance, and car drifting to emerge as central to my research. At the outset I wanted to study Islamic groups and was not aware of the importance the urban environment, youth groups, and car drifters would later have for my work. While hanging out with religious activists who longed for virtue and order, I eventually found out that individuals who were labeled as "deviant" were not only more entertaining to follow, but also extremely revealing, in their awkward trajectories, of Saudi society and the way power was exerted over – and within – it. I was diverted from my first project by a series of blockages and by the defection of my contacts. Initially convinced that the responsibility for these cul-de-sacs lay in my own inexperience and alienation from my object, it took me a while to understand that my project was intrinsically difficult and that these mishaps revealed at least as much as they concealed. Fieldwork was a dialectical enterprise, and the topic of my research changed considerably during the years I spent pursuing it.

The first mishap occurred as I was exploring the possibility of conducting part of my fieldwork among Bedouin populations in Upper Najd, a few hundred miles west of the capital. Upper Najd (*'uliat najd*), the huge region between Riyadh and Mecca, is part of what geologists call the Arabian Shield (*al-dir' al-'arabi*) and opposes its multicolored crystalline formations to the beige monochrome and sedimentary cuestas of Lower Najd (*safilat najd*), where the capital is located. (See Map 1.) Between the Nefud Desert, the Jebel Tuwaiq, the Wadi Dawasir and the Hejaz, the mountains of Upper Najd reach altitudes ranging between 2,000 and 5,000 feet and are encased in a huge plateau that gently slopes down eastward. With its crests, its deserts, its volcanoes and its mesas, this contrasting world was the hinterland of Riyadh since the city became the capital of the Al Sa'ud in the mid-nineteenth century.

During my first stay in the country, I had made a few good friends among Bedouin migrants coming from the Arabian Shield. In December 2001, Bjad had walked in my small office with his younger cousin, who had freshly arrived from his hometown (*dira*) and was willing to learn French. Bjad soon invited me to his home, a cramped apartment he shared with six brothers and his cousin, where I spent innumerable evenings. In his mid-thirties, witty, pleasantly unstable, and unbelievably generous, he was born into a Bedouin nomadic family, the eldest of a long series of brothers and sisters. His father, who received a stipend from the National

MAP 1. Saudi Arabia.

Guard, had settled down only a few years earlier in a dramatic valley that Bjad visited every now and then.

During weekends and holidays, Bjad introduced me to the steppes and plateaus of Upper Najd where he had spent most of his life. With his brothers and the occasional relative from other villages, we drove along sandy paths in the middle of nowhere, camped near gaping craters, cooked goat stews on tiny stoves, and shivered at the evocation of the genies and spirits who, according to many anecdotes, loved to pester men and women of the steppe. Upper Najd exerted a powerful fascination on me, and I even considered Bjad's facetious idea of becoming a shepherd at his father's service. On the yellow and pale green flat plateau, surrounded by brown extinct volcanoes and in the company of the few remaining nomads who were scattered here and there in the vast sun-dried open space, I would eventually learn the melodious Bedouin dialect I so craved to fully understand. The end of my teaching appointment in Riyadh and another teaching job in France terminated this project.

During the years I spent away from Riyadh, from 2002 to 2005, I kept a close contact with Bjad and a common friend of ours, Sa'b. When I came back to the city in 2005, Bjad, who was about to get married, was busy moving on to his new life, and I spent most of my free time with Sa'b. In his mid-twenties, Sa'b was a graduate student and lived with relatives who had also migrated from the steppe. Tall and slender, he was proud of his stature and extremely vain about his looks. Sa'b invited me to stay with his family for a few weeks while we were looking for an apartment to share. He wanted to take the opportunity of my arrival to put some distances between his relatives and himself and – as he put it – to drastically "change his way of life": get up earlier, work on his papers in the morning, eat right, and exercise.

A few weeks after my arrival in Riyadh, Sa'b and I drove to his village in Upper Najd, 200 miles to the west, to attend Bjad's wedding celebration. Faithful to my desire to explore the steppes, I thought it would be an excellent occasion to assess the potential of longer fieldwork in the village, where I could study local Islamic groups and the relations between youth and their parents. I wanted to examine the role local institutions (the mosque, the religious group, the school) played in intergenerational relations. I had met young religious activists in Riyadh, and wished to study a rural settlement where – I thought – social relations would be more easily accessible than in the complex urban environment of Riyadh and would present themselves in a nutshell. I naively hoped that close kinship-based relationships would allow me to explore a more compact society than Riyadh's, which many blamed for its distant, alienated social relations.

Another factor spoke in favor of rural fieldwork: Bjad, Sa'b and their brothers and cousins were among the waves of migrants that had come to Riyadh from the steppes and highlands of central Arabia. Spending a few months in their village sounded like a good way to get a better grasp of the recent history and current social stratification of the city. A large share of the capital's population moved back and forth between the city and their home villages, where they spent weekends and holidays. For many students, soldiers, employees, and small businesspeople, Riyadh thus was not only "the big city" with its mysteries and attractions. With its pens and its corrals, its large horizons and its vast skies, it was also an extension of the patch of scorched earth on which they were born and where they were entrenched in dense social networks. To understand Riyadh, you had to know the steppe and its people.

We set out to Sa'b's village in his car on a warm winter day. We would spend the night at his parents' before continuing on our journey to the village where Bjad was celebrating his wedding. Bjad's village was a colony or "sanctuary" (*hijra*). Sanctuaries were agricultural settlements created in the 1910s and 1920s by the Bedouin who joined 'Abd al-'Aziz Al Sa'ud, the founder of the Saudi kingdom. Wary of the mighty nomadic tribes who were the key of military power in central Arabia, eager to check their power and assert his own, sedentary leader 'Abd al-'Aziz sent religious missionaries (*mtawwa'*, pl. *mtawi'a*) to the steppes and convinced many nomadic tribes to fight for him in return for material and spiritual reward. Some tribes agreed to settle in colonies set up around wells, in places suitable for agriculture, and to form an informal army, called the *Ikhwan*, or Brethren.[11] The word *hijra* has many interrelated significations. It means that Bedouin migrated (*hajaru*) from their nomadic and – in sedentary eyes – unruly way of life to the security and stability of a settled life. Like the Prophet Muhammad, tribesmen were expected to do their Hegira (*hijra*) and to transition from an irreligious environment to the abode of Islam, a sanctuary (*hijra*, pl. *hujjar*) where they would lead productive lives and learn the principles of true religion.[12]

This first wave of sedentarization was followed by a second in the 1950s and 1960s, when the nomadic economy collapsed and oil-funded state policies were designed to help Bedouin households settle down and enter the agricultural business.[13] Many communities were created at this time, including the village of my friend Sa'b, where we arrived in the late afternoon. The village was situated in a shallow valley alongside a seasonal river (*wadi*). About a hundred houses were scattered on both sides of the main road while a school, an administrative center (*al-imara*, literally "the principality"), and several shops were located between the dry riverbed and the road. Two mosques served the community, the first one in the most densely built area and the second one in the newest

FIGURE 2.1. A sheep and goat market in Upper Najd, 2009. Copyright © Pascal Menoret.

neighborhood to the north. Saʻb explained to me that economic activity was centered on state employment at the village's school and *imara* and in the nearest town and on subsidized agriculture and livestock farming. (See Figure 2.1.)

On the riverside about twenty palm groves, several vegetable gardens and a dozen alfalfa fields lined the ephemeral waterline with square patches of greenery and bundles of palm trees. On the side of the steppe, about twenty corrals were populated with goats and camels. Several heads of families also received a stipend from the army or the National Guard: since its creation in 1932, the Saudi state had endeavored to enroll Bedouin tribesmen in the military to better control them. In the 1970s, "the only channel of upward mobility open to the nomads [was] through the military, but even here they make up the mass of the troops and only a few of the officers."[14] The Bedouin had been marginalized by the state and tended to meet a glass ceiling in all branches of activity.[15]

2.2. Loyalists, Islamists, and Jihadists

Shortly after our arrival in the village, we were invited for coffee and tea by a relative of Saʻb's. We walked into his "fire place" (*msheb*), a low, rectangular cement room in the courtyard of his house. *Msheb* literally means fireplace, and by extension the room around it, designed to entertain guests away from the main house where the women stay. As was the case in most houses I visited there was no *msheb* in the women's part of this house, but – according to Sa'b – a room designated for female social gatherings. The *msheb* was the place where generosity, manhood, and manly ethics (*muruwwa*) were flaunted in the public gaze. In its contemporary usage, *muruwwa* conserved the classical meaning of "chastity, good nature . . . , dignity and compassion . . . , merit [and] good conduct," to which it added a layer of mundane masculinity. Having *muruwwa* meant being energetic, courageous or simply having guts.[16] With its carefully crafted script and its well-defined roles, masculinity was a spectacle performed in the absence of women and in which men were both actors and spectators. The all-masculine atmosphere around the hearth didn't mean that women were totally invisible, however. In the steppe like in Riyadh, gender segregation was not equally and absolutely enforced. Women were actively shaping not only their own spaces but also the rare spaces they shared with men, and were participating in the very definition of masculinity and virility.[17]

Two dozen men were sitting on the carpeted floor, their backs to the wall and their elbows on cushions, while the host was installed next to the fireplace, in the corner opposite the door, busy with his coffeepot (*dalla*) and teakettle. He was preparing the beverages that two of his sons, both in their teens, carefully poured into tiny white porcelain cups (for coffee) and small transparent glasses (for tea). The custom was to drink but a few cups of the pale green cardamom-flavored coffee before slowly sipping one glass of red sugary tea. After the cup was finished, the *gahwadji* or coffee-boy immediately refilled it, unless you delicately shook it between your thumb and finger or shut it with the palm of your hand, indicating that you did not wish any more coffee. The boy would then rush to the fireplace and pour a glass of tea. The bitter coffee was usually accompanied by dates, whereas the sugared tea was sipped alone, sometimes with crunchy pieces of *eqt* or dried cheese.

The *gahwadji* had to fill all empty cups to show the host's generosity; to fill only a third of the handle-less cup with coffee so as not to burn the guest's fingers; to remain alert, following the guests' every movements and watching the host out of the corner of his eye; and, above all, not to let a drop of the precious beverages fall on the rug. To me, sipping coffee and tea in the company of elderly gentlemen was especially interesting because the entire range of male participants were all gathered together in plain sight. But for the same reason, it was often an ordeal: I struggled to follow the conversation while remaining as dignified as possible, my six feet four inches uncomfortably folded on the floor, my every movement scrutinized by a dozen pairs of eyes and sometimes commented on for days. When it came to good manners, the Bedouin were as fastidious as the Parisian bourgeoisie.

That night, a group of elderly gentlemen were listening to Abu Sa'b, my friend's father, crack joke after joke, letting out short, dry outbursts of laughter while holding his large feet with his left hand. Abu Sa'b was in his seventies, but his strong, muscular body; his energy; and chatter could have fit somebody half his age. He raised goats and cultivated a few acres of land with the help of an agricultural loan from the state. Like many villagers, he also received a meager stipend from the armed forces. According to his son, he was straightforward, despised worldly goods and was well known in the village for his cynicism. After we sat down on the carpet, a tiny coffee cup in our right hands, the *shiyab* or elders started showering me with questions under the amused gaze of Abu Sa'b: what was I doing in the country? Did I know the tribes? Was I a Muslim? Did I want to become one?

While remaining silent, Abu Sa'b didn't miss a second of the inter-action, his eyes flashing from guest to guest. He was probably trying to understand what manner of strange bird his son had brought home. With a hesitant voice, rather embarrassed by the straightforwardness of the inquiries and the peculiarities of the elders' dialect, I explained that I was studying Saudi youth and working under the umbrella of the King Faisal Center in Riyadh. I knew little about the tribes, but enough to admire them and wish to learn more about them. I was not a Muslim, and the eventuality of my conversion was, after all, not in my hands, but in the hands of God.

After this inspection – the first of many others – we had a light din-ner at Abu Sa'b's. Sa'b and I then slipped out of the long, grey cement house into the cool night. We drank more coffee and tea with Sa'b's friends. They also pressed me with questions that had to do either with Islam (was I going to convert?) or with the elders (what did I think of them?). Everybody apparently expected me to praise Islam and to blame the elders, whom they deemed "backward" and "narrow-minded." An appreciation of Islam coming from the mouth of the *franji* (pl. *franj*, the Frank) in these times of global criticism of the latest monotheism seemed particularly piquant. *Franji* was the word used to describe the invad-ing hordes of French and Englishmen that, centuries ago, had abducted

Palestine. It was now used to describe Europeans in particular, and Westerners in general.

On our way back home, Saʻb explained that as a result of intergenerational strife, the elders had lost their authority in the village and were challenged in their customs and beliefs by the youth, whose number was considerably higher. (Abu Saʻb alone had twenty-three children from four different marriages, and sixteen of his children were still living under his roof.) If one also factored in a no less profound divide among the youth themselves, between those whom Saʻb called "extremists" (*mutatarrifin*) and the others, middle-of-the-road, whom he labeled "mere Islamists" (*mujarrad islamiyin*), there were the ingredients for a tense but fascinating situation. Several of the "extremists" had recently joined the ranks of the Iraqi resistance, and one of them had reportedly been killed by U.S. troops, adding to the sense of martyrdom and rage felt by the group.

The elders, the "mere Islamists," and the "extremist" youth were enmeshed in conflict. They met in separate places and avoided mingling with each other. Three of Saʻb's half-brothers were among the "extremists": they convened every day at the mosque and sported untamed beards and shortened *thawbs*, which not only referenced the Prophet Muhammad's ways but also distinguished them from other villagers. The respect due to elders was – if it had ever existed – a thing of the past. Elders were living on the stingy generosity of state salaries and loans and were unable to provide guidance to the youth, who faced a tough choice: either emigrate to the big city to compete on a tight job market or stay in the village and live a frugal and isolated life. The irony was that although a large number of offspring was believed to reflect a man's virility and status, numerous children could also undermine their father's ability to ensure employment and harmony in his household.

According to Saʻb, intergenerational strife was not to be found in Bjad's village, "because *they* are true Bedouin," recently sedentarized families who had stuck to their customs. As for Saʻb's kin, state-subsidized agriculturalists for two generations, they had – again according to him – lost their Bedouin ways, which Saʻb characterized as independence of spirit, generosity, and a strong attachment to the tribe's ethics or *slum*, a set of courteous manners that, handed over (*sallama*) from generation to generation, ensure peace and reconciliation (*salam*). In Saʻb's eyes, the current intergenerational strife and the break in tradition had a lot to do with the impact of state policies on the steppes: manhood and generosity had given way to state-encouraged vulnerability, greediness, and religious extremism. His village, highly subsidized by the government but lacking dynamism and economic prospects, was prone to internal conflict.

The local crisis seemed to be representative of the wider Saudi picture, where despite the authoritarian lid put on political activities, several groups were engaged in a debate over notions of authority, power and legitimacy. The religious tradition produced by the Saudi state in reference to eighteenth-century reformist Muhammad bin 'Abd al-Wahhab, was "a religious discourse used by political authority against society and a weapon wielded by society against this authority."[18] The general narrative about Saudi Islamic politics was that Al Sa'ud had built their state with British and American help[19] to the initial dissatisfaction of the 'ulama of Najd, whose later acquiescence had been lavishly elicited and rewarded, in particular after the 1973 oil boom.[20] This allegiance had proven to be a double-edged sword and younger generations had turned the top-down religious discourse into a tool of resistance. This turn of events had triggered the apparition in the 1960s and 1970s, in high schools, universities, and mosques, of the Islamic awakening (*al-sahwa al-islamiyya*) movement. According to one of its main activists, sheikh Salman al-'Awda, the Islamic awakening was "concerned with *inkar al-munkar 'alanan* (disavowing the abominable in public)..., a political act that [was] guided by religious interpretation"[21] and targeted perceived deviances, from the nonobservance of religious precepts in public to the rulers' corruption, mismanagement of state affairs and abuses of authority.

The difference between Islamic officialdom and the Awakening movement could be illustrated by both camps' attitude toward the Koranic commandment to "promote virtue and prohibit vice." The Koran enjoins believers to form "a community inviting to all that is good, promoting virtue and prohibiting vice" (3:104). One of the signature features of the Saudi religious tradition was to turn what the Koran describes as a collective task into a narrow state monopoly, exerted by appointed 'ulama and, more specifically, by the "Committee for the Promotion of Virtue and Prohibition of Vice."[22] Nicknamed by Westerners the "religious police" and *al-mtawi'a* or *al-hay'a* by Saudis and Arab residents, the committee policed public spaces, enforced strict gender segregation, and made sure businesses closed down during the five daily prayers. Sheikh Salman al-'Awda questioned this monopoly: to him the promotion of virtue was a collective responsibility, not the task of a police force. During the electoral campaign preceding the 2005 municipal elections, Sheikh 'Awadh al-Garni, a prominent Awakening activist, went as far as to interpret the Koranic injunction as a justification for democracy: "Through its criteria

and its values, the community (*al-umma*) will entrust its representatives
with its ambitions and its dreams. If society for instance refuses to elect so-
and-so and sees so-and-so more fit for the post, society, through its vote,
exercises its *right to promote virtue and prohibit vice.*"²³ The municipal
elections, shut down by King Faisal in 1964, had been revived by Crown
Prince 'Abd Allah in the early 2000s; the Awakening eventually won a
majority of seats in the main cities of the country.²⁴

The third strain, besides the state loyalists and the Awakening activists,
was those whom Sa'b called "extremists" and whom other Islamists
described as radicals (*hizb al-ghulat* or fanatic party)²⁵ or, in reference
to the 1980s' Saudi-funded anti-Soviet Afghan guerrilla, "jihadists." Following Osama bin Laden, this movement had excommunicated the rulers
and criticized the alliance between the Al Sa'ud, the United Kingdom,
and the United States, and had launched several attacks against Western
military and civilian sites within Saudi Arabia, before supporting the
Iraqi resistance. It is this movement that had taken root in Sa'b's village and was challenging well-established notions of authority. In the
1990s, the young veterans of the Afghan war had similarly "returned
with their own sense of worth achieved as a result of participation in a
real life-threatening experience." This transformation had "emasculated
their fathers, who had already been undermined by the religious discourse
of acquiescence and the authoritarian state that nourished and perpetu-
ated this discourse."²⁶ As I went to sleep that night, in the rudimentary
men's reception room of Abu Sa'b's house, I was excited in a way I hadn't
been since the beginning of my fieldwork. The village not only harbored
colorful figures, like a healer who – according to Sa'b's brothers – cured
tonsillitis by ironing out his patient's feet. It also seemed perfectly suited
for a study of youth, religious activism, and intergenerational politics.
Yet my presence, which brought together factions that usually tended
to ignore each other, had caused friction in the community, putting the
continuation of my work in jeopardy.

2.3. Down and Out in Najd

The next day, we were invited for lunch by Sa'b's uncle in the courtyard
of his house, under the gentle January breeze. The meal was attended
by what to my standards was a huge crowd: approximately fifty people
of all ages, all male, were seated on a gigantic rug around a *kebsa*, a
pyramid of fragrant, steaming rice topped with big chunks of meat. Our
host courteously sat me next to him. Everybody was smiling, and the

youths that Sa'b had described as "extremists" the previous day greeted
me politely. Yet I could not help but feel uncomfortable and nervous.
The children, seated behind me on their own rug, started throwing small
pebbles at me. I turned around and tried to give them a frowning stare,
while our host admonished them to stop annoying me. I was feeling more
and more uneasy. In spite of the cool temperature, the tropical sunshine
was powerful and I soon had to go to Sa'b's car to get my headdress.

During my short absence, one of the two "extremists" had engaged
Sa'b's uncle in front of the whole attendance by quoting a verse of the
Quran: "Don't take my enemies and yours as friends by showering on
them your affection,"[27] reproaching him for befriending me, an unbe-
liever, and urging him to invite me to convert to Islam. Sa'b could have let
his uncle respond to this remark. But, being my friend and feeling insulted
by proxy, he decided instead to throw himself in the conversation and told
the young man, "Bullshit" (*kalam fadhi*). The conversation immediately
heated up. "*Kalam Allah kalam fadhi?*" (Is God's word bullshit?), asked
the "extremist," infuriated and ready to fight back. "Of course not. What
you say is bullshit." The second bearded youth joined the conversation,
urging Sa'b in turn to start preaching Islam to me. Sa'b answered: "This is
none of my business." His language soon became more cutting: "You are
interested in nothing, no wonder that you became extremists. You don't
even deserve the honor of being spoken to. Now shut up and keep quiet."
At that moment, I was coming back from the car. Seeing me approach,
his uncle put an end to the dispute, saying, "He is our guest; respect him
as such." I sat down under the general gaze, oblivious of the words that
had just been exchanged.

After lunch, Sa'b proposed that we go for a drive around the village. I
didn't know yet what had happened at the end of the lunch (Sa'b told me
the story later that day), but I longed for a break from the tense atmosphere in the village. We crossed the desolate plateau whose emptiness
was interrupted here and there by acacia trees and extinct volcanoes,
and pulled over near a pool of rainwater where we exchanged jokes and
took pictures. During our absence, the outcomes of the lunch's confrontation were unfolding in the village. The two youngsters who had argued
with Sa'b met with his "extremist" brothers, and they all knocked on
Abu Sa'b's door, bitterly reproaching him for having hosted an unbe-
liever under his roof. The argument between father and sons turned into
a tragic struggle between tribal spirit and *muruwwa*, embodied by Abu
Sa'b, and religion and purity, championed by his sons. The debate was
so heated that Sa'b's mother, although not easily unsettled, called Sa'b

on his mobile phone and urged him not to come back to the village that night. She had a premonition that the whole story would turn bad. Sa'b summed up his father's position for me:

SA'B – If my father is forced to choose between the rules of hospitality and the rules of paternal love, he will choose hospitality, and will not hesitate to take arms, if necessary, against his three deviant sons. As a matter of fact, my father has seen worse than this, he is an *'ilmani*, a secularist, and he sticks to his tribal customs.

Sa'b told me everything later that day, during Bjad's wedding dinner. I was grateful for his frankness, as everybody else had carefully avoided mentioning to me the conflicts in the village. We were now in the *hijra*, sitting around the fire in Abu Bjad's courtyard, dozens of miles away from Sa'b's village, oblivious to the gathering around us of venerable elders and clumsy teenagers dressed to the nine. The night had brusquely fallen on the village's white houses, and the breathtaking landscape of granite peaks, sand dunes, and elephant-like pinkish rocks had vanished from sight. Sa'b's story was slowly sinking in, from the brief confrontation during lunch to the alarmed phone call of his mother and his father's reaction. I was in shock and chose to keep to myself for a while. Sa'b continued his conversation with one of Bjad's brothers who was garrisoned on the Iraqi border, and had repeatedly opened his door to Iraqi resistance fighters on the run. As I distractedly listened to the conversation, I could not help but think that the occupation of Iraq was not only a distant international and regional catastrophe, but also a very personal tragedy that had strong repercussions on people around me.

To honor Bjad's family, I had followed Sa'b's cousins' advice and dressed up in full Saudi garb: white robe (*thawb*) and red checked head-dress (*shmagh*) maintained by a black rope (*'igal*). Apparently impressed by my borrowed skill with draping the headdress around my head, the groom told me how "the elders [were] telling stories" about it. One of his uncles told me approvingly "*ta'arrabt!*," "You Arabized yourself!" But not even this jolly remark cheered me. I smiled politely, but my mind was elsewhere: I was obsessed by the scene at lunch, and was looking for a way of understanding what, in my first and decisive interaction with Sa'b's community, had gone wrong. If I was *franji* and if the *franj* were waging war in the Middle East, how could I pursue my fieldwork in Saudi Arabia? In the many times I entered the company of Saudis later in my stay, it was probably not as a stranger: I had many friends and was received as if I were kin. Yet for many of my interlocutors I was still an enemy, and going native would not change this fact in any way.

When we came back to his village, late at night, Sa'b's mother was waiting for us behind the metallic door of their house's courtyard. Draped in a beautiful red and yellow veil that covered her from head to toe and left her face exposed, she was in total panic. "Your brothers have weapons," she told Sa'b, twisting her wrists, "and they have been on the lookout since this afternoon." She implored us not to stay in the village a minute longer and to immediately drive back to Riyadh. Abu Sa'b was not to be informed of our presence either, for his sense of honor would compel him to refuse to let us leave, which would only make the situation worse. We drove back in silence, each one of us absorbed in his thoughts. The village situation was fascinating, but too fluid and too threatening to be investigated.

Among the many reasons why my fieldwork in the highlands could not take off, Sa'b's trajectory and personality certainly played an important part. He was a wonderful informant, but obviously not the best ally. Although he was willing to help me understand his village and the various groups that composed it, his own position within his society was too peripheral to make him a convincing door opener. It took me a long time to understand that Sa'b was not as accepted in his village as his father's status and reputation would have suggested. In the eyes of the villagers, he was what Kabyle mountaineers in Algeria call the "house man" who during his childhood and adolescence had "brood[ed] at home like a hen at roost."[28] He was seen as a mama's boy, spending too much time at home reading books and listening to the Saudi national public radio. Even with his position as a graduate student, he was not as highly regarded as his elder brother, who became a *"duktur,"* an MD, someone who heals and earns a comfortable income, or his younger brother, who made money trading goats. Instead, Sa'b was in the process of becoming a *"dukhtur"* – as Saudis ironically say with a fricative *kh* –, a PhD, someone who *iatfalsef*, philosophizes with no tangible result, looks down at people and chases after a modest salary in a public college.

I had to face the facts: albeit chivalrous, his attitude during the lunch at his uncle's had ultimately deprived me of my access to the village. Such was the interpretation of his closest cousin, a forty-something independent-minded individual who, like most of Sa'b's family, worked in the armed forces. As we were discussing the events, he told me that Sa'b had an old disagreement with his half-brothers, who were born of the third marriage of his father. Sa'b was constantly disparaging them and his sharp tongue had offended them more than once. In turn, cloaked in the religious garb that bestowed upon them the dignity they felt deprived of, they had reframed their relationship to Sa'b as a crusade, and called him *'ilmani*, secularist. Next to *hadathi* (modernist) and *librali* (liberal) in the Islamists' glossary, this term described those Westernized intellectuals who were seen as supporters of a "cultural assault" (*ghazu thaqafi*) on local norms and customs. According to Sa'b's cousin, if I had visited the highlands with another villager, someone who – like himself – truly respected local customs, I would have been able to continue my fieldwork.

A few days later, as we reflected back on our trip, Sa'b tried to explain his position. After he had had a car accident a few years ago, his three religious half-brothers had prayed he would burn alive in his car. They revealed this odious attitude to him, and he cut off all communication with them. I felt overwhelmed. After no more than a few weeks in the country, I was already entangled in a family quarrel that reflected the deteriorated climate of a society where "Islamists" were accusing "secularists" of treason, and "secularists" were in turn pointing the finger at the Islamists' "extremism." The rift dividing Saudi society in 2005 cut across Sa'b's own family. One of his brothers who worked for the army had simply walked out of his post one day, pronounced the whole Saudi state irreligious (*kafir*), and was now living in the steppe, away from everything but his goat pen and the local mosque. Another brother would be arrested by the secret police a few months later, on the allegation of his participation in an Al-Qaeda plot (three other youths were arrested with him under similar charges). Sa'b's family had only been allowed to visit him in 2009, four years after he was detained.

Dhaifallah, Sa'b's charismatic younger full brother and a college student in Riyadh, could communicate with all sides. Unlike his elder brother, he had spent most of his life outside, among men, in the pen or around the fireplace, and took care of his social capital: he esteemed everybody and his reputation was impeccable, especially among the elders. According to Sa'b, he was the only one in the new generation who embodied the real Bedouin character: courage, generosity, frankness, and a robust sense of humor. He was appreciated even among the most radical Islamists. The fact that he was one of the most attractive youths of the village also played a role. He so wittingly praised the old ways that everybody seemed thankful to him for being both traditional *and* appealing. I would have been happy to have him become my main informant in the village. Yet he remained reticent and preferred to bury himself in his studies, only occasionally meeting me for coffee or a meal – I doubt he could have walked very far with "the Frank" in tow anyway.

A cousin of Bjad's had yet another take on the story of our flight from the village. In his mid-thirties, married and the father of five children,

he lived off a modest stipend from the National Guard in the *hijra* we
had visited. In his view, physical or verbal violence toward Westerners
was a natural reaction to the current aggression against Arab and Islamic
countries, from Palestine to Afghanistan to Iraq. He himself not only
understood, but also supported this violence, although – from another
point of view – he would personally guarantee and protect my security
"as a guest" in Upper Najd. According to him, the main issue was not
Sa'b's relationship to his half-brothers, but my very position in the country as a Westerner with a notebook and a voice recorder at a time when
Westerners with guns and drones were patrolling neighboring Iraq and
Afghanistan and supported the Saudi and Yemeni repression efforts. With
or without Sa'b, with or without Dhaifallah, my fieldwork in the highlands of Najd, in a village where many of the youth were boiling with
rage and dreaming to fight in Iraq, was doomed from the very beginning.

2.4. Activism and Frustration

Our misadventure in Upper Najd showed me that I had to draw a line
between my friends, who like Sa'b were often too similar to me to be
efficient intermediaries, and my fieldwork allies. Instead of walking in the
open and presenting my work in front of large assemblies, I had better
keep the number of these allies low enough not to be too vulnerable.
The durability of my fieldwork was, paradoxically, linked to my ability
to reduce rather than multiply the number of my interlocutors. I had
to constantly walk a thin line, meeting enough people to understand
what was going on around me, while trying to limit my contacts to a
nonthreatening close circle of informants and allies. The situation was
daunting: I had three years to reach out to valuable interlocutors in a
society in which building up networks was often a lifelong task.

In 2002, one of my informants, 'Adil, who in high school belonged to
an Awakening group, had introduced me to one of his schoolmates, Fahd.
At only seventeen, there was a somber look about him, as he dragged an
overweight body crowned by a bearded face that he seemed to inten-
tionally make terrible. Constantly frowning and pouting, he sported a
disdainful attitude and an air of restrained violence that starkly contrasted with his insightful remarks and brilliant mind. Born in Riyadh,
Fahd was the last son of a retired state employee who had emigrated to
the capital from a small town in Lower Najd. Socially, physically, and
psychologically speaking, he was the exact opposite of Sa'b, as sedentary,
plump, and principled as my friend was Bedouin, slender, and versatile.

Now twenty-one, a college dropout and the author of several short stories, he worked in a small company and was trying to move from his previous Islamic circle to a more highbrow crowd of young journalists and writers. It is 'Adil and Fahd who helped me start my fieldwork in Riyadh, before I realized that my presence was more of a liability than an asset for them and that they were not socially strong enough to assist me further.

Fahd was reluctant to dwell on his activist period. His hesitation became apparent when, instead of helping me to contact his former companions, he introduced me to his new circle of friends, a *shilla* or group of young intellectuals who gathered several evenings a week in a private rest house (*istiraha*) on the outskirts of Riyadh. In a context of widespread repression, small, informal groups were safer than large, official gatherings.[29] *Shilal* (pl. of *shilla*) served as the launching pad of many collective actions. Composed of ten to thirty individuals who had known each other for a long time, these gangs of close friends and relatives were united by a common goal and served as a second, men's home outside of the actual household in which it was commonly understood that women – one's mother, wife, or sisters – had the upper hand. Everybody belonged to a *shilla*, from the teenager to the princes, and spent an extended amount of time with *al-'iyal* or *al-shabab*, the "buddies" or "youth." Both terms applied equally to skinny adolescents and pot-bellied gray-haired men, as long as they collectively pursued a common goal.

Most *shilal* were purely recreational. A group of close friends would rent an apartment or a rest house, sometimes equipped with a small swimming pool, a volleyball net, or a soccer field, and would buy a television set, a video game console, or a Ping-Pong table in order to spend time away from the strain of work and family. There were *shilal* of businessmen, artists, investors, princes, writers, poets, teachers, and policemen – even the King belonged to a *shilla*. Within them information was shared, news were spread, opinions were shaped, decisions were made, opportunities allocated, and reputations built or destroyed. It is within *shilal* that individuals accumulated symbolic capital, that is, "all the manifestations of social recognition . . . which make up a social being that is known, visible, famous, admired, invited, loved,"[30] and strove to convert it into action and power despite a forbidding environment. These small networks bridged the gap between private and public, personal and political, individual and collective. In the absence of independent clubs, associations, societies, unions or parties, away from the larger tribal structures one could find in the steppes and the countryside, these informal spaces of sociability were in a way the backbone of urban society.

I was now meeting regularly with Fahd's *shilla* of young writers and journalists, ideally placed to hear the latest gossip and follow social debates. The 2005 municipal campaign was in full swing, and I wandered around the city from electoral office to campaign tent, on the lookout for any information that would help me understand the election's dynamics. In the evening, away from the agitation of the streets, the hours I spent with the *shilla* were a welcome diversion. Almost all its members had passed through Islamic groups and they showed a remarkable interest in politics as well as a strong commitment to debate. Their attitudes and opinions struck me as being extremely fluid. One of them in particular, still sporting the young zealots' stern style with a long beard, short-ened robes, and an authoritative attitude, would praise Che Guevara and Quentin Tarantino in a stentorian voice that sounded more appropriate for a Friday sermon than for an after-dinner conversation.

I was received with ceremony and was invited to share my views, but the ice was never fully broken. Their politeness was both spotless and chilly, and I was always interrupting the natural flow of their discussions. I also longed to observe an Islamic group, not former Islamists who were about to become part of the country's intellectual elite. I slowly realized that Fahd was inviting me to assert his own position. He was the youngest and one of the most active members of the group; he would order dinner and set up the tent, next to the rest house, that they used as meeting space, dining area, and playroom. The first one to come and the last one to leave, he would serve the others, clean the tent, and cater to their every desire. Each evening was for him a feast and an occasion to show his social and organizational skills.

During an interview he agreed to record with me,[31] he tried to explain his commitment to Awakening groups and to his *shilla* by his sentiment of personal failure: "All my brothers are teachers, all of them." He looked embarrassed, paused, and continued: "All, except me. I studied in college but . . . I haven't made it. My little brother is in college too. He wants to become a teacher." I began to comfort him, but he giggled my commis-eration away and pointed to his new intellectual friends and his desire to become a writer himself: "But hey, I am the one who tries new stuff. My brothers are too sensitive, super judgmental and think that every new thing comes from the Devil. I am the retarded one, the black sheep at home." After a short silence, he added in a tone half-disheartened and half-defiant: "I am a stranger among my brothers, in a way."

This eccentricity made him an interesting interviewee. After I had stopped the recorder at the end of the interview, he spontaneously explained why he had agreed to meet me, using the same pompous, slightly patronizing tone he had sported during our conversation. I then rushed to my car and scribbled what he said in my notebook:

FAHD – I am helping you because I want to give you a more precise idea of our society, even if it is a bad idea [to do so]. So that you carry it to the West. You spend a fair deal of energy to understand how we live, and I think that helping you is the right thing to do. You must carry to the West an exact idea of us, so that people no longer fear us but know who we are. Because the West will act more intelligently and more fairly if it knows us well. Power and ignorance? I prefer power and knowledge.

I was still regularly meeting with 'Adil. Quick-witted and shrewd, he had a social background similar to Fahd's. His father had come from a small oasis of central Najd and worked as part of the support staff of the ominous "Committee for the Promotion of Virtue and Prohibition of Vice." 'Adil was born in Riyadh but frequently spent weekends and holidays in his village, in a valley north of the city. Like Fahd, he was very interested in my project and promised he would help me. During his years in Islamic Awakening groups that gathered in high schools and mosques, he had become an observer more than an actor, a position that made him in my view an outstanding interlocutor. In one interview he agreed to record, he explained that his de facto position was the result of a conscious decision:

'ADIL – My goal is not to conduct research on those [Islamic] groups. And over the last years, especially last year, I had the feeling that I was getting tired for nothing. Why? Because I don't want to become an Islamic activist . . . I have no goal! And if you walk around like that, with no goal, it means that you have a problem. I took all this as a story, to keep myself informed, that's all. Like I told you: the others are in the field and I am watching them. It's not even like I am in the public, no. I am watching them from outside the stadium. Because once you get into the game, you get in trouble. You can enter the field if you are prepared to act like that. I am not.
PASCAL – You didn't want to become the ball . . .
'ADIL – I don't want to become the ball. I am prepared, I could be one of them without any problem. But it's not what I wanna do, and I don't think I could be really useful anyway. I prefer to watch from a distance.

Sometimes, just like Fahd, he would interpret his outsider position as a personal failure. "I wanted to become like them, but I couldn't make it," he confided one day. I liked 'Adil's detachment. Despite his distance, he felt emotionally close to his fellow activists, and shared the Islamic groups' worldview: to him and to them, the Muslim world was under attack and all Muslims had to resist. The bottom line in his view was political and we often discussed the massive American arms sales to the country, linking them to Saudi Arabia's current difficulties, from widespread corruption to militant violence. One day, after we had chatted about the different groups that opposed the royal family, he bluntly told me, "I am scared of reading Osama Bin Laden, because I know he will convince me."

'ADIL – Look, it's hard for me to say that I'm a reformist, you know why? Because it's useless to fix a wreck. Are you gonna dive in the ocean to fix the Titanic? It's not possible. Although the Titanic represents unbelievable riches, right? It's useless to try to fix it, although it represents a lot for those who built it, and they would certainly have been happy to get it back afloat and fix it. But it's useless: it's a wreck! Whereas if you're aboard a ship that has a few problems, like, I'm ready to cut my arms and legs to fix it, I'm even ready to sacrifice my life so that twenty thousand can live, no problem. Our problem here . . . is that our ship is lost! Reform is impossible . . . except if . . . there will be a possibility for reform only if we launch a new ship . . .

PASCAL – Which will be . . .

'ADIL – A radical change. Because I really think that this ship of ours, now, is lost. I mean, we are in a society with no politics, and it oppresses me, really, we have become a society with no state, I mean.

What would he have done with revolutionary convictions in a country where power was restricted to a narrow circle of senior princes, where any sign of dissent was tantamount to a crime, where politics was banned, where the state itself – in the Weberian sense of a rational and legal entity – was missing? It was wiser not to get too intellectually and emotionally involved and to maintain the only position he apparently took pleasure from – observation.

Unlike Fahd, who had left his Islamic commitment behind, 'Adil still belonged to two distinct Islamic groups. The first one was composed of a dozen individuals who in high school had frequented the same circle of Koran recitation (*halqa tahfidh al-Qur'an*) and the same Islamic awareness group (*jama'at al-taw'iya al-islamiyya*). Koranic circles were groups of students who gathered in a mosque around a leader, generally a college student, to memorize the Koran and discuss Islamic norms and culture. Based in schools and convened by seniors or by teachers, Islamic awareness groups were more exoteric and open to artistic, cultural, and athletic activities. (See Figure 2.2.) These informal spaces of socialization attracted students through various activities, from sports to theater

FIGURE 2.2. A summer camp run by Islamic activists, 2006. The Koranic quotation above the stage reads: "Are they equivalent, those who know and those who don't?" (39:9). Copyright © Pascal Menoret.

to summer camps, and formed a powerful network from which several Islamic groups drew resources and followers.[32]

    'Adil's companions were college students who regrouped every week in a rest house, not far from the *istiraha* where I spent my evenings with Fahd's *shilla*. Besides their meetings, they also ran religious extracurricular Islamic awareness activities in various high schools of the city. Everything seemed to be leading to a first contact. But when 'Adil put the idea on the table, the student in charge of the group abruptly refused. "If we got pulled over while we're with him, what will the police say?" he asked 'Adil in order to justify his decision. "And what wrong are we doing?" replied 'Adil. His concern was left unanswered, and the group's members all abided by its leader's decision. "The guy is a moron," he concluded. Given the climate of repression, I thought the "moron" had a point.

    'Adil's second group was even harder to approach. Mostly students at the Islamic University of Riyadh, its members were both more radical in their religious views and less involved in the daily functioning of the

Islamic movements. Like a few other radical groups, they had withdrawn from what they perceived to be a sinful and irreligious society. True to their convictions, they lived in an apartment, cut off from the surrounding world, and felt nothing but disdain for it. Even other Awakening groups were contemptible in their view: they had labeled "secularist" (*'ilmani*) 'Adil's other Islamic group after it ran internal elections. They equally shunned loyalist circles and despised the Committee of Senior Clerics (*hay'at kibar al-'ulama'*), who was the supreme religious institution in the country. Playing with words, they mischievously nicknamed it the Committee of Senior Clients (*hay'at kibar al-'umala'*).

All of 'Adil's attempts to introduce me to his fellow Islamic activists failed. He was not discouraged, however, and thought that I would be interested in the ongoing war between Islamic and secularist students at Riyadh's university, where he was an undergraduate student. The nearest opportunity to visit the university was to see a theater play during the "end-of-year ceremony of the student affairs department." The celebration happened against the backdrop of a heated confrontation between Islamic and secularist students over the "stipend question." Each Saudi student was entitled to a monthly stipend (*mukafa'a*) of approximately 800 riyals (about $160), a welcome help in a city where lodging and transportation, given the housing crisis and in the absence of a public transit system, could be extremely pricy. The administration of the university was supposed to pay the stipends every month, but the payments were often delayed and students hadn't received a riyal for a while. Young Islamists claimed that the university was investing the students' money in the booming Riyadh stock market. The secularist students, who for 'Adil were the long arm of the government among students, accused in turn the Islamists of politicizing the student body and of threatening public security.

The debate was exacerbated by the fact that, according to 'Adil, one of the armed militants recently arrested by the police had been a member of the university's Islamic group, a story that gave some credence to the secularists' allegations. In the meantime, the "student affairs department," an Islamic fiefdom inside the university, was ironically forced to align itself with the general anti-terrorist mood. The play Islamic activists presented that night was entitled *Who Made Terrorism?* and was preceded by anti-terrorist anthems. The "student of the year" then gave a speech. Tall and emaciated, his eyes staring at us from the depth of cavernous orbits, he delivered a lengthy panegyric of the "student affairs department." His speech was as empty as it was powerful, and his incandescent oratorical style raised thunders of applause among the students. 'Adil whispered in my ear that the "student of the year," who used to study in his high school, was a declared partisan of al-Qaeda.

The plot of the play was deceivingly simple: after a violent argument with his father, a young man, Salih, was expelled from his house and, turning to the audience, conversationally recounted his tribulations with the university. He pronounced a violent diatribe against the professors, whom he crudely described as arrogant and ruthless, and against an administration that gambled with the famous stipends while students walked around in rags. Interrupting the play, the students began to chant, "One week . . . Two weeks . . . One month . . . Two months . . . " "All the performances mention the stipends issue. Islamists have to talk to the students' guts if they want to attract them," 'Adil said. The play resumed. Roaming the empty streets and lamenting the meanness of the world, Salih encountered a terrorist, dressed like a film noir villain and displaying a comically menacing attitude. The terrorist pitied Salih and pointed to a comprehensive solution to all his problems: pulling a plastic gun out of his jacket, the actor handed it to Salih and, with a grandiloquent gesture, pointed to one of the deans who, tight-lipped and straitlaced in his formal black cloak, was seated in the first row. The audience burst into laughter. A few seconds before he pulled the trigger, Salih realized his mistake, threw out the weapon, and begged his father – and the dean – for mercy.

"Even the Boy Scouts' plays are better," 'Adil wryly commented. "Here the audience laughs at the actors more than they laugh with them. And did you see how few people clapped their hands at the end?" After the curtain fell, as if to echo 'Adil's remark, the students booed and whistled away a last antiterrorist anthem. The dean stiffly walked out of the amphitheater, which emptied after him. The following day, 'Adil told me that an Islamic activist and two professors had reprimanded him for having introduced "a Westerner, an infidel" to the university. I was an "intruder" (*dakhil*) who had nothing to gather from the student affairs department's activities, and they threatened to denounce him to the dean for having brought an unauthorized person to the university. 'Adil sadly told me we had fired our last bullet while attending the play: he was now unwilling to take more steps toward helping me out. Ending the conversation, he whispered in a contrite voice, "I now feel even less powerful than before."

2.5. Surveillance and Repression

As I got closer to the groups I had set out to observe, I thought I was entering port. But I was blown back into the open sea, so to speak. Unlike current activists, ex-activists were extremely easy to talk to, especially when they were writing anti-Islamist articles in the printed press owned by the royal family, and were ready to entertain me with lengthy stories about the evilness of political mobilization. A journalist I met in Jeddah was known for having experienced the whole gamut of Islamic positions, from peaceful activism to his engagement in the most militant movements and to repentance. As soon as I mentioned my interest in the Saudi political scene, he rehearsed a well-known orientalist story, explaining that just as Islamists had been religiously indoctrinated into opposition, rehab would "deprogram" them and teach them how to renounce their extreme ideas. I quickly became annoyed by the turn of the conversation and probably made my point a bit too clearly, as he never answered my calls despite having agreed on meeting me the next day. Ex-activists were accessible, provided that you were willing to passively listen to the state's gospel. But they provided few insights into the Islamists' relationships to political conditions, state repression and the wider society.[33]

'Adil's friends' reluctance to meet me and to engage in a fieldwork relationship had a lot to do with the regional context. Most of the people I met probably thought that I was a spy on the payroll of a Western intelligence agency. 'Adil told me that to his friends, my knowledge of Arabic and of recent Saudi history were highly suspicious: at the time of my fieldwork, French intelligence agents were operating in Riyadh and anthropologists participated in U.S.-led counterinsurgency operations in Iraq.[34] Talking about Awakening activist Sa'id bin Zu'ayr who, jailed three times, was arguably the country's most famous political prisoner,[35] one of my informants lost his temper during an interview. Nawwaf, twenty-six, was a white-collar employee coming from a sedentary Najdi background and had participated in various banned street demonstrations in 2003 and 2004.

NAWWAF – They proposed to free him after eight years in jail, and he refused to sign the confession (*ta'ahhud*) [they had prepared in exchange for his liberation]. He cussed and said: "I won't put a drop of ink on your paperwork." They'd just asked him to sign. "I have been jailed with no reason, it is an insult to my human dignity." His relatives even met [interior minister] Prince Nayef. "Tell us why he's in jail," they said. "Why eight years? Tell us why." And he replied: "He'll get out only if he signs."
PASCAL – (*Admiring tone*) What an intransigent character.
NAWWAF – (*Thinking I am being sarcastic, with an icy voice*) Well, you'll find intransigent characters everywhere these days. (*Silence.*) You think he's at home now, living a comfortable life? Before *you* go to sleep, the secret police (*al-mabahith al-'amma*) explore under your bed before you get in it. Are you happy

with your life? What intransigence are you talking about?...Inspections, arrests and security checkpoints won't make your life more secure. Because of these checkpoints, your penholder, there (*pointing to my desk in exasperation*), can become a bomb.

Other people feared that I might be followed by the secret police, and did not want to run the risk of being suspected or accused of treason. The surveillance of the secret police, as well as the looming fear of being imprisoned and tortured, induced a climate of widespread terror. Meetings were canceled at the last minute, phone calls were left unanswered, and promises were broken on a regular basis.

I had vaguely known that the interior ministry's secret police department was monitoring my actions, but I hadn't been certain of this surveillance. One incident brought it into plain sight. In the summer of 2006, I started studying the Ministry of Education's summer camps, which many interviewees described as important spaces for youth politicization. With the help of the King Faisal Center, I obtained all the necessary authorizations from Riyadh's Department of Education and began visiting a number of schools, looking for a camp where I would stay for the whole summer. In exchange for this favor, I was asked to write a report on the summer camps for Riyadh's Department of Education. One of the teachers had written a short piece in a local newspaper about my project, and I naively thought that my show of goodwill and this bit of publicity would help my integration into the schools. As I should have expected, the effect was quite to the contrary.

After a thrilling week in Riyadh's extremely heterogeneous public system, ranging from run-down inner-city schools to state-of-the-art institutions in the richest suburbs, I ran into the vice-manager of the Department of Education, who put an end to my fieldwork, despite my paperwork having been signed and stamped by his superior. He made his decision after a conversation that lasted several hours and was a parody of a police interrogation. According to him, I had hidden my actual motives and was trying to give a distorted image of the Saudi educational system. Conscious of the unwanted attention Saudi schools had attracted for their reported opposition to change and alleged role in radicalization,[36] he not only banned me from visiting more summer camps, but also filed a report to the emirate of Riyadh. His complaint reached the secret police, and the officer who was in charge of my case came to the King Faisal Center, asking to meet me. I was not in and the explanations provided by the center's secretary general must have been convincing enough: he closed the file and sent a positive report to the emirate. By that time, summer camps were naturally over and my hope to conduct observation and interviews had evaporated.

I wish I had met "my" officer. Approximately my age and reportedly well mannered and educated, he had been following me for the past two years. His surveillance was not without fault. He thought, for instance, that I was married, an odd assumption I could perhaps explain. A colleague of mine, who was conducting fieldwork in Riyadh, had spent a month at my place. During her stay, she had had a dramatic effect on my way of life, persuading me, for instance, to finally buy a fridge. Like a Saudi bachelor, I ate outside and bought fresh drinks from the *baqala* (corner shop) next door: I had never felt the need for such a luxury, even though summer average temperatures were in the upper 110s. She had also shamed me into removing the ugly colored plastic wrap that the previous tenant, a Saudi doctor from Jeddah, had glued to the windows to keep out of the neighbors' sight. Together we bought beautiful curtains that the doorman, an affable Sri Lankan in his late twenties, installed. She finally opened the door to a stray cat, and I paid the doorman to feed it when I was traveling. In essence, she turned my spartan dwelling into a comfy home.

The doorman had the key to my place and was perhaps working with the secret police, like many underpaid domestic workers in the city. "My" officer may have relied on his testimony – or on somebody else's – to assess my marital life. Although pervasive, surveillance was neither perfect nor predictable, a fact that didn't make anybody more comfortable. Quite to the contrary: you never knew when or how the police would interfere in your life. Followed by the secret police, how could I explain to my Saudi contacts that it was safe to meet me? Did this surveillance mean that I had crossed the line between fieldwork and political involvement? In Arabic, fieldwork was called *'amal maidani*, an expression that also meant civil activism. Did that imply that, just like political activists needed protection, I needed a godfather to continue my research?

In the summer of 2005, Sa'b helped me meet the sheikh 'Abd al-Ilah, who was to become an important fieldwork ally. He had been an active participant in the reform movement that, demanding more transparency from the state and more rights for citizens, mobilized in mosques and universities during the 1990–1991 Gulf War. Launched by academics, religious sheikhs, judges, Islamic activists and students, it was hard to decide whether the reform movement was more Islamic or more secularist. This is how Nawwaf, who was a teenager at the time of the war, remembers his family's reactions to the protests:

NAWWAF – When I was in middle school, something happened that made me come of age. In 1993–1994, the creation of the Committee for the Defense of Legitimate Rights (*lajna al-difa' 'an al-huquq al-shar'iyya*) made a lot of noise in the media, you were forced to hear about it.... After that, you had the crisis of Burayda [a city 200 miles north of Riyadh], with demonstrations, sit-ins, and the crackdown on the sheikhs. It was a huge shock: those are religious sheikhs!...How can they be arrested and tortured by the state?...But the elders looked at them as if they... "Those, there, they studied in the West, they were influenced by the West, they are secularists (*'ilmaniyyun*), they came back [to Saudi] with Western ideas."

Sheikh 'Abd al-Ilah was a decade older than Nawwaf. In the early 1990s, he had participated in drafting two important petitions that were sent to King Fahd, the *Letter of Demands* (*khitab al-matalib*) in 1991 and the *Memorandum of Advice* (*muzhakkirat al-nasiha*) in 1992. He had also participated in the creation in 1993 of the Committee for the Defense of Legitimate Rights, a political association that was banned shortly after launching.[37] During one of the interviews he agreed to record with me, he explained that he had helped cement a political alliance between three competing groups, the Islamic Awakening groups, some (rare) members of the Islamic establishment, and secular-minded intellectuals and professors. As a result of his activism, he had been arrested in the 1990s and spent half a decade in jail. Sheikh 'Abd al-Ilah clearly understood the ramifications of my fieldwork, and his position as a middleman between several communities made him a crucial ally.

On our first meeting he strongly criticized the double standards of the Saudi political and religious establishment: the religious clerics appointed by the state advocated armed militancy outside Saudi Arabia while forbidding any sign of dissent inside the country. Violence outside and submission inside had in his view pushed Saudis in conflicting directions, triggering a political crisis whose ramifications were obvious, from the Jihad in Afghanistan and the 9/11 bombings in the United States to militant violence inside Saudi Arabia in 2003–2004. The ban on politics and the very tight lid kept on civil activism (*'amal maidani*) had led even liberal-minded intellectuals to conclude that armed violence was the solution. He would certainly have agreed with Madawi Al-Rasheed who wrote, "in the absence of other means of expressing difference, criticism or disagreement with the ruler, excommunicating him becomes the only possible mechanism; violence becomes the only means of changing the situation."[38]

Surveillance was gradual and irregular, and repression could reach unexpected corners of everyday life. In its routine security operations, the state did not only rely on an army of plainclothes officers and informers. It also relied on ordinary citizens, who for the sake of tranquility carefully scrutinized their neighborhoods. Some of my informants complained about this neighborhood watch and the fact that local residents had not only their "eyes upon the street,"[39] but also their hands on the phone receiver and were ready to call the police on suspicious-looking strangers. Informants and friends deplored the "suspicious gaze" (*nazhrat al-riba*) that met any unexpected encounter, whether in the street, in the workplace, or in the realm of ideas. People – especially if they were young, female, or foreign – were deemed guilty until proven innocent; ideas were considered corrupt until proven useful. This "social control" (*al-zhubt al-ijtima'i*) was the topic of numerous publications,[40] and public speech about the city of Riyadh often implied the notion that young people were out of hand, and threatened society and the state.

The Riyadh Municipal Council convened in public more than a year after the 2005 elections. During this first session, several middle-aged male Riyadhis pointed to the necessity of a tighter regulation of places where youth gather: cafés, soccer fields, public gardens, and sidewalks. An Islamic member of the council, 'Id al-Suwaylem, blamed girls who "offer themselves to boys" and mentioned the perils of gender mixing in public spaces (*ikhtilat*). Middle-class family men and their representatives seemed unaware of the already pervasive enforcement of stringent norms, in particular at the hands of the "Committee for the Protection of Virtue and the Prevention of Vice."[41] This control ensured that Riyadh was a notoriously dull city, where what seemed natural elsewhere was explicitly forbidden. Walking with an unrelated woman or taking pictures in public could easily land you in jail if caught by the police. If the cops were not around, you could still run into trouble if a righteous neighbor or passerby denounced you. It is what happened to a man who, a few minutes after he started photographing the beautiful view of downtown Riyadh from my street in Sultana, was arrested by the police, his car left on the sidewalk for weeks.

If after investigation the police did not find anything wrong with your behavior, they could still refer you to the religious police for further inspection. That's what almost happened to Sa'b and I after we were caught picnicking on a public lawn in the central business district. An officer of the National Guard approached us, searched us, and, ultimately, called the religious police. "I have nothing against you, but *they* will surely find something," he said menacingly. The religious police could charge us with indecency or even prostitution: What could a Westerner be doing with a young Saudi in a park after sunset? Before he could reach them on the phone, however, another National Guard, walking out of a hotel nearby, recognized Sa'b, who often spent his evenings writing in the lobby and knew some of the security personal. After the National Guard, pointing to Sa'b, said, "He's a journalist, there is nothing against him," the officer backed down from his threat.

I was taken aback by how quickly a banal check could escalate into the most unpredictable – and unpleasant – outcome. Repression was not exceptional or restricted to cases of political activism: it was the horizon of most activities and everybody, everywhere, was liable to experience it firsthand or to inflict it on others. No wonder that some of my interviewees, like Fahd, for instance, pointed to long periods during which they kept to their houses, met nobody, and were solely "preoccupied by themselves." An encounter with the police, a car accident, or simply the feeling of being under surveillance often pushed them to become downright housecats (*beytutiyin*). Meanwhile, the public spaces of Riyadh were collectively produced as threatening, and most people were reluctant to leave the protective shell of their homes and their cars.

Repression was naturally worse when it came to political dissent. Every Saudi I met during my three years of fieldwork, and with whom the conversation passed the level of banalities, knew at least one person who had been abducted by the security services and was often detained in unknown locations, for an unknown reason and an unknown number of years. According to the Saudi Civil and Political Rights Association, one out of six hundred Saudis was in jail because of their opinions or political activities.[42] Like Sa'b's half-brother and his friends, people simply disappeared one day, and information about them, when available, passed through word of mouth. If you were arrested for minor political reasons – most often a critical comment posted on the Internet or your relationship with another "suspect" – the police had you sign a pledge not to do it again (*ta'ahhud*). A relative would be ushered to the police station, sometimes witnessing your confession before bringing you home, temporarily free and belonging to a bleak category: political suspect. Recidivism and graver offenses were treated with far less leniency. To sign a political petition, demonstrate in the street or be caught in the company of other suspects was punishable by jail time with or without hearing. The prospect of a trial was no less grim than the deprivation of one's rights. As the

Saudi judicial system was based on confession, which was extracted by torture or by threat of torture, physical violence was the true foundation of the law.

Torture and mistreatment loomed large over each encounter with police agents and were used more intensively in political investigations. Sheikh 'Abd al-Ilah described the interrogation sessions he had witnessed during his jail term:

SHEIKH 'ABD AL-ILAH – Interrogations (*tahqiqat*) lasted for about six months....I wasn't tortured myself but I witnessed torture sessions, I visited the places where torture was carried out, I heard the shouts, I heard my friends, my neighbors, some were tortured every night...to extract information....They were particularly harsh on the younger detainees, to have them snitch on their comrades...But everybody could pass in their hands, [one of my colleagues] for instance was submitted to extremely vicious torture sessions, extremely vicious ones! He got the worst treatment...as if they wanted to break his righteousness (*himma*), in a way. He was the only leader [of the opposition movement] to be tortured. But among the youth...most of them have been tortured.

Investigators didn't need to torture everybody, as horrendous stories travelled fast among activists. One ex-activist told me how in the 1990s accounts of torture leaked from the political prison of al-Ha'ir, in the south of Riyadh, and scared him into fleeing to Yemen across the mountains. Two events had particularly unnerved him: prisoners being dragged behind a car until death and others being skinned alive, sewn up, and skinned again. Repression was both gruesome and haphazard, and this uncanny combination of brutality and arbitrariness prompted an extremely tight control of society and individuals.

Repression allowed for a considerable amount of personalization in the relationship between the state and the individual, the psychological effect of which were at least as destructive as impersonal and bureaucratic political violence. In 1993, in the heydays of the protest movement, 'Abd al-Ilah had written a straightforward public letter to Interior Minister Prince Nayef, in which he predicted the end of the royal family's grip over the country, going as far as to quote King 'Abd al-'Aziz's famous saying: "We conquered this country by the sword, only the sword will take it back from us." Whether he remembered this feat or not, Nayef took personal care of the sheikh once he was released and applied for a commercial license:

SHEIKH 'ABD AL-ILAH – When we got out of jail, we realized that the atmosphere had totally changed. The freedom level had decreased in an unbelievable way, everything was completely under control, it was totally depressing. It was like we were in a clogged tunnel.... Police surveillance was very tight, you couldn't even think about any form of religious preaching (*da'wa*)...total control. Surveillance, censorship, travel bans, even work bans. I was banned from working.... I went to the commercial court and applied for a license to open a business. The judge refused without giving a reason. I then sent a friend of mine to ask if anything was wrong, and the judge said: "The case is crystal clear, I can do nothing. If he brings a paper from the secret police (*al-mabahith*), I'll give him his license." I called the director of the secret police, I told him my story, he replied that he had never heard of anything, and that the judge had to write him a letter. I went back to the judge, who refused: "It would be detrimental to my allegiance to the state if I tried to help *someone like you.*" (*Said in a comical tone; we both laugh.*) I informed the director of the secret police and he told me: "Write the Interior Minister" [Prince Nayef, the King's brother]. I sent him a letter, and all I received was a formal order banning me from opening a business, stamped by the secret police. The director of the secret police then told me that I needed to meet the Interior Minister in person. But I had nothing to tell him, why take the pain to meet him? I just wanted my commercial license . . . But the director told me: "You must meet him." So I asked for an audience, which was granted. The atmosphere was conciliatory, and the minister assured me that state security was more important than anything else . . . that state punishments had to be taken seriously . . . Finally, he told me: "See? I give you my permission to open a business. Now go back to the court." And this time, they gave me my license.

The judge had no autonomy: he needed the permission of the secret police to act, and he could jeopardize his career by simply writing an official letter on behalf of an ex-political convict. The director of the secret police himself could not act without an order from the interior minister. The matter had thus to be decided by the personal interaction between Sheikh 'Abd al-Ilah and Prince Nayef, who at the time was the fourth person in the state. The prince reminded the sheikh that state procedures and state security were no light concern: the license application had to go all the way up to his desk, and personal contact overruled other decisions.

Meanwhile, Nayef introduced 'Abd al-Ilah to his network of protégés and clients: the commercial license was traded for a certain degree of political allegiance. The fiefdoms created by senior princes in the second half of the twentieth century were not only of an economic nature and linked to oil rent distribution.[43] They were also political and based on the various repression tools devised by the royal family since the mid-1960s. The outcome was positive for Nayef, who lost a potential opponent and gained an ally in the Islamic activists' community. From 'Abd al-Ilah's point of view, the outcome was mixed: his personal networks now extended to the palace, but he had renounced political opposition.

2.6. Violence and Fun

As I left the sheikh's office, tightly gripping in my hand the notebook in which I had recorded several names and phone numbers, I had the distinct feeling that I was at a turning point in my fieldwork. Confronted with political ambiguities, I surely needed the sheikh's political support. The difficulties I encountered during my fieldwork were not only of a political nature, however. Rereading my field notes, I am struck by the memories of long, empty days and the difficulties of meeting people on an everyday basis. This emptiness and the steady feeling of powerlessness that permeated my days were no accidents in my fieldwork: they were constitutive of it and as such warrant analysis.

"*Al-Riyadh, khara*," "Riyadh, piece of shit," would exclaim two Syrian friends after an excursion to the coast of the Gulf, as the immense grid of avenues emerged in the twilight, a shimmering chessboard nonchalantly dropped on the plateau by some giant. Although Saudi interviewees and informants did not abhor of Riyadh quite as much, they recognized that the city had little to offer if one was not closely connected to the royal family or part of the oil-rent distribution networks that have been analyzed under the rubric of "segmented clientelism"[44] and that some informants, including Sa'b, described as feudal (*iqta'i*). Riyadh was seen as a selective El Dorado where only a handful became rich, while the majority of residents, parsimoniously financed by the state or their employer, struggled to cover astronomic housing, transport and living costs.

Sa'b's cousin was a good example of the difficulties of navigating an opaque economic environment. He had come to Riyadh to work in the armed forces but after a few years had bought two minimarkets that he operated with underpaid imported labor. He had traded in stocks until 9/11, when the markets had become unpredictable. He then retreated to the sheep trade, which according to him was the only business where he could find, in his own words, "risk-taking, trust, and profit" (*tajriba wa thiqa wa rizq*). The sheep trade steadily rewarded entrepreneurship and self-confidence, whereas more "modern" but far less transparent sectors, from real estate to the stock market, were riddled with corruption and nepotism.

The difficulties of finding one's "bread and butter" (*luqmat 'ish*) – in Sa'b's cousin's words – were redoubled by the atomization of society. Riyadh was a gigantic suburb where families and individuals lived scattered in individual houses and small apartment buildings, far away from each other but under the surveillance of the state. In the face of massive state intervention in economic life, from wages, loans, and subsidies to commercial monopolies, tribes had lost their economic raison d'être, which for anthropologists of Bedouin life was to ensure a sustainable livelihood for their members.[45] In Riyadh, besides mosques, malls and roads, there were very few public spaces, and they were tightly monitored. The secret police and the ministry of Islamic affairs controlled the mosques, planting plainclothes officers and informers among the believers and laying off dozens of undesirable imams if necessary. Saudi Arabia was one of the rare Muslim majority countries where, for fear of political mobilization, mosques were closed outside of prayer times. Malls were not more welcoming, and private security companies filtered out and chased bachelors and members of the lower classes. Even streets were repulsive and pedestrian-unfriendly; large and busy, deprived of shade, difficult to cross, their asphalt nearly melting under a scorching sun, they were abandoned to cars, trucks and taxis.

Social segregation expressed itself in various ways, including access to cars (which in the absence of public transportation were key to personal mobility) and housing (most households didn't own their house and had to rent shabby units far away from workplaces). The northwestern parts of the city, elevated and exposed to the northern breeze, were bourgeois and costly whereas the southeast of Riyadh, an area with rapidly decaying neighborhoods built from the 1930s to the 1950s, housed the lower classes and labor migrants. (See Map 2.) Gender segregation was even more pervasive, splitting society into two halves that met only in the intimacy of homes and the high-end work environment of hospitals and some companies. Everywhere else, women and men were not supposed to interact. Wherever there was the slightest possibility of an encounter – in malls, on sidewalks, in cars – women had to be draped from head to toe in a black cloak called *'abaya*, their faces concealed by a *khimar*. Women were subjected to the authority of a male guardian (*mahram*), who was a direct relative. They were officially banned from driving.

A third – generational – segregation divided urban society. Overwhelmed by its own fertility, Saudi society erected barriers between families (*'awa'il*) and bachelors (*'uzzab*), who were commonly perceived as troublemakers, delinquents, and molesters.[46] Real estate companies restricted bachelors – typically rural migrants and students – to housing in certain streets, where two- or three-story cement buildings lined squalid sidewalks. Restaurants, cafes, and malls were systematically divided in two sections, families and bachelors; in many places, young single males

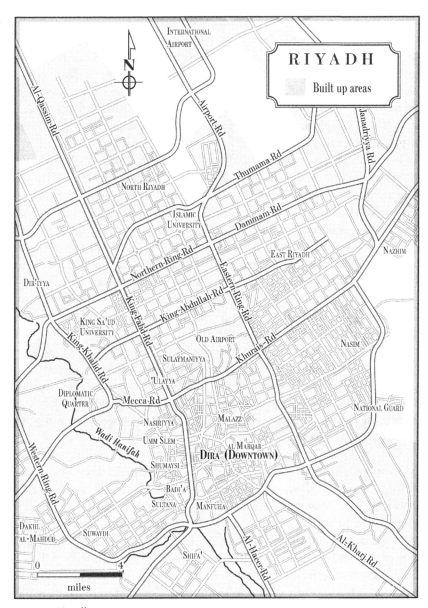

MAP 2. Riyadh.

were simply undesirable. Marriage was a strong divider between reputedly stable families and single males who were feared as unruly and
disruptive. High divorce rates unsettled this picture, but access to women
was still conceived as a pacifying tool. Newlyweds were known to

disappear for months on end, absorbed by their discovery of normative intimacy, and to reappear only with sprouting *kurush* (bellies) and
tamed spirits. I had myself observed handsome, dry-humored, and revolutionary Bjad become, once he got married, an average-looking, calm,
and submissive pater. Part of my own predicament I undoubtedly owned
up to the fact that, notwithstanding the secret police's marital fantasies, I
myself was a bachelor whose professional interest in other people's lives
could easily be misinterpreted as awkward or inappropriate.

I shared my first apartment with Sa'b. We had found a spacious three-
bedroom unit in Sultana, an old neighborhood in the southwest of Riyadh.
Old Sultana, originally an industrial suburb of the city, was a mere succession of workshops and stores where you could buy a variety of presum-
ably stolen car parts, from radios to wheels, bumpers, tires and antennas.
New Sultana, where we lived for six months, was a recent suburb built
along the Wadi Hanifa, a dried riverbed that for millennia had been the
backbone of lower Najd and had now been turned into an environmen-
tally friendly theme park by the Riyadh municipality. Our apartment
overlooked the Wadi, thick with palm trees and gently curving around
the neighborhood of Badi'a across the river. From our windows we could
see old Riyadh, whose twin towers – the Khalidiyya, built in the 1970s –
loomed in the distance, above the lush palm grove that was reportedly
owned by the emirs of Qatar since the eighteenth century. Toward the
north of the city, more recent skyscrapers were often hidden by sandy fog
during the day, and became visible only at night, loaves of iron and glass
glowing above the city.

Our building was reserved for families, but the landowner, Abu
Muhammad, raised the rent by 20 percent and decided that because I was
a Westerner, I was allowed to live in a family apartment. After six months,
however, Abu Muhammad asked us to leave the premises. He coarsely
explained that the families around us had complained about the "disorder" we stirred and the "visits" we received in our apartment, and said
that we had better leave of our own accord before they called the police. I
contended that Sa'b and I hardly ever entertained guests at home and that
because Sa'b was leaving Riyadh, I would be alone in the apartment. We
had never seen our neighbors, and I suspected some misunderstanding.
But he had already made up his mind and I could not talk him out of his
decision. Sa'b had found a job in another university and was about to
leave Riyadh anyway. I decided to move into a smaller apartment, closer
to the central business district and to the King Faisal Center.

This first summer of my fieldwork felt oddly empty and vaguely menacing. I was so broke that I could no longer afford to rent cars, and

borrowed a 1982 Chevy Caprice from a professor at one of Riyadh's universities. He had imported the car from the Midwest in the 1980s and had religiously kept it in his garage ever since, using it from time to time for shopping. On the very day Abu Muhammad expelled us from our apartment, cops pulled me over on King 'Abd Allah Road, as I was driving the vintage Caprice to the center of Riyadh with Sa'b and his cousins. As Sa'b explained to me, they could not understand why a Westerner would want to drive a drug dealer's car in the company of three intimidating Bedouin. Parking the rather conspicuous vehicle in front of the apartment building was probably at least partly responsible for my sudden disgrace among the neighbors.

Sa'b's move coincided with a period of increased hesitation in my work and I soon became overwhelmed with a feeling of isolation and powerlessness. All the information I needed, all the informants I could work with, all the stories I wanted to hear were there, just a phone call away. Yet before I met Sheikh 'Abd al-Ilah, an invisible wall was keeping me away from them. I felt punished for an unknown crime, Tantalus starving an arm's length away from food and water. I could not put a name to the terrible sense of paralysis that gripped me until I heard Sa'b's brother Dhaifallah complain about being *tafshan*. Sa'b had just left Riyadh, and Dhaifallah and I would roam the streets for hours on end in his Toyota. Speeding along the thoroughfares, he would randomly honk his horn and hit the steering wheel with his fists, shouting, *"Ana tufshan!"* (It sucks!).

Being *tufshan* involved not only feeling disgruntled by a specific event. It also related to a whole family of sentiments, encompassed by the noun *tufush*, which literally means "escape" and was used by interviewees to characterize the subtle and incapacitating torpor I recognized as having paralyzed me for months. On January 22, 2006, a year after I settled down in Riyadh and six months after Sa'b left the city, I wrote this short and desperate field note:

I am overwhelmed by a sense of a general loss of time, of *tufush*, of neverending procrastination, that which classical Islamic theology denounces as *irja'*: postponement, expectancy, and fatalism. Yet it is here and now that everything begins, and I will probably regret having lost all this time, all these contacts, all these opportunities.

Dhaifallah's word choice opened unsuspected perspectives. I soon discovered that during the last three decades, *tufush* had become one of the targets of both Saudi sociologists and Islamic activists. Wary of the increased free time that had resulted from the 1973 oil boom and the emergence of a consumer and leisure-based society, sociologists, criminologists, and religious activists were voicing their fears. Convinced that idle hands were doing the devil's work, they had filled pages of reports, scientific articles, and newspaper pieces and had pronounced conferences and sermons on the necessity to find solutions for the terrible emptiness that gripped society.[47] They were looking specifically at younger generations, more likely in their view to misuse their free time (*waqt al-faragh*) and to break down the fabric of society.

Local sociologists usually translated the colloquial form *tufush* into the more standard words *faragh* and *malal*, "vacuum" and "boredom," respectively. This linguistic shift was a source of misunderstandings. The state-funded war on delinquency would focus on idleness without trying to understand what young people meant when they talked of *tufush*. Rather than a psychological void or ennui, *tufush* suggested a feeling of social impotence that overwhelmed ordinary Saudis when they recognized the incommensurable distance between the economic opportunities of Riyadh and their own condition of unemployment or low income, broken families, and poor housing. *Tufush* was better understood as the feeling of being deprived of social or relational capital in a city that could only fulfill every dream if one had a useful connection (*wasta*), a patron, or a godfather. It was the recognition of the invisible wall I so often experienced.

Tufush was also a peculiar notion of time, which "is really experienced only when the quasi-automatic coincidence between expectations and . . . the world which is there to fulfill them is broken,"[48] when one feels a mismatch between subjective hopes and objective chances and is reduced to one's own forces. Being *tufshan* meant to be confronted with the thickness of time, with impossibility as materialized in emptiness, boredom, and desperation. A few weeks after my enlightening conversation with Dhaifallah, Rakan added his own understanding of the notion. Being *tufshan* was to be in one's corner, bored to death, knowing that the city was full of possibilities and realizing that, whoever one could ask for help, these possibilities would remain out of reach. It was the sense of worthlessness that gripped you when you had lived long enough in the capital to have had your efforts and aspirations repeatedly rebuffed. Being *tufshan* was to experience in one's everyday life a sense of the huge "discrepancy between what is anticipated and the logic of the game in relation to which this anticipation was formed, between a 'subjective' disposition . . . and an objective tendency." This discrepancy between one's own abilities and actual opportunities, between ambitions and odds expressed itself in the relation to time and gave rise to "waiting or impatience . . . , regret or nostalgia . . . , boredom or 'discontent' . . . , a dissatisfaction with the present that implies the negation of the present and the propensity to work towards its supersession."[49] *Tufush*, or the awareness of social inadequacy, was a revolutionary sentiment.

Nawwaf, who had participated in street demonstrations in support of political prisoners in 2003 and 2004, analyzed this sentiment as "indifference" (*la mubala*) to the consequences of one's activism. He was recounting his political education, between his male socialization in his family and his curiosity toward the early 1990s reform movement, and mentioned his own ability to ask bold questions and tread in forbidden territory:

PASCAL – And this boldness, this self-confidence, where did they come from?
NAWWAF – From indifference [*min al-la mubala*]. The thing is that the government had this style, it managed to give people the illusion that the secret police were everywhere in society, the illusion that walls had ears. But it isn't true. I would tell people that it was a lie, you see. "Don't believe the government." It is ourselves who created fear.

Nawwaf had grown indifferent to both state propaganda and the consequences of his own actions. Dissatisfied with the situation, having acquired a clearer vision of the competing forces, he used his indifference as a lever and set himself in motion. To explain why he and others took to the streets in 2003, Nawwaf said that "the situation hasn't changed much, it is people's nature that has changed. They became indifferent (*la mubaliyun*), they were like: I don't care." Indifference and carelessness were potent political sentiments and didn't necessarily signify passivity or apathy.

Tufush encompassed the discontent or rage (*ghadhab*) that some of my interviewees, including Fahd or Rakan, were regularly pointing to in our conversations and which resulted of their increased awareness of their social and political surroundings and of their own fragile position within them. Rage overwhelmed young Saudis when they realized that Riyadh, the wealthiest city of the Middle East, where all dreams could come true and all projects could be achieved, was regulated by favoritism and bribery. This sensation of social impotence was not an incapacitating feeling, however, and the realization of being socially expendable was actually a liberating experience.

Still in his car, I had asked Dhaifallah to elaborate on the difference between *tufush* and boredom. "Boredom (*malal*) means a vacuum, it means nonexistence," he said, whereas "*tufush* is what drives you to do anything and everything. It is what pushes you to become a *'arbaji*, a hooligan." According to a satirical anonymous text circulating on the web and entitled "Escapism in the Science of Hooliganism," *tufush* was what makes you "sell the entire world for the price of a bicycle wheel," and "deal with the whole universe as if it was a cigarette butt and step on it."[50] *Tufush* was the reckless laughter of one who cares for no one and nothing, a radical attitude that Sa'b, Bjad and Dhaifallah had repeatedly displayed in sign of independence and high spirits. It was a feat of destructive humor, which "is not directed against isolated negative aspects of reality" but targets "the finite world as a whole."[51]

Tufush wasn't specific to Saudi Arabia or to the early twenty-first century. It was similar to the "free and easy . . . desperado philosophy" bred by the *Pequod*'s whalemen in Herman Melville's *Moby Dick*. Far away from all humans, surrounded by the perils of the open sea and forced to follow their leader's foolish pursuit of the white whale, their "odd sort of wayward mood" came along with their "extreme tribulation" and "in the very midst of [their] earnestness:" "There are certain queer times and occasions in this strange mixed affair we call life when a man takes this whole universe for a vast practical joke, though the wit thereof he but dimly discerns, and more than suspects that the joke is at nobody's expense but his own."[52]

Tufush was a specimen of Melville's "general joke": a realization that the world was meaningless and risible. According to the origin of the word, it meant the random movements of a drowning man trying to escape his somber fate. *Tufush* was the last burst of the drowning man, a way to express one's ultimate detachment and humor while risking being swallowed up and overcome. My informants were not onboard a three-mast ship chasing the white whale. They were living in Riyadh and struggling with their very own Leviathan. As I followed their tribulations, the city itself, with its thoroughfares, its neighborhoods, and its sidewalks, its somber moods, and its fits of rebellion, had become a central character in my work.

3

City of the Future

A city made for speed is made for success.

– Le Corbusier

3.1. Saudi Suburbia

Another rest house, another *shilla* of young Saudis hanging out in a tent in the east of Riyadh. Half a dozen men in their early thirties were watching a soccer game on a old television set in a small room covered with a grubby carpet and littered with tin plates and plastic cups. Outside, a brief and dramatic winter storm was pummeling the volleyball field directly in front of the tent.

After months of wandering about, and thanks to Sheikh 'Abd al-Ilah's help, I had eventually fallen in with a group of Islamic activists, young professors, and lawyers with whom I had more in common than field-work: as a former philosophy teacher, I somehow belonged to the family. Thamer, my main contact in the group, taught religion in high school and we often reflected on the similarities between Islamic studies in Saudi Arabia and high school philosophy in France. Both disciplines were crucial to the identity of a strong centralized state that used ideology to assert its own authority. Both were often reduced to pedantic and dry catechisms, inflicted on crowded classrooms of overwhelmingly bored and sneering students, under the distant gaze of the ministry's inspectors. Thamer valiantly tried to turn his courses into lessons on freethinking and liberty, introducing the students to novel ways of dealing with the sacred texts and reading with them authors who, like Malika Oufkir and Naguib Mahfuz, were considered deviant by mainstream Islamists.

A friend of Thamer's rushed into the tent, shaking the rainwater from his robe, a stack of paper in his hand. After quick salutations, he showed us what he had discovered that day: a friend working downtown had given him a copy of a rare document, the official act by which the king had granted one of his brothers a huge stretch of land north of Riyadh, near the town of Banban. The city was expanding northward and the real estate market was thriving thanks to booming oil prices, a sustained demand for housing and easy access to state-guaranteed loans. The northern lands represented the future of Riyadh and the new owner would probably acquire a colossal fortune in the years to come. "Those lands could accommodate the whole population of Kuwait," commented someone. The motivations for the royal decree were obscure. Did the king want to compensate his brother for a political or economic loss? Was he paying back an old debt or honoring an old promise? He had given him such an amazing opportunity that various social circles in Riyadh were probably buzzing with the news.

The situation was not in itself novel: since the creation of the country in 1932, princes were regularly endowed with political and economic fiefdoms by their primus inter pares, the king. The Saudi economy was organized along a series of captive markets and commercial monopolies, of which senior princes took the lion's share with impunity. The Al Sa'ud had earned the nickname of Al Shubuk ("the fences") for the hundreds of miles of wires they had deployed in the middle of nowhere to keep intruders and developers off their empty lands. The fences represented the future wealth of royal absentee landowners, who eagerly followed the evolution of the urban growth and waited for the time the city's sprawl would reach their properties. In the absence of a free press or of political checks and balances, word of mouth was the only available source of information. If the whole country was the business of the Al Sa'ud family, its inner workings were as elusive and discussed as a family secret.

Sighing at the ease with which princes got away with nepotism and corruption, someone mentioned the second caliph of Islam, 'Umar b. al-Khattab, celebrated for his frugality and for curbing the power of the Meccan aristocracy.[1] Hearing the second caliph's name, Thamer dryly commented: "*Those* were true Arabs." One of his friends, in utter disbelief, silently gestured as if to wave away disheartening thoughts. "What can we do against this, really?" asked the latecomer, who had unsettled the peaceful soccer evening with his depressing piece of news. Nobody answered. After an embarrassed silence, someone raised the volume of the television again and the gathering quietly went back to normal.

The legal documents he had brought with him, however important, were of no use: they could not be published in any of the local newspapers, which belonged to the royal family. They could not be posted on the web because the secret police, using the IP address of his computer, would soon track down the author, threatening and harassing their way through his networks of friends and relatives if necessary. One could only start a rumor, drop it like a bucket of water on arid soil, and hope that something, no matter how tiny or irrelevant, would grow out of it.

Peering at the princes' business through the thick decorum that surrounded the royal family, knowing what they were doing, and yet being totally powerless to act on it: this subtle form of despair epitomized what *tufush* was about. As a result of his own fits of desolation, Thamer would regularly bury himself in work or isolate himself at home for several months in a row, acting as if the whole world had suddenly fallen off its axis. Then one day he would reemerge, smiling softly and, slightly embarrassed, tell a tale of how busy he had been with his family. Because he was divorced and the only son of a middle-class couple living in northern Riyadh, the pretext did not hold up well. He knew it and would apologetically put the blame on his tribal identity: "We are like that in my tribe: *mizajiyin*, moody, mercurial." The truth was easier to tell, if not to confess: he had been irrepressibly *tufshan*.

In this chapter I tell the story of the transformation of Riyadh from a snug pedestrian city into an open-ended and car-centered suburbia shaped by princes, planners, and developers. Contrary to the narrative of development promoted by the Saudi state, this transformation was not a peaceful and linear evolution but a fast-paced and dramatic shift marked by conflicts and expulsions. Until the 1960s the city had grown organically, like the peels of an onion, through the addition of neighborhoods around its core, signaled by the Fort Musmak, the grand mosque and the central market. (See Map 3.) In a few years, between the late 1970s and the early 1980s, Riyadh suddenly leaped far beyond its limits and left the banks of the Wadi Batha and the Wadi Hanifa, two dry riverbeds between which the walled city was contained since the eighteenth century. Whole neighborhoods were emptied of their inhabitants, who moved en masse to the north and the east of the old city, in tract houses that had been organized in superblocks along a grid of perpendicular six-lane highways. In the north of the city, where the king's brother had received his royal handout and where I had been following 'Ajib for a night, developers and car drifters were the masters of the game: developers were constructing

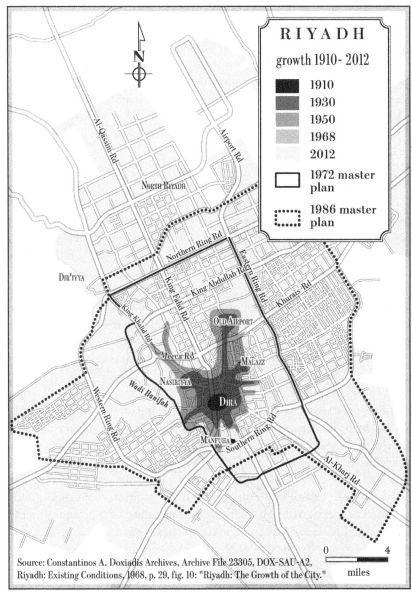

MAP 3. Riyadh Growth 1910–2012.

miles of straight asphalt that drifters used as a playground, far away from
people's eyes, private security guards, and police patrols.

This leap to suburbia left behind the winding, shaded lanes, graceful
mud-brick houses and crowded markets of the old Riyadh, which were
progressively populated by Arab, African, and Asian labor migrants. (See

FIGURE 3.1. Street scene in downtown Riyadh, 1968 (Constantinos A. Doxiadis Archives,[2] copyright © Constantinos and Emma Doxiadis Foundation).

Figure 3.1.) In his novel *Crossroads of Darkness*, Muhammad al-Muzaini follows the trajectory of a young man who in the 1970s joins the Islamic movements and trades friends and family for the "absolute subordination to the religious sheikh."[3] Toward the end of the novel, frustrated with the sheikh's authoritarianism, he leaves the religious group and comes back to his father's house, only to find the neighborhood in a state of turmoil. The municipality is opening new streets and compensating those homeowners who lost their dwelling. People are leaving for the north of Riyadh. Banks are offering loans, and blueprints are exhibited, contemplated, and commented on in the old city's courtyards and alleys. Peering at the plans his father proudly displays, the narrator realizes that his time with the Islamic group kept him away from the development of the city, a manifold event that proves more decisive and eventful than his own "attraction to the Brothers."

On the night of his return, he is awakened by shouts and cries: one of their neighbors has been murdered and it turns out that the culprit is none other than the victim's brother:

Here's the story: the man had sentenced his own brother to death and he slew him at a close distance from his house.... He wanted to avenge himself because of his brother's purchase of an old nondescript house, which was among the many whose owners were entitled to compensation. The view of the money that poured into his brother's pocket like a flood filled him with anger: it would lead his brother from sorrow, hunger and destitution to a world of youthfulness, health and brilliance. These wicked thoughts could not part his mind and he was eager to shed blood ... He stabbed his brother to death and ran away.[4]

In the street, as he witnesses the neighbors' distress and follows the police's investigation, the narrator comes to understand "the meaning of the blue lines on [his] father's glossy plans":

They were part of a master plan for a future in which men would become exhausted and indifferent, a future that planted in their minds disgraceful desires, prompted by appetites long suppressed and only recently unearthed. I asked my brother about the houses whose owners were compensated. He told me that our house was one of them and he started counting the other houses, the closed and silent homes that had been deserted by their inhabitants. The huge, monstrous void that people had left behind hissed under the wind's caress ... Neighborhoods die. They are slain just like that guy's brother.... People's stories vanished ... as they are waiting for the exodus, waiting for the compensation committee with their plans that enclosed promises of unexpected riches.[5]

In the last pages of the novel, 'Ayyush, an old woman who refuses to leave (and whose very name means "alive"), witnesses the destruction of the neighborhood and of her own house. She sees the multiple colors of everyday life vanish, day after day, into the faded brown of the mud bricks. She takes refuge in a room left untouched by the bulldozers and is eventually swallowed, after a torrential winter rain, by a mud flood.

In my research, the life and death of Riyadh's neighborhoods similarly took precedence over my initial interest in Islamic groups. A tiny market town in the first years of the twentieth century, Riyadh was probably now, after Cairo and Baghdad, the third-most-populated city of the Arab world and a major commercial and political hub. With more than 5 million inhabitants, it was by far the most populated city of the Arabian Peninsula. An imported workforce had turned it into a remarkably diverse city, with Bangladeshi, European, Egyptian, Filipino, Indian,

Lebanese, Pakistani, North American, and Yemeni neighborhoods, ethnic restaurants and markets, underground churches and temples, and hidden discos, bars, and brothels. Its streets and highways, night after night, were the theater of a car insurgency of sorts. It is car drifting that sparked my interest in the way the city had been designed and its infrastructure built.

Unlike Cairo and Baghdad, Riyadh was not located on a major waterway: sprawling on the isolated limestone plateau of Najd, the city was far from the coasts and the Wadi Hanifa would remain dry save for a few days every year, when winter storms caused flash floods that swept the riverbed. Like the most recent U.S. cities, Riyadh was connected to the world through its airports, its railroad and its highways. The transarabian highway that ran from the Red Sea to the Persian Gulf bisected the capital and operated as a border between its oldest neighborhoods to the south and the new city to the north. Named "Mecca Road" in the West and "Khurais Road" in the East, it crossed King Fahd Road, the main North-South axis of the city, in a huge cloverleaf interchange. This was the geographical center of Riyadh, busy with cars and trucks rushing in all directions. The interlacement of overpasses and tunnels had been named Midan al-Qahira (Cairo Square), although it wasn't what urban planners called a square and was far removed from Cairo's thriving public spaces. Quartered by roads running from the Red Sea to the Gulf and from the Mediterranean to the Indian Ocean, its center empty but for the swishing of vehicles, Riyadh was now a city on the highway, designed for the car and made for speed.

3.2. Doxiadis and Containment Urbanism

Riyadh's extension was planned between 1968 and 1972 by a Greek architect, Constantinos A. Doxiadis (1913–1975). "The first global urban planner" according to Rem Koolhaas,[6] Doxiadis had already designed Islamabad, parts of Karachi and Baghdad, al-Bayda (Libya), Tema (Ghana), and Eastwick (Pennsylvania) when the Saudi interior ministry commissioned him to design the master plan of Riyadh. The document was published in July 1971, two years before the 1973 oil boom triggered an unprecedented bonanza in the country and irreversibly modified the Saudi system of power. Revised and adapted after the boom, the Doxiadis master plan formed the backbone of Riyadh's development and provided most of the notions central to the organization of the city's space, in particular the central open-ended axis, the superblocks, and the modernist idea, borrowed from Le Corbusier, that successful cities were designed for rapid traffic and speed.

Born in 1913 in Bulgaria to Greek parents, a few years after the country's independence from the Ottoman Empire, Doxiadis emigrated with his family to Athens when he was a toddler. Doxiadis's father, Apostolos Doxiadis, became the minister of relief in 1922 and was given the task of organizing the reintegration of 1.5 million Greek refugees fleeing from Asia Minor after the fall of the Ottoman Empire and the Turkish-Greek war. In the 1930s, Constantinos (he went by "Dinos" among friends and family) studied architecture in Berlin and started his career in Athens as an architect and urban planner. He built himself a reputation during World War II in the resistance to the Italian occupation of Greece. It is reportedly during his wanderings on the Albanian front that he first formulated his idea of "ekistics" (the "science of human settlements"), a neologism by which he meant that urban planning had to be less dependent on architecture, its stars, and its fads; more open to the social and natural sciences; and closer to social and economic planned development.[7] Deemed a science and no longer a technique or an art, urban planning was taken out of the public debate and confided to the rule of experts.

After the war, his approach was criticized by fellow architects and urban planners as "mystique," "clichéd," or "salesmanship."[8] Yet his role in the post–World War II reconstruction of Greece and his links with the World Bank, Harvard University, and the Ford Foundation ensured that his ideas had a steady international audience. In 1945 he became the Greek deputy minister of reconstruction, in charge of the aid provided by the Marshall plan to the country. In the post–World War II years, he was already a partisan of self-help housing and homegrown solutions instead of costly public programs, a position that he would defend during most of his career as an urban planner. He advocated a pro-U.S., rural Greece whose population should be kept in the countryside to avoid urban growth and to limit economic, social, and political crises.

In 1953, Doxiadis created his own architectural and urban planning practice, Doxiadis Associates (DA). It gained a worldwide reputation for its urban planning operations, which were inexpensive, attentive to basic needs and used an attractive vocabulary of low-rise buildings, pedestrian paths, and urban parks. DA was particularly active in the Middle East, the region at the border of the Western and the Eastern blocks, where he collaborated with the United Nations and the World Bank on housing, reconstruction and urban planning programs in Syria, Jordan, Iraq, Lebanon, Iran, Pakistan, Saudi Arabia, Sudan, and Libya. Doxiadis's most celebrated projects were the 1958 master plan of Baghdad and the creation of Islamabad, the new capital of Pakistan, in the 1960s.[9]

For the *New Yorker*, his Greek background made him a convenient agent of pro-U.S. overseas development. "Free of the imperialist stigma" attached to North American and Western European experts, he was nevertheless running "his firm with northern (or 'western') efficiency."[10] His projects were closely followed by U.S. media outlets, in particular NBC and the *New York Times*, probably because, from the turbulent borders of the Western world in Iraq, Iran, and Pakistan to the racial frontiers of Eastwick (Pennsylvania)[11] and Detroit, urban planning operations were crucial to the definition of American identity as a hegemonic power.

Extremely controversial for his involvement in Cord War urban containment strategies, Doxiadis was more productive as an urbanist than Le Corbusier or Walter Gropius, his celebrated colleagues at the Congrès International d'Architecture Moderne (CIAM). Whereas Le Corbusier adopted an artistic and sophisticated persona from his Parisian atelier, Doxiadis projected the more reassuring image of a manager and an engineer. He believed that the city of tomorrow was to be built by Anglo-Saxon science and technique, not by Francophone inspiration and pose.

Doxiadis was primarily concerned with rural migrations and the political consequences of rapid urban growth. In the Middle East in particular, he promoted a containment urbanism that would lead urban dwellers to happiness. "Healthy, happy cities create healthy, happy people," he wrote in a 1959 letter to the Ford Foundation.[12] His planning efforts were seen in the United States as preventing rural migrants to cities from falling into cultural alienation and politicization and as ensuring the stability of conservative political regimes. He himself saw his work as creating "for the less developed nations a way of life and a pattern of thought that would lead them to 'identify themselves with the West'."[13] Urban planning would prevent urban unrest by raising standards of living, creating the conditions for prosperity and fostering the development of consumption-based economies.

In 1950s Baghdad, with the help of Egyptian architect Hasan Fathi, Doxiadis designed cozy neighborhoods for the Iraqi lower classes, adorned with "gossip squares" that were intended to "promote social cohesion by recreating a village environment."[14] These urban hamlets were celebrated by the *New York Times* as anticommunist devices: recreating "the close family and tribal relationship the rural Arab knew in this ancestral home" [*sic*], they were supposed to prevent his "conversion by communist agents."[15] Urban villages were less susceptible to allow for the constitution of an Iraqi proletariat.

Iraqi elites thought that Doxiadis's housing projects would not only thwart social unrest but also showcase the modernity of the Iraqi institutions and promote "a welfare state able to rival the Communist developmental model."[16] Meanwhile, a gridded plan of wide and straight avenues scattered the inhabitants in dispersed, low-density superblocks along the Tigris, making it easier for the state to monitor and control urban spaces. The very year Doxiadis's plan for Baghdad was published, the Iraqi monarchy was overthrown by a nationalist coup. A neighborhood planned by DA would be built by the new regime after the Greek consultant left Iraq and christened Madinat al-tawra (Revolution City), before being renamed "Saddam City" and, lately, "Sadr City." In Iraq not more than in Greece Doxiadis's urban design helped prevent later unrest.

After his assignment in Baghdad, Doxiadis participated in the Harvard Pakistan Project, an economic planning mission cofunded by Harvard University and the Ford Foundation. In 1959 the government of Ayub Khan commissioned DA to create the country's new capital. The "Abode of Islam" (Islamabad) was to succeed Karachi, deemed too "Indian" and not "Pakistani" enough to preside over the destiny of the newly created nation.[17] The master plan Doxiadis swiftly delivered in May 1960 was titled "The City of the Future" and showcased the main concepts of his urban planning theory. The city was no longer static, but mobile: renamed by Doxiadis "Dynapolis," the contemporary city had to be planned to avoid congestion and other growth issues.

Whereas "the static city of the past" didn't need to accommodate mobility and growth, contemporary cities grew from a center that was gradually choked by overuse and growing traffic. The "ideal Dynapolis" would be "a parabolic settlement," built around a central spine that could grow indefinitely and serve as the administrative and commercial lifeline of the whole community. (See Figure 3.2.) Not tied to an old core, the "city of the future...can expand and always be ready to create a new center and new neighborhoods."[18] "Dynapolis" was to the static city what a do-it-yourself kit is to a finished item. Even after the foreign experts had left the country, it was susceptible to expansion by planners, developers, and bureaucrats.

Doxiadis's idea of a "dynamic city" answered the preoccupations of the sociologists of the school of Chicago, in particular those of Ernest

from the static city to the ideal Dynapolis

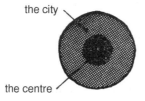

a. the static city of the past

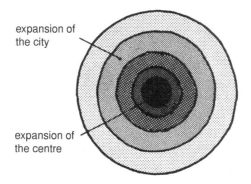

b. the static city which now grows into a Dynapolis

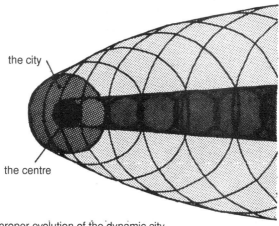

c. proper evolution of the dynamic city
   the ideal Dynapolis is a parabolic settlement
   with uni-directional growth.

FIGURE 3.2. "From the static city to the ideal Dynapolis" (Constantinos A. Doxiadis Archives,[19] copyright © Constantinos and Emma Doxiadis Foundation).

Burgess, who in his canonic essay on "The Growth of the City" studied the spatial consequences of urban development. As the city center ("the loop") grows, the surrounding areas are increasingly devoted to traffic and mobility. This "zone in transition," located between the center and the residential periphery, attracts to its slums various outsiders, "migrants" and "hobos." Mobility is the "pulse of the community" and the engine of growth; but where it is the greatest, social organization breaks down and "areas of demoralization, of promiscuity, and of vice" develop.[20] Doxiadis shared Burgess's diagnosis and decided to accommodate mobility instead of fighting it. The center would become mobile and grow along with the city. The city around the loop was replaced by the city along the motorway.

The second notion that Doxiadis fully developed in his master plan for Islamabad was the "human sector" or "superblock," a notion already implemented in Iraq. The domination of car traffic made it necessary to reaffirm the human scale. The notion of city block was to Doxiadis a notion of the past, and had to be replaced by the idea of sectors or superblocks that were closed to through car traffic and designed around pedestrian circulation. On both sides of the central spine, sectors would be self-contained 1.2 miles squares, and each resident would be able to reach their center, with its services, schools, and shops, in less than fifteen minutes on foot. Established on the human scale, the superblock was to be surrounded on all sides by highways. Cars were a necessity, "but we must separate man and his car"[21] in the space of the city, protect islands of human traffic in the ocean of mechanized circulation, and isolate the scale of the machine and the scale of man.[22]

Along with Le Corbusier's Chandigarh and Lucio Costa's Brasilia, Islamabad was a high modernist city, that is, a city engineered from above, away from public debates, by a coterie of urban planners whose function, in Doxiadis's eyes, was similar to that of a "strong conductor ... responsible for everything within Islamabad."[23] Yet Doxiadis's modernism was more sophisticated that the dystopian visions of his elders. Whereas Le Corbusier and Costa advocated the death of the street and of the square, replaced by roads, highways, and mammoth esplanades, Doxiadis sought to restore the human scale within the city's sectors, by way of "gossip squares," as in Baghdad, or of shaded pedestrian streets, as in Islamabad. A second difference with Le Corbusier arose from his precise observation of local architectural and urban practices, disregarded by modernism as backward or a thing of the past ("the donkey's path" in Le Corbusier's parlance). Unlike the formalist designs of

Le Corbusier and Oscar Niemeyer, Doxiadis's high modernism aimed at picturesqueness and *couleur locale*.

The master plan of Islamabad was criticized on several accounts. As in Brasilia, far from encompassing the whole spectrum of the capital's residents, the plan didn't provide for low-income housing. The City of the Future was, ironically, also a city of slums, a situation that was heightened by the fact that construction workers were housed in temporary camps with substandard conditions of life. Several shantytowns sprouted within the grid, whereas neighboring Rawalpindi, where Doxiadis's plan was never implemented, became a sprouting informal city.[24] Like the cities built by the British in imperial India, Islamabad reproduced the dichotomy between the indigenous town: Rawalpindi, with its informality, its disorder, and its noise, and the imported capital, with its wide avenues, its silence, and its hierarchical space. Separated by a green belt and by army barracks, both cities were linked by a highway, which prompted the bon mot: "Islamabad is five minutes from Pakistan."[25]

His work in Islamabad gave Doxiadis an edge in an Islamic world that, in the 1960s, was looking for an identity, between the perceivable U.S. interest in seeing a conservative front emerging on the southern border of the Soviet bloc and the postcolonial affirmation of nations such as Pakistan and Saudi Arabia. It is Albert J. Meyer, the administrator of the Harvard Pakistan Project, who recommended Doxiadis to the Saudi royal family in 1962. Visiting Riyadh for the State Department's Agency for International Development (USAID) program, Meyer mentioned Doxiadis's name during a conversation with the Saudi Finance Minister, Prince Musa'id bin 'Abd al-Rahman, one of King Sa'ud's uncles. Musa'id wanted to invest in a "municipal development program" and a "country-wide master plan," as well as help Riyadh "improve . . . its public image."[26] Dramatic urban growth and massive rural migration had put municipal planning and urban security high on the royal family's developmental agenda, immediately after water, agriculture, roads, and education.

After his conversation with Musa'id, Meyer reported to the State Department that, "despite [the] usual Saudi obstacles, [there was some] enthusiasm for development," which was "partially genuine" and "partially [due to the] fear [of] Nasser and Arab socialism." Meyer argued that, in urban planning as in economic development, an appropriate course of action was to involve "private institutions backstopped by [the] US government."[27] In a special report to USAID, Meyer explained that "in Iraq, too strong alignment with the Nuri government [which was overthrown in 1958] was fatal to the US assistance effort."[28] None of this was to be ventured in Saudi Arabia, and Doxiadis Associates, along with private institutions such as Harvard University, the Ford Foundation, or the American University of Cairo, were to step forward.

It took five years for DA to get a foot in the door and secure a contract with the Saudi government, despite the Greeks' readiness to accept all kinds of jobs, from the construction of airports, silos, hotels, and military cities to the design of campuses and water and agricultural systems. The first representative of DA in the country, 'Abd al-Mun'im al-'Aqil, was arguably King Sa'ud's personal bodyguard, and created a trade company after his royal patron was overthrown in 1964 by his half-brother Faisal. After the coup, his relations with the deposed monarch seem to have been an obstacle to his performances as an intermediary, and in 1966 Doxiadis found a more efficient intermediary in the person of Jordanian General 'Ali Abu Nuwar. A businessman with extensive connections, he had succeeded Glubb Pasha as head of the Arab Legion and had himself attempted a coup in 1957 against the young king Hussein of Jordan. Abu Nuwar introduced Doxiadis to 'Abd Allah al-Sudayri, the Saudi deputy interior minister for municipal affairs. After Abu Nuwar agreed on an emolument of 2 percent of DA's remuneration for his services, Doxiadis signed the contract for the Riyadh master plan on Christmas Day, 1967.[29]

As in Islamabad, Doxiadis envisioned the transformation of Riyadh into yet another "City of the Future," a title that soon adorned the cover of glossy Saudi publications.[30] His team of architects, planners, and economists moved to Riyadh in the first weeks of 1968, where they opened an office in the recently built al-Malazz neighborhood. Very soon, however, the DA team was asked to join a task far less noble than their survey of Riyadh's existing conditions. Just like dozens of urban renewal projects, the story of Riyadh's master plan began with an episode of eviction and deportation.

3.3. Bedouin Removal

They say: "If we return to the City, the strongest will expel from there the weakest."

– Koran 63:8

On February 22, 1968, a month after his arrival in Riyadh, one of Doxiadis's employees, Nicolas Efessios, alerted his colleagues in Athens of an unexpected issue, "the removal of some 60,000 Bedouins from

FIGURE 3.3. A slum on 'Asir Road, in the southeast of Riyadh, in 1968 (Constantinos A. Doxiadis Archives,[31] copyright © Constantinos and Emma Doxiadis Foundation).

settlements in areas...North-East of Petromin to more suitable locations."[32] Prince Salman bin 'Abd al-'Aziz, the governor of the Riyadh province since 1963 and the capital's strongman,[33] wanted to send the "Bedouin" back to the desert, where a special ghetto would be built for them. Because the city counted around 300,000 inhabitants, the Saudi administration was in fact preparing for the deportation of one-fifth of Riyadh's population.

Categorization of the outcasts wasn't clear, however. Although the administrative literature of the time depicts them as "Bedouin," they most likely came from settled as well as nomadic background and were "people coming from the countryside,"[34] the epithet of "Bedouin" denoting their otherness and the vague threat they evoked among urban dwellers. Riyadh's residents would cast Bedouin as out-of-place, unruly, and untrustworthy,[35] a set of stereotypes that has survived to this day. More important, they were residing in slums located in the very areas that showed the sharpest increase in land value. (See Figure 3.3.) The city was expanding to the north, in the direction of Petromin (the General Organization of Petroleum and Minerals), the royal palace, and the airport. The immense stretches of arid wasteland around Riyadh acquired a value, and slums slowed the maturation of the real estate market. The Riyadh municipality was ordered to clear these highly profitable lands and to open the way to bulldozers. As a preliminary task to the planning of the new Riyadh, the Greek consultants were to lend a hand in the cleaning up.

From their first assignment in 1967 until the late 1970s, the Greek experts periodically advised the government on its "Bedouin development policy," a euphemism devised in 1975 by the Saudi interior ministry to refer to measures aimed at controlling the rural populations and turning them into productive and subservient citizens.[36] For months on end the deportation and housing project would be a thorn in the planners' side. The project was followed closely by the main princes of the royal family and put the DA team, from the very first days of their presence in Riyadh, under a close and probably unwanted scrutiny. During conversations with DA experts, Salman pointed to a relocation site a dozen miles southeast of the city, not far from a camp of the National Guard and under the polluted wind of a cement factory.[37] The Riyadh municipality, headed by a minor Al Sa'ud prince, 'Abd al-'Aziz Al Thunayyan, was apparently less confident than Salman and asked the Greeks to "examine the suitability of the site." A month after it started working in Riyadh, the DA team was already ensconced in a family quarrel.

The issue was thorny for yet another reason: it challenged the urban planners' modernist assumptions. In the 1950s and 1960s, slum removal and collective housing schemes were one of the ways through which planners engaged in urban renewal in places such as the United States, Western Europe, or South America. Doxiadis's team agreed on the necessity to remove the slums from the central areas of the city, where land prices were on the rise and new avenues were planned, and to find alternative housing solutions for their inhabitants. But they were also uncomfortable with Salman's idea of purely and simply deporting the Bedouin outside of the city proper. A solution had to be found within the city's limits.

Areas of unauthorized shacks and ramshackle temporary dwellings have rapidly increased during the last years in Riyadh. Main concentrations of these can be found north of the Petromin, west of the ministries along Mataar [Airport] road, northwest of Nassiriyah [the royal palace] and south of Omar ben Khattab road. Others exist southwest of ['Asir] road and east of Manfuhah, near the manufacturing areas, as well as in smaller clusters in other sectors of the city. Most of these shacks are of recent construction and have been put up by people migrating to the capital from agricultural areas and desert oases.... These dwellings, of which a large number are unauthorized..., are the cause of unhealthy conditions and unrest. They definitely bring serious problems to the development, servicing and management of the city. Substandard housing poses a major problem to the city and should be solved. The replacement of this category of housing must be foreseen in a rational way related to employment possibilities thus providing for the integration of the new communities within the city structure.[38]

The Greeks agreed on the fact that slums were "the cause of unhealthy conditions and unrest" and had to be cleared (they didn't explain how unrest manifested itself, however). Yet they opposed Salman's deportation plan on hygienic, social, and economic grounds. On July 18, 1968, they visited the proposed site with an employee of the capital's Town Planning Office and concluded that because it was "adversely affected from the dust of the cement factory,"[39] the site was unsuitable for housing. According to the modernist idea of zoning, or the separation in space of the city's diverse function (housing, commerce, industries, administration, culture, etc.), industrial areas couldn't be confused with residential areas. A few months later, they developed this argument in a letter to Deputy Interior Minister 'Abd Allah al-Sudayri:

It is not advisable to allow the creation of a residential community within an area of manufacturing and industrial uses. [It] would result first in improper and unhealthy living conditions for its residents and in their physical and social isolation within an alien environment. Second, it would cause an artificial increase of land prices... The adequate integration of the new settlers... require[s] that the selected site... should... be properly related to employment areas, it should be satisfactorily covered by existing central civic services and should not be isolated from similar residential sectors of the city. It is therefore indicated that the new residential community for the establishment of Bedouin population in the area of Riyadh should not be set within the anticipated industrial areas.[40]

In the experts' view, functional segregation (between residential and industrial zones, for instance) was not to be confused with social segregation (between various classes or income groups). Residential areas had to be diverse enough to allow for an integration of several groups. The Greeks thus devised a middle-of-the-road solution: removing the slums from the central areas of Riyadh and displacing their inhabitants, but only to rehouse them within the city limits.

Although principled, the experts' intervention did not change much to Salman's project. They called for the creation of low-cost housing communities east and west of the Dirab Road, which connected Riyadh to Upper Najd, to Mecca and Jeddah, in the Shifa' and Shubra areas, in places which were adjacent to previously built areas but still removed from other residential neighborhoods. The "Limited Income Neighborhood"

(*hayy al-dakhl al-mahdud*), which during my fieldwork was known as a
Bedouin area, a high-crime zone, and a *tafhit* stronghold, was eventually
planned in the late 1970s by the French firm that upgraded Doxiadis's
master plan.[41]

In the east of Riyadh, a few other neighborhoods similarly accommodated rural migrants, including the stern housing project bearing the
bucolic name of Nasim (the breeze), which was planned in the mid-1970s
and was even more peripheral, at a distance from both the city center and the new residential neighborhoods. Bedouin residents and rural
newcomers were politically isolated, socially singled out and spatially
marginalized in ghetto-like areas, which resulted in durable economic rel-
egation. By that time, however, the Greeks had washed their hands from
any involvement in Bedouin displacement and rehousing schemes. As the
"Bedouin issue" repeatedly resurfaced, consuming the experts' time and
energy, an order came down in 1969 from DA's head office in Athens,
enjoining them to keep their distances, unless a "separate assignment"
and a new contract were negotiated with the interior ministry.[42]

In late 1960s Riyadh, displacing populations was a novelty. Until then,
the state had tended to legalize informal neighborhoods and to grant
formal land titles to their residents. The story of the shacks that had
sprouted up west of the Nasiriyya royal palace is characteristic of the
way the slum issue was dealt with before the urban renewal projects of
the late 1960s. "Built of mud and wood" on plots with no legal status,
the Nasiriyya slum was inhabited "by officers, soldiers and workers"
who worked in the palace area. In 1961, King Sa'ud himself formally
granted the lands to its residents and created a "committee comprising
a representative of HRH head of the National Guard, a representative
of the royal properties and an engineer to define the number of plots,
[their] owners and sizes, and see [that] no harm or disorder occur in
Nassiriya."

The committee decided that the informal constructions "cause[d] no
harm in Nasiriyah." Its members recommended that, for the sake of both
security and aesthetics, a tree-lined road be built between the palace and
the slum, and decided that "the height of all the buildings must not exceed
the height of the [palace] wall." When granted a plot, residents would
have to build "good looking buildings"; as for "wood and mud houses,"
they were composing "a bad scenery to the communities" and therefore
had to be "eliminated." Slum residents were not expelled, but were asked
to upgrade their dwellings with the help of the royal palace. The gesture
was part of King Sa'ud's series of good-will policies toward the tribes and

the army, and was characteristic of an era during which the city grew organically around its core, with no central planning or policing.

After Faisal's 1964 coup, the palace's attitude toward slums drastically changed. The new king and his entourage envisioned several development plans whose prime effect was to increase the distance between the state and ordinary Saudis. The city of Riyadh had to be organized around economic and strategic concerns, and the day-to-day arrangements of the past were broken. The administrators implementing the 1961 land compromise were also dragging their feet. In 1968, seven years after the lands had been formally granted to the residents by the previous King, the Minister of the Interior, Prince Fahd bin 'Abd al-'Aziz,[43] was still in the process of requesting lists of dwellings, building sizes, and owners from the municipality of Riyadh. At this point, the Greek experts were once again asked to step in and assess the slum situation. A report sent in 1970 from the Town Planning Office to deputy interior minister 'Abd Allah al-Sudayri sums up the advices they gave to the ministry:

1. It is possible that Nasiriya becomes a main governmental and diplomatic mission center . . . 2. It is not advisable [to leave] these kiosks and mud houses on [al-Ma'zhar] road, which is considered one of the main roads in Riyadh. 3. Buildings in this area do not fit with the high prices of lands. 4. It is better for the government to find a more appropriate place . . . to move these houses to. Since most of the . . . inhabitants work in Nasiriya, the following points were clarified: 1. A community close to Nasiriya must be found, being near their work, and . . . at the same time up to their social standard and income. It should not be on main roads . . . 2. Every family in these communities will be granted a plot, proportional to the one used by them at present, and be given a good compensation for their house, so as to build a new house on the new plot. 3. For the approval of the government on the above mentioned, the area will be surrounded by 4 streets with widths between 20–30 m, and a green area on its sides to be as a boundary for this area.[44]

Slum removal, not upgrading, was ultimately the solution devised by the urban planners. If the recommendation was halfway between the generous solution imagined by King Sa'ud and the ruthless deportation scheme proposed by Prince Salman, the result was dramatic. Not only were Bedouin residents treated like a disposable and movable quantity, but urban planning also emerged as a way to manage populations. Streets were built to identify, isolate, and control certain categories of residents; green spaces were used as boundaries; Bedouin communities were to be built far from the main roads, the general traffic, and the public's gaze.

It was not the first time that entire communities were marginalized. After the creation of the Kingdom of Saudi Arabia in 1932, when Riyadh started growing, outsiders to the city were not allowed to settle within its fortifications. Slaves of African origin who worked for the royal family created the "quarter of the slaves" (*hillat al-'abid*), which after King Faisal abolished slavery in 1964 was dubbed "quarter of the free" (*hillat al-ahrar*). Northern Najdis from the Qasim area, an ancient commercial crossroads on the pilgrimage route between Baghdad and Mecca, were also forced to camp outside of the walls. They progressively developed the "quarter of the Qasimis" (*hillat al-gusman*) on the left bank of the Wadi Batha. Between their neighborhood and the walled city, Qasimis created a market of their own, whose reputation later eclipsed that of the old market: did not most of the newcomers come from 'Unayza, a town dubbed by travelers "the Paris of Najd?" In the 1940s, in order to house rural migrants, the municipality erected the first planned neighborhood of the city in Manfuha, where gridded streets and uniformly designed housing were both cheap to build and easy to police.[45]

In the 1950s, the municipality knocked down the walls of Riyadh and opened several thoroughfares through the maze of winding streets to connect the old city center to the new neighborhoods. After the ministries were moved from the Red Sea port of Jeddah to Riyadh, where they lined the straight avenue leading from the old fort to the airport, the state planned the neighborhood of al-Malazz or New Riyadh (*al-Riyadh al-jadida*), to the northeast of the city, to house civil servants and their families. Old Riyadhis saw this extension as a foreign and bizarre entity, as illustrated by the following story, recounted by literary critic 'Abd Allah al-Ghazhzhami:

A man living in Dakhna, in the old Riyadh, often missed the communal prayer at the mosque. The people of the neighborhood (*jama'a al-hayy*) came to him and told him that he who does not pray with his neighbors may as well leave Dakhna and find a new home for himself in Malazz.[46]

Riyadh's residents had lived for centuries in multi-families houses built around a central courtyard and along narrow zigzagging streets. (See Figure 3.4.) The large streets of Malazz, laid out on a grid, and the individual villas enclosed with gardens and walls were foreign to the local sense of place.

Malazz was inspired by the Aramco Home Ownership Loan Program and by the planning of al-Khobar and Dammam, from the 1930s onward, by American engineers of the oil company.[47] The Aramco Loan Program,

FIGURE 3.4. The courtyard of a mud-brick house in Riyadh, 1968 (Constantinos A. Doxiadis Archives,[48] copyright © Constantinos and Emma Doxiadis Foundation).

designed in 1951 to alleviate housing shortages and remedy the emergence of shantytowns around Dammam and Dhahran, failed to attract workers to new suburban developments built next to the oil plants, and native Riyadhis looked at Malazz with suspicion.[49] Despite initial misgivings, planned neighborhoods and suburban villas soon became the standard of what it meant to live a "modern" life:

The [Malazz] development signaled a departure from the old *laissez-faire* attitude and heralded a new era of government intervention in the land and housing market as a major supplier, financier and subsidizer. The villas were sold to government officials on long-term loans. The planners followed the gridiron network with a hierarchical street network comprising a 180 ft.-wide highway bifurcating the new suburb, major roads of 100 ft. in width, collector streets of 60 ft. in width, and service passageways of 30–45 ft. in width.[50]

From the 1970s onward, individual villas financed by government loans and individual cars running on public roads would be generalized to the whole city of Riyadh. As in the post–World War II United States, suburbanization was prompted by a mix of public policies, of technological advances and of consumerist measures, and the capital's various functions and populations were progressively planned outside of the walled core, zoned outward on the flat, vast plateau surrounding the city. Like Los Angeles in the eyes of Lewis Mumford, Riyadh was on its way to becoming an "anti-city."

3.4. Mobility and Slums

Palatial edifices and fearful slums are the strange, complementary features of modern cities.

– Ebenezer Howard

Rural and foreign migrants were even more loathed by the inhabitants of Riyadh than the bureaucrats coming from Jeddah. Massed in hastily built slums made of wool tents, tin shacks, and wooden barracks, rural migrants were already a significant presence in the 1920s' Riyadh. From the 1960s onward, they literally flooded the city in search of jobs. The regular increase of the state's oil revenue and the centralization of political and economic power lured many from rural areas to Riyadh. Severe droughts also affected the central region of the country in the 1960s, decimating the cattle and forcing many nomads to settle and, ultimately, to migrate to big cities.[51] The nomadic economy, based on herding and seasonal agriculture, was further threatened by the legal abolition of the tribal territories (*dira*), the nationalization of grazing lands and the emergence of wide socioeconomic disparities among fellow tribesmen, between the happy few who had invested in subsidized agriculture and the innumerable others who fell into destitution. Rural migrants were in effect economic and ecological refugees.

In 1925, 1953, and 1968, land property regulations gradually deprived the Bedouin tribes of their economic function, which was to organize and regulate the nomads' access to grazing lands and wells.[52] In 1925, the legal notion of tribal territory (*dira*) was eliminated. From now on, every tribe could theoretically have access to water and land everywhere in the country, regardless of previous tribal boundaries. The former tribal lands were nationalized in 1953, and in 1968 a new decree regulated the Islamic notion of land revitalization (*ihyia' al-mawat*), according to which land belongs to whomever cultivates it or builds on it.[53] This last regulation officially aimed at fostering agriculture and channeling state subsidies to the most productive Bedouin and farmers. In reality, it deprived many Saudis of their livelihood and triggered unheard of inequalities.[54] Only the already well-off and well-connected could afford to invest in agriculture and the poorest Bedouin and peasants, who could no longer claim the legal protection of their tribes, had to flee to the cities. The reform of land tenure was in effect a process of expropriation and proletarianization.[55]

From the 1950s on, Bedouin and peasants not only settled in villages and small towns, but also migrated into the bulging cities of Riyadh, Jeddah, and Dammam. At some point during the 1960s, rural migrants came to outnumber the original inhabitants of Riyadh: in 1968 they were 54 percent of an overall population of 281,000.[56] This swift demographic change worried the Al Sa'ud, as Doxiadis himself witnessed during his first visit to the city in November 1968. During a 30 minutes meeting at the royal palace, King Faisal, "while talking about Riyadh, was mainly concerned about water, inadequate housing and slums" and "social conditions" in general.[57] A few days after the royal audience, a high-ranking civil servant spelled out to the Greeks the actual position of the King and of the senior princes:

Do we want actually Riyadh to become a big city? Do we want to encourage unreasonable concentration of people in big cities? Government policy regarding regional development, concentration or not of people in big urban areas, development of rural areas and provincial centers, comes before the preparation of planning or engineering projects.... His Majesty the King [does] not favor the development of Riyadh toward the [north] or [northwest], as this takes the city away from sources of water into areas which are dry and sandy. His Majesty [is] cautiously skeptical on the idea that Riyadh would become big, with population ranging at 1.5 million. This would necessitate more security measures, [a] bigger police force, etc.[58]

The galloping urbanization of the country was experienced as an ordeal, and the Al Sa'ud were watching the rapid transformation of their capital with growing displeasure and anxiety. Regional development, or the channeling of services and populations to secondary towns in order to relieve the capital, was discussed in decision-making circles. However, as Doxiadis explained to the Mayor of Riyadh a few months later, Riyadh "might be strengthened even more by virtue of its central location if the south and north of the country [are] developed.... Madrid was small when Spain was centered on the Mediterranean. It grew in importance when the Atlantic coastline and the north of the country developed."[59] Because of the country's centralization, there was no way out of urban growth in the capital.

Security and police were King Faisal's main concern. In the oil-producing eastern province of al-Hasa', strikes and demonstrations regularly targeted the operations of the American oil company Aramco and leftist groups challenged the political monopoly of the royal family. In the central province, student unrest and army unruliness were seen as a serious threat. The Arab Cold War in the 1960s opposed socialist and nationalist Egypt, Syria, and Iraq, on one hand, to pro-U.S. Saudi Arabia and Jordan, on the other hand. This regional rift threatened to run through Saudi society, between partisans of the throne and the unionists, soldiers, and nationalist activists who admired Egyptian president Nasser, were listening to Radio Cairo and demanded economic and social reforms. A year after Doxiadis started working in Riyadh, plans for a series of coups were reportedly uncovered, and repression targeted leftist and Nasserist activists in the army.[60]

The Al Sa'ud feared that the social imbalance represented by rural migrations would translate into a political challenge to their rule. In 1962, Albert J. Mayer, Constantinos Doxiadis's godfather in Saudi Arabia, had taken this threat seriously. If the Al Sa'ud were obsessed about "Nasser's Arab socialism, with its threat of subversion," to him the main impediment to the Saudi regime was elsewhere. It was the Bedouin, with their long history of opposition to sedentary polities and their geographical mobility, first in the steppes of Central Arabia, now in the form of labor migrations to the cities. Geographical mobility could turn into social blight and political mobilization:

Economic change in Saudi Arabia will most certainly offer a growing series of challenges to the establishment. The Kingdom seems to be mounting a toboggan at the top of the chute. As the destruction of the Bedu [*sic*] economy goes inevitably onward, the establishment will face not only the problems of dealing with the Bedu as displaced city-dwellers, but also threats to the kingdom's potential stability.[61]

In order to keep the Bedouin in the countryside, King Sa'ud attempted to turn them into agriculturalists in the Wadi Sirhan, near the Jordanian border; the project was by and large a failure. King Faisal's very own settlement project in Haradh was initiated by the U.S. oil company Aramco and the Ford Foundation, and engineered by the German consulting firm Wakuti International. According to an American anthropologist studying the Haradh settlement scheme in the 1970s, the "project was initiated during the early 1960s when many Saudi Arabian nomads had suffered badly from a prolonged drought... This same period also witnessed an acceleration in the growth of the major cities of the area," and the state took this opportunity to engage in a gigantic experiment in social engineering.

A report submitted to the government by the Ford Foundation stressed the main objectives of the project: to undermine "Bedouinism," since "two elements – saving and investment – [that are] vital for economic development are not part of the Bedouin system of value." Settlement and agriculture would operate "a series of changes from... kinship to citizenship,... nomadic pastoralism to modern farming,... individualism to cooperative participation, [and] tribal participation as a kinsman to national participation as a citizen."[62]

It wasn't clear what distinction was made between "cooperative participation" and "tribal participation," and why the former was more valuable than the latter. What was clear was that the royal family was invested with a new *mission civilisatrice*. A Saudi 1963 report describes "the great revolution started by the late King 'Abd al-'Aziz," which was "spreading civilization in the desert." "Civilization" entailed settling the Bedouin in houses, developing agriculture, "drilling wells and building mosques."[63] The Bedouin hinterland was now the target of an internal colonization enterprise that, under the guidance of U.S. and German experts, fostered rural displacements and urban squalor.

Agricultural settlement projects failed to attract as many people as intended. After completion of the al-Haradh project, "no more than two minimal lineages of the Al Murrah [tribe] could be characterized as active participants in the program and very few other nomads were associated with the Settlement Project in any way other than as low-salaried wage laborers." Reproducing the stereotypes that Aramco had inherited from European colonialism and from labor hierarchies in U.S. mining towns, agricultural engineers on the al-Haradh farm called Bedouin laborers "*kulya*, coolies." This racial hierarchy translated into steep wage differences. "The laborers... received monthly salaries that ranged between 300 and 500 Saudi riyals while their Bedouin foreman received approximately 1000 Saudi riyals. The Palestinian and Jordanian supervisors made several times this amount, with the European employees making many times as much."[64] No wonder that agricultural labor, although presented by U.S. and German experts as leading to settlement and civilization (two notions that are encompassed in the Arabic word *hadhara*), was not deemed attractive by most nomads, who preferred instead to emigrate to the cities.

Together with economic growth and employment opportunities in the cities, the construction of more roads and the accelerated import of cars increased Bedouin and rural geographic mobility. Once dispersed in all corners of the steppe, Bedouin mobility was now converging on a few locations. As more and more Saudis moved from the countryside, municipal agents at first tried to prevent their settlement en masse, but soon realized that they had to make do with the idea that rural "migrants are shaping the culture of the city as much as they are adjusting to it."[65] In the Saudi sociological literature of the subsequent decades, the notion of "ruralization of cities" (*tarayyuf al-mudun*) translated a mounting malaise toward rural migrations.[66]

Most migrants came from small towns, villages and nomadic encampments, and had no economic or cultural capital. "Illiterate and unskilled," they "suffered from widespread unemployment."[67] Desperate for work, they found employment at the royal palace, the national oil company Petromin and the new ministries, around which slums soon sprouted. Migrants would be hired as construction workers, guards, and soldiers or as bus, taxi, and truck drivers. Some more fortunate became gamekeepers (*khwi*) for the royal family. They tended to live alone and send remittances to their families back home, waiting for a good opportunity to bring them to Riyadh.

Described as unruly, unpredictable, and volatile by Saudi technocrats and experts, slum dwellers were seen as a threat to the established way of life of the sedentary population. Saudi bureaucrats overlooked the fact that rural migrations had been largely generated by the consistently anti-tribal policies of the state and by the failure of agricultural development. A 1963 report describes how, in their "tents and cottages [*sic*] made of tin and pieces of wood..., [the Bedouin] practice their own customs and traditions," to the apparent dismay of the urban population, which looked at the newcomers with fear and disgust. The "Bedouin" caused "trouble [to] the security and health departments" and presented "many moral... problems."[68] Promiscuity, immorality and vice were deemed endemic in the slums, where women and men mingled freely and showed little reverence for the powers that be. Demography was looming and innumerous rural bodies – young and untamed, sexually aroused and

politically undisciplined, pressed in growing slums – were seen as a threat
to order and morality.

Paul Bonnenfant, an anthropologist who lived in Riyadh in the 1970s,
described the parallel economy of slum building:

By 1975 many workers had specialized in wood recycling and in the production
of standardized panels, which they sold to whomever wanted to quickly build
a shack: prefabrication methods applied to slums, so to speak. In 1980, a tin
shack with adjusted plank costs 4,000 to 5,000 riyals. Walls and interior ceiling
are often covered with paperboard (refrigerator's boxes for instance) to avoid
draughts and keep dust out.[69]

Slum dwellers were building their homes at a time when development
experts, including Doxiadis, advocated self-help programs. By the end
of the 1960s the mayor of Riyadh, 'Abd al-'Aziz Al Thunayyan, started
advocating for a "low cost project" to house the rural migrants, which
DA experts relabeled a "pioneer project" and was none other than Prince
Salman's Bedouin removal plan:

People coming from the countryside take a piece of land and start building their
shacks, their 'cottages' as the mayor called them, and then the owners or the
government protests; the Mayor stops them and the people wonder why the
government does not let them build.... The Mayor concluded that he needs a
low cost project as he called it and in order to be able to proceed with it he needs
a ... "feasibility study for a pioneer project."[70]

In 1968, shanties composed 20 percent of Riyadh's housing stock,[71] and
the streets of Riyadh were a perpetual traffic jam. Rural migrations and
economic growth stretched the capital beyond its housing and transportation capacities, and the resulting crisis pressed the royal family to devise
long-term solutions and reshape the city. The influx of migrants triggered
a severe housing crisis and sparked heated debates among civil servants
and foreign experts over land ownership, car traffic, social housing, and
the state's responsibility to its poorest citizens. These debates between
DA experts and Saudi decision makers elicited in turn strong responses
among petty landlords and landowners.

3.5. Land Is Political

From their first weeks in the country onward, the experts were confronted
with the general opacity of the city and its society. Riyadh had no detailed
map, no census, and no land register, none of the basic instruments of
municipal governance. DA had to use 1964 British air photos to map

the area as it was in 1968. Even simple tasks, such as taking pictures of streets and houses, proved tedious and triggered aggressive reactions from the residents. During a time of government crackdown on socialist and nationalist unrest, and as the real estate market was beginning to grow, the Greeks had to obtain official authorizations from the Interior Ministry before trying to take photographs. An additional frustration was the poor collaboration of secretive offices and reluctant administrations. DA was introduced to the Saudi public in *al-Yamama* magazine as the qualified planners of "Detroit City in the USA,"[72] a title that apparently didn't help dissipating local hesitations. The feudal structure of the municipality, with its intricate networks of patrons and clients, was not easy to decipher, and rare were the employees who voluntarily opened their drawers and archives.

In view of "the natural reluctance of the indigenous population to be interviewed by foreigners,"[73] DA's household survey of Riyadh was conducted by Saudi employees of the finance ministry, who visited 5 percent of the city's households, or 2,571 families out of 51,200. They drew a map based on the British air photos to locate the households, and asked questions about the household members (sex, age, profession), the description of the dwelling, and the family's transportation means, habits, and itineraries. A roadside survey was conducted in parallel to the household survey. It was necessitated by the "unacceptable traffic situation" in a city whose narrow streets were not prepared for a soaring number of cars. In a letter to Benoît Joubert, UN adviser to the telecommunications ministry, DA transportation engineer John Frantzeskakis explained that a "mathematical model" would be built to "estimate future travel generation," and that projected car use growth would "constitute the basis for the proper dimensioning and further design of the transportation network of Riyadh."[74]

Cars were to become the measure of the new city, and the planners took individual motor vehicles and their centrality as facts of nature. The new middle and upper-middle class, enriched by commerce, state contracts, or official positions, was importing more and more vehicles from Europe and the United States, and the bloated streets of Riyadh were a perpetual traffic jam. (See Figure 3.5.) Despite repeated letters to the municipality, DA was unable to obtain precise figures about the import of cars or the number of vehicles in the city, probably because such figures simply didn't exist.[75] But the road survey, which was "completed without any accident" and under the supervision of the traffic police,[76] provided the data necessary to the planning of Riyadh's future traffic pattern.

الـريــاض ـ ازدجــام حـــركــة الـمـــرور

RIYADH – TRAFFIC CONGESTION

Traffic congestion is a usual phenomenon along King Saud (Batha) street. Drivers wait patiently in long queues during rush hours while traffic officers try to regulate a traffic much higher than what can be properly accommodated by this street under its present condition.

ان ازدحـام حـركة المرور هو ضى' بالوف فى شارع الـملـك ـ مود المعروف بشارع "البطحاء" • ويتنظر السائق دوره فى المرور ليصبر فى صفوف طويلةمتلاحقة اثنا' ساعات الازدحام بينما يحاول شرطى المرور تنظيم حـركة المرور التى تعتبر أكبر كثيرا ما يستطيع هذا الشـارع بحالته الراهنة ، استيعابه من الـسيارات بصورة لائقة مأمنه •

FIGURE 3.5. Traffic jam on Batha Street in 1968 (Constantinos A. Doxiadis Archives,[77] copyright © Constantinos and Emma Doxiadis Foundation).

In DA's surveys, Riyadh comes across as a city whose population, thanks to successive waves of migration, is massively young and male. The city absorbs considerable resources without producing much, a trait the Greeks associate with cultural deficiencies among the Saudi population, described as traditionalist and opposed to change. "The Saudis in Riyadh, as descendants of a pastoral people, consider heavy muscular exertion as something not only unpleasant but also unfit for human dignity,"[78] the experts write, without quoting the figures that allowed for such sweeping generalization. 42.4 percent of the capital's residents were civil servants, but inequalities of income were blatant: "almost 50% of the private households earn less than 15% of the aggregate personal income."[79]

The Greeks unsurprisingly refrained from linking these inequalities with the concentration of power and wealth into the few hands of the main princes and their clients. Rather, they saw social and economic behaviors as expressing cultural and "traditional" patterns. Inward

looking, centered on the family cell, and built around the mosque, this
"focal point of the community,"[80] Riyadh was to the Greeks an ideal-
type of the ethereal "Islamic city" whose spirit Doxiadis had already tried
to capture in his descriptions of Baghdad. This alleged pervasiveness of
backward-looking habits rendered the intervention of the state and of
foreign experts all the more urgent. Saudis had to become productive and
progressive citizens.

Doxiadis presented his first report on "Existing Conditions" to the
king at the University of Riyadh in October 1968. Prior to the royal audience, during which King Faisal expressed his distaste of urban growth,
Doxiadis took a flight over Riyadh and the surrounding plateau. The
interior ministry hadn't been able to secure a plane and, once again, it
was a British company, Airworks Services, that helped DA achieve an
overarching vision of the city by providing a plane for free. Although
Doxiadis had had a positive meeting with defense minister Prince Sultan,
the defense ministry refused to allow him to take aerial pictures of the
city. The bird's-eye view Doxiadis was gaining couldn't be stored for ulte-
rior uses: it had to be enjoyed on the spot, and the Greeks took precise
notes during their seventy-five-minute trip.

"The flight was made following a radial pattern" and surveyed seven
major axes, each time "starting and ending at the airport:" Airport Road
to the old center, Mansura Road to the south, Kharj Road to the southeast, the Eastern Province railroad to the east, Khurais Road to the northeast, Dir'iyya Road to the northwest, and Mecca Road to the southwest.
"In every direction the flight was continued [past] the last developments
which could be noted, flying at an altitude of approximately 150–200
meters [500–650 ft] from the ground." It was a good opportunity to
survey the space outside the city and assess the options for growth.

On four of the seven routes the Greeks noticed the existence of camps
of the National Guard, who were watching over the main accesses to
the capital (the Hejaz Road, the Qasim Road, the Khurais Road, and the
Kharj Road). To the east of the city, cement factories and workshops composed an industrial landscape with slums growing haphazardly around
the plants. To the west, Prince Sultan's palace, King Sa'ud's sons' palaces,
and a number of other royal residences surrounded the city with a luxurious belt of gardens and pools. The flight flattened the capital, erasing
what had appeared as obstacles on the ground. "From the air, the hills
of the east of Malazz as well as those of the south-east of the industrial
area did not seem as big or difficult . . . The terrain was, as known, barren
and sandy all around, except for Wadi Hanifa,"[81] which confirmed the

planners in their decision to design the new Riyadh away from the Wadi's gardens and palm groves.

The bird's-eye view was deceptive, however. Once the Greeks came back to the ground and after Doxiadis flew back to Athens, visibility was once again blurred by the difficulties of everyday operations in Riyadh. Contrary to what the flight above Riyadh had suggested, there was no superseding point of view from which the city and its inhabitants could be made visible. The "God's eye view, or the view of an absolute ruler"[82] that was supposed to be the vantage point of the urban planner, was a view of the mind.

Municipal agents were stingy with information because they often didn't have any access to it either. They expected that the Greek experts would give them "a clear and real picture of the city," a snapshot that would allow to better control it. In the eyes of the Mayor, "careful organization [would] give land . . . its exact value"[83] and turn the desert around Riyadh into a quantified resource. This goal proved hard to achieve, however. As they proceeded to survey the slums, halting the construction of new dwellings or the renewal of existing ones, municipal agents were met with incomprehension and growing anger.

Mayor Al Thunayyan had told Doxiadis he was powerless in the face of haphazard growth: "Many people are building everywhere. They ask for permits, which they are given, but [we do] not know whether they should really build there, or whether they should go higher up. . . . I cannot stop the people, there are no regulations, no zoning." Doxiadis's answer had been technical and consistent with the expert's instrumental perspective on land ownership. We will "provide for [regulations]," he had told the Mayor. "In our preliminary plan, we will propose basic articles of law helping you to proceed with such cases." Perplexed, the mayor had pointed to the religious nature of the land ownership law. Doxiadis had replied, his expert's faith undisturbed: "We will have later the advice of specialists in Islamic law, of lawyers in the capital who will help us face these problems." Still unconvinced, the mayor had pulled out his last card, and "said that when [Doxiadis] saw His Majesty [he] would have to speak on existing work and on new permits."[84] Land was such a sensitive issue that building permits and cadaster were to be discussed with none other than the King himself.

Land was political, and this was the main reason why the city was transparent to neither planners nor administrators. (See Figure 3.6.) Land was preempted by the princes, distributed to their clients, subdivided into plots, exchanged against political acquiescence. Land was

FIGURE 3.6. Visit of a Saudi delegation to Doxiadis Associates in Athens, 1969.
Doxiadis is in the middle, wearing a white shirt with no tie (Constantinos A. Doxiadis Archives,[85] copyright © Constantinos and Emma Doxiadis Foundation).

sometimes given away, as the Mayor one day confessed, "to avoid political problems."[86] As a result, the cadaster was a well-kept secret. In
January 1969, after a meeting with the Mayor, Nicolas Efessios reported
that "plots of land have been sold and others donated by [the] government to people in the city,"[87] and this was as detailed as the information
would get. A few months later, after the order was given to the municipality to "give [the experts] all existing information," Efessios wrote
again to Athens that information on land ownership was still "scant and
vague."[88]

Unable to achieve an overarching view of Riyadh, the experts were
often turned by the Al Sa'ud into private real estate advisers. In June 1969,

the most senior member of the royal family summoned the Greeks to his palace. 'Abd Allah b. 'Abd al-Rahman Al Sa'ud, born in 1893, was King 'Abd al-'Aziz's younger brother and King Faisal's uncle. He had fought in the conquest of al-Hasa and of the Hejaz, ordered the destruction of Bedouin settlements during the repression of the 1929 Ikhwan revolt, and gave the decisive green light for the deposition of King Sa'ud in 1964. After a genial introduction and some general questions about the master plan, the old warrior "enquired more particularly about the anticipated development around his lands, situated from kilometer 4 to kilometer 7 on al-Kharj Road," in Mansura. The experts exhibited the plan, which showed four streets connecting the land to the main axes of the city. The prince did not protest against the expected noise and pollution. He explained, "The two freeways..., when constructed, will enhance the development and value of his area." The most important member of the royal family after the king seemed more interested in his own piece of land than in the master plan. No wonder the prince "seemed satisfied" in the end. The planners prepared "for him a map showing the boundaries of his land and the proposed major roads around it" and gave away strategic information about the future of his personal wealth.[89] This was not 'Abd Allah b. 'Abd al-Rahman's first coup. In 1949 he had twisted the arm of Bechtel executives to have them build him a castle at a fraction of the construction cost.[90]

Others princes followed and consulted the Greeks about their shares in the capital's real estate market. The king's son, 'Abd Allah al-Faisal, requested a subdivision of his land from DA in preparation for future development.[91] Princess Sara, one of King 'Abd al-'Aziz's daughters, voiced her concerns about the Riyadh-Qasim highway, designated to run along her land, and obtained a significant reduction of the right-of-way.[92] Prince Fahd b. Sa'ud, son of deposed King Sa'ud, was less shrewd. Presenting himself as the owner, he asked for an exorbitant compensation for the Abu Mahruq Hill in al-Malazz, which the municipality wanted to turn into a public park. "Commonly used by people who climb its slopes to offer evening prayers and enjoy the view of the city and the evening breeze," the hill was considered one of the main natural landmarks of Riyadh. It was also an infamous slum. The Greeks objected that "the title of the land and the exact boundaries of the ownership" were not "defined by any legal document." The prince confessed that the hill wasn't his property and belonged indeed to the public realm. Unashamed by the public display of his duplicity, he threatened to develop it in order to claim its property under the 1968 land regulations, which granted ownership to whomever cultivated a land or built on it. It was ultimately decided that, because the prince had "not made any use of the land since the [alleged] date of taking possession," his claims were not legitimate. The hill was later turned into a park.[93]

3.6. "Mecca-Oriented Roads"

By 1971, the Greek experts' mission had dramatically evolved. From mere consultants they had become actual urban planners, who were opening new roads, widening existing avenues and participating in day-to-day planning operations. In the old center and in the buffer zone between the center and the new neighborhoods, they expropriated landowners and froze land acquisition and building permits. In the winter of 1970, DA approved the subdivision of various princes' lands, among whom were 'Abd Allah bin 'Abd al-Rahman and 'Abd Allah al-Faisal. News of that preferential treatment perhaps reached individual landowners' ears; they started resisting expropriation. The outcry was such that the municipality waived any responsibility, indicating that it didn't have "the authority to stop issuing building permits."[94] DA was brandishing the threat of slums to demonstrate the necessity to act now: it was either top-down planning or the mayhem of shantytowns and unruly subdivisions. The experts also tried to rub landowners the right way and mentioned that the "government [would] invest considerable sums . . . which [would] benefit the individuals . . . and raise the value of land." They urged everybody to cooperate "both for the benefit of the individual and that of the whole city."[95]

The fiercest battle was waged by local residents against the extension and widening of Prince Faisal bin Turki Street, known under the nickname of Khazzan Street. Perpendicular to Batha Street, this important thoroughfare ran between the old city and the Murabba' Palace. Its facades were about to be bulldozed by SAUTI, the Italian subcontractor in charge of the widening of the capital's streets (euphemistically called "beautification"). Landowners reached out en masse to the municipal administration to stop the operation. In January 1970, during a meeting at the municipality, young architect Charalobos Bislanis dismissed local resistance and declared that "the further expropriation of five meters [would] not be difficult in that particular area of the city where there [were] only mud houses." The mayor's answer was chilly: municipal agents would "try to convince the landowners to set back the ground floor" but warned of complications.[96] DA proposed to compensate the loss of ground space by the authorization to build higher.

A few weeks later, the mayor confessed that he had been "pressed by the higher authorities and landowners": the answer was no. Landowners who also owned shops didn't want to lose any space at the street level and had demanded state compensation. The Greeks were stuck between the landowners' resistance, the state's stinginess and the impotence of the municipality. Forced to endorse the landowners' position, plan a much narrower avenue and to abandon the elegant, shaded galleries that would have replaced sun-drenched sidewalks, Bislanis refused to sign the official memorandum.[97] The same scenario happened in other locations, in particular Washm Street and Medina Street, where landowners also opposed the widening of the pavement and the redesign of sidewalks and facades. All sides were clinging to their rights, and the common good mentioned by the experts remained an abstraction.

Widespread opposition to the master plan wore down the patience of the Al Sa'ud. Because many princes, civil servants, and landowners were challenging the urban planners' authority, Salman created a Master Plan Commission in 1971, which became the High Commission for the Development of Riyadh (*al-hay'at al-'uliya li-tatwir madinat al-riyadh*) in 1974. The commission had full power over the master plan. Salman's goal was to silence the critics, put an end to the homeowners' insurrection, and start implementing the master plan and the road network. Its eight members, including the mayor, the deputy interior minister, a representative of the landowners' committee, and a DA architect, met twice a week under the chairmanship of Salman. They would sometimes be transported in helicopter above the city, probably to take some distance from what was happening on the ground.

The Greeks were less than pleased with the creation of the commission. "Unfortunately another committee has been formed here on a higher level," one of DA architects reported to Athens. "[It] is again going through the master plan and the final community designs that we have submitted."[98] The first decisions of the commission were experienced as a rebuff. The right-of-way of the main thoroughfares was reduced, the existing subdivisions along the main axes, which the Greeks wanted to freeze, were approved, and the building regulations (height, surface) were revised. Very little remained of the decisions put forward by DA.

Opposed by homeowners, contradicted by civil servants, and manipulated by princes, the master plan slowly became a hammer without a master. The plan was not a unilateral scheme imposed from above by a technocratic fiat. It was rather being devised at the crossroads of the princes' strategies, the engineers' ideals, the developers' greed, the administration's maneuvers, the homeowners' legal guerilla attacks, and the Bedouin's calm encroachment. The plan was not the "dictator" or the "despot" of which Le Corbusier had dreamed. It wasn't designed "well away from the frenzy in the mayor's office or the town hall, from the cries of the electorate or the laments of society's victims."[99] It was negotiated in the brouhaha of people's and administrative committees, challenged by homeowners' petitions and revised along princes' pressures.

In 1971, Doxiadis finally presented the master plan of Riyadh, which was answering the two most "urgent problems faced by the city:" the "regulation of transportation according to a rational roads' network," and the "provision of urgently needed housing."[100] (See Figure 3.7.) The main idea of the plan was to transform the existing hub-and-spoke urban pattern, centered on the old mud-brick city, the Musmak fort, and the grand mosque, into the linear model Doxiadis had theorized as "Dynapolis." Large 1.2-mile square superblocks separated by wide, perpendicular freeways were designed around a central spine that prolonged Batha Street toward the new neighborhood of al-'Ulayya. Running between two parallel thoroughfares roughly oriented northwest-southeast (the future King Fahd and 'Ulayya Avenues), the "Doxiadis Axis" became the new business and administrative district. Military and industrial zones to the east and recreation parks to the west completed this snapshot of the city's future. The Bedouin housing project, a tiny outgrowth along the Mecca Road in the southwest, was linked to the city proper by an administrative buffer zone.

DA experts had assigned specific functions to each zone, clearly separating residential, industrial, commercial, and administrative neighborhoods. The business and administrative district was no longer a fixed area in the middle of the city, potentially bloated by the expansion of its surroundings. The center itself was designed to grow linearly, and only this "linear growth pattern" would allow Riyadh to "avoid the future strangulation of the existing center," which was to become a touristic and picturesque landmark. The Musmak fort, several palaces and whole areas would be protected and landscaped to serve as a reminder of the rich architectural tradition of central Najd, and as a model for the design of the public spaces and residential housing. The central spine was roughly oriented in the direction of Dir'iyya, Al Sa'ud's first capital in the eighteenth century, which in 1818 had been bombed by the Egyptians on behalf of the Sublime Porte. The plan bridged between past and present, and experts were expected to suture the wounds inflicted on the city by former dominations.

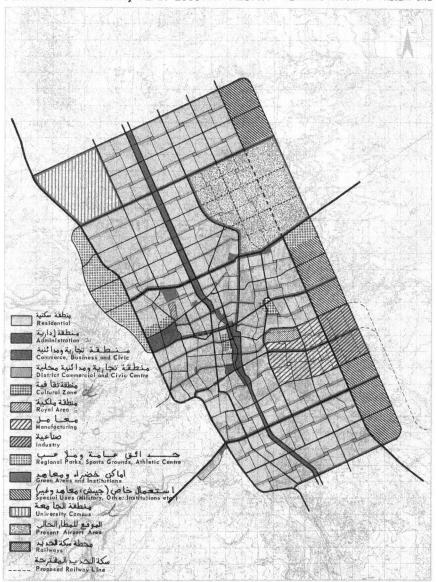

FIG 9

المخطط الرئيسى، السنة ٢٠٠٠م ١٤٢٠هـ ـ الإحتفاظ بموقع المطار الحالى

FINAL MASTER PLAN, YEAR 2000 A.D.-1420 A.H.   RETAINING AIRPORT IN PRESENT SITE

D - SAU - A 30010 / 330

DOXIADIS ASSOCIATES · CONSULTANTS ON DEVELOPMENT AND EKISTICS   مؤسسة دوكسيادى ـ مستشارون فى شئون التنمية والاكستكس

FIGURE 3.7. The 1971 Master Plan of Riyadh, with the central axis running through the grid of superblocks and the royal palace to the west (Constantinos A. Doxiadis Archives,[101] copyright © Constantinos and Emma Doxiadis Foundation).

Traced "through open areas," the plan was primarily designed to "cater to the requirements of continuously increasing traffic."[102] Wide, straight thoroughfares would "facilitate an easy and quick movement from one part of the city to the other" and "divide the area of the city into well defined and manageable sectors."[103] Doxiadis had pledged to King Faisal that the new capital would "save the child, the old and the crippled from the dangers caused within the cities by the invasion of machines,"[104] and the master plan mentioned "the introduction of a bus network on adequate routes."[105] But DA didn't investigate further the creation of a public transportation network, and left untouched the existing system of collective and individual taxis. Massive car imports and the widespread fears caused by rural migrations, slums, social polarization, and mounting crime confirmed the domination of individual vehicles, which were reputedly safer than public transit. Riyadh was condemned to worship the automobile, imported and commercialized by powerful families, and desired by all as a sign of prestige and social status.

The master plan expressed this cult of the car in an odd way. The general orientation of the city toward the northwest allowed its lateral streets, roughly oriented southwest-northeast, to face Mecca and the direction of prayer (*al-qibla*). These "Mecca-oriented roads" made of Riyadh, as Doxiadis boasted in his letter to King Faisal, "a symbol for a Moslem city" and a place "governed by the spirit of Arabia." "We have been happy to find out that the overall topography has allowed us to direct the main streets toward Mecca,"[106] even though the Town Planning Office criticized the "many awkward and unnatural shapes"[107] caused by this orientation. The planned city was similar to an immense mosque facing Mecca. To the west, the royal palace was like an imam leading the prayer ahead of the various residential, administrative, commercial, industrial, and military zones. On wide, straight, smooth asphalted roads, Riyadh was communing in the worship of cars and speed.

Beside traffic and mobility, the master plan addressed the urgent problem of housing, to "accommodate...lower incomes" and provide "new residential areas" in lieu of the widespread slums.[108] Although the various functions of the city were spatially segregated, social classes would mingle in the new residential areas. "Special segregated housing colonies for different occupational or economic groups should be discouraged," and neighborhoods should instead be "composed of various representative segments of Saudi Arabian society." The Greeks assigned various building types and heights to each neighborhood, in which villas and apartment blocks, properties, and rentals, would be found lining the same streets.

Riyadh remained a deeply segregated city, however. The slum issue "cannot be solved only by the creation of new housing communities in other parts of the city." Yet DA experts planned the Bedouin housing project outside of the city proper, against their own warning that "isolated specialized communities tend to accentuate differences, thus creating barriers and social friction."[109]

Residential neighborhoods were designed as self-sustaining "population units" or "communities," complete with "shops, schools, mosques, parks, etc." and "richer in variety and content than the present day building stock."[110] Within each superblock narrow lanes were limited to local access and pedestrian circulation while through traffic and long distance trips were pushed to the periphery. DA experts tried hard to indigenize the superblock solution that Doxiadis was implementing everywhere. The sector's "sizes and basic dimensions . . . are inherent to the rhythm of Riyadh, which must be respected," they wrote. They claimed sectors were reminiscent of "the idea of Murabaa [*sic*] which is a basic traditional element in the city."[111] The *murabba‘* or quadrangle was not a "traditional" urban repertoire, however, but the name of King ʻAbd al-ʻAzizʼs new palace, and referred to the building's regular plan, as opposed to the irregular urban pattern of old Riyadh.

Inspired by free-market principles, the Greek experts advised the royal family not to get involved in public housing programs. Housing was to be provided by the private sector, whose investments would be guided by clear and transparent planning regulations. Two reasons were invoked. First, in these pre–oil boom years, there was a "financial impossibility" for the government to provide "subsidized housing in large enough numbers for all who need a dwelling," especially when private homeowners or companies were ready to invest. Second, the plan was intended to educate Saudis: "A man who pays for his own house acquires pride in ownership and matures with the responsibility he undertakes which makes him a socially stable element in society."[112] Public housing would infantilize its beneficiaries, turning them into potential troublemakers and agitators. Private housing was a better way of localizing and controlling individuals.

Over the three decades that followed, the automobile and housing markets became, along with public sector salaries, the main channels through which the oil rent was distributed. In the terms of the plan, individual responsibility and accountability were to replace the haphazard relationship between tribesmen and royal patrons, made up of an exchange of gifts in return for allegiance. In reality, Saudis became dependent on the bureaucracy, real estate developers, car dealers, and homebuilders.

Because developers and importers were closely linked to the royal family, the old allegiances did not disappear. Far from Doxiadis's dream to help produce a society of free individuals, the master plan helped Saudi elites streamline their domination. The extension of Riyadh allowed princes and businesspeople who invested in land development and car import to tap into the incomes of civil servants and middle-class households. Financed by public sector salaries and milked by clients of the royal family, the middle class had become a resource for big business and a source of overall stability.

Agricultural experts had turned land and water into resources that could be planned, developed, and tapped. In a similar way, urban planners converted the lands around Riyadh into a resource for those powerful enough to have access to it. The Doxiadis plan allowed landowners and developers, princes, and businesspeople to subdivide barren lands, assess their value, turn them into properties, and exchange them on the real estate market. The organization of space along "big avenues, straight, leading [people] to those places where we want them to go,"[113] turned out to be a vital tool in the creation of a manageable society of consumers. Driving from their homes to shopping malls, mosques and government agencies, Saudi citizens would be distracted from burning political issues by the dream-come-true of a Westernized, family-based way of life. Close to the freeway, hygienic, and individualized, financed by responsible fathers with the help of government loans, and protected by high walls from the envious gaze of neighbors, the single-family tract house epitomized Saudi modernity.

During their assignment in Saudi Arabia, DA experts were confronted with hazy situations, resistances, and obstacles. They had to explain and reassure, to explore and defuse, and to guide and reject. Their overall attitude vis-à-vis their Saudi counterparts was a mixed bag of condescension, irritation and fascination, and they often resorted to arguments of authority when it came time to solve misunderstandings or disputes. Their snooty attitude was partly based on their feeling superior to a society that they saw as unproductive, disorderly, and prisoner of its traditions. They took their developmental mission very seriously and asserted their role with an authority that was a model to be followed by the local bureaucracy.

"Basic infrastructure projects ... cannot be examined and accepted or rejected" by any kind of cost-based or economic argument, DA experts wrote in the *Final Master Plan*. "No urban system can function properly without them, and the only pertinent question ... is not whether they should be undertaken at all, but when they will be undertaken." The experts' technical knowledge was out of discussion. "One can discuss priorities, but not the projects as such. One can discuss the economic feasibility of alternatives for satisfying the need, but not the need."[114] The plan or chaos: DA drew its legitimacy from this dramatic binary set of alternatives. Development would soon lead to a firmer grasp of the state on people's lives, and to an increased control over society. Instead of opening up political decision making to participation and consultation, foreign expertise had reinforced the top-down nature of political authority. Not only had the state's power increased; its very nature had changed. It had become close to infallible.

4

The Business of Development

Those parasites and pickpockets aren't satisfied with anything less than taking over the land itself.

– Abdelrahman Munif[1]

4.1. Parking Crisis in Sulaymaniyya

In the narrow street of the Sulaymaniyya neighborhood where I moved after Abu Muhammad terminated our lease, I witnessed on a small scale how the space of the city could become a contention site. The street where I found a one-bedroom apartment was sandwiched between the military hospital and the military airbase headquarters. It was framed by large decaying villas and new apartment buildings on one side and the long, stern wall of the hospital on the other. With its mixed housing and its proximity to public services and highways, this part of Sulaymaniyya was home to a transient population of civil servants and medical workers, mainly Saudis and Arabs but also increasingly Filipinos.

As a result of long hours spent at home, waiting for my informant's phone calls, setting up appointments, writing down my field notes, or simply trying to avoid the midday sun, I followed the activity on the street below my window more closely than in suburban Sultana. There was more to be observed, too. Sulaymaniyya was livelier than the banks of the Wadi Hanifa and the street was bustling with traffic, especially in the early morning and early afternoon when the tide of cars came in and went out with the beginning and the end of the official workday.

Sulaymaniyya had been developed in the 1950s and 1960s between the Ministries Quarter, the old airport and the high grounds that in the 1970s became the new central business district, al-'Ulayya. Its central location and the age of its buildings made it ideal for migrant workers who did not mind living in vintage houses from the 1960s as long as the rent was cheap and the commute convenient. A few doors away from my building, the Center for the Enlightenment of the Migrant Communities (*markaz taw'iyya al-jaliyyat*), which dealt with the task of calling non-Muslim foreigners to convert and ensuring new recruits were doctrinally ortho-dox, was often busy with meetings and festivities. Saudis progressively moved away from the street because its location and diverse built envi-ronment had attracted a mixed population. They were probably also put off by the fact that it served as an additional parking lot for the military hospital and was jammed with honking and idling cars from early in the morning until mid-afternoon.

Congestion became worse with time, and passed all expectations when the municipality decided to overhaul the sidewalks along the military hos-pital. As in most streets of Riyadh, sidewalks were an occasional extension of the buildings. Landlords decided whether or not to build them and as a result, walking along most streets was a steeplechase. Sidewalks had var-ious sizes and heights and most often disappeared abruptly, prompting one to walk in the middle of the road, regardless of the speed or prox-imity of passing cars. Although our street was clearly not a renowned hangout, the municipality decided to outfit it with all the accoutrements that were found in Riyadh's most elegant avenues. (See Figure 4.1.) A redbrick sidewalk was built with trees, streetlamps, and wide, individual-ized parking places. Construction lasted for four lengthy months during which the street, already barely accessible, became a maddening place. A meager team of certainly underpaid Yemenis and Pakistanis worked at irregular hours and received the occasional visit of their boss, a tired Saudi in his fifties.

Since parking had become almost impossible, some of my neighbors installed in front of their spot two poles linked by a chain with a lock, sometimes with a sign: "No parking." Locks were only cosmetic, because poles could easily be carried away. The point was to appropriate public space, and the whole thing was a way of stating: this is mine; do not go any farther. This did not settle the matter, however, and many vis-itors to the hospital or the airbase tried to remove the chains and take the spots. If the residents witnessed the violation, they would point in indignation to the lock as proof that the spot, although public in theory, was reserved for their private use. One day, a Filipino nurse almost hit a Saudi driver who had tried to take his place. He seemed oblivious to

FIGURE 4.1. A sidewalk along King 'Abd Allah Avenue, 2007. Copyright ©
Pascal Menoret.

the risk immigrants faced when they threatened nationals and repeatedly
defended his piece of asphalt as if it were his livelihood. Meanwhile, fists
were brandished, insults were exchanged, tires were punctured, and the
street had descended in pandemonium.

During these months of construction and upheaval I listened to customers' gossip at the local grocery store. People claimed the work cost
much more than its actual value, and that a wealthy and influential member of the municipal team was pocketing the difference, probably aug-
mented by a commission. Confronted with what they framed as political
violence and corruption, local residents could not petition or address
the municipality – a frustrating and vaguely threatening institution. They
could try to collectively devise a way to better use public space, but the
daily, massive tide of cars from outside the neighborhood made any organization irrelevant. Most incoming cars catered to places of power such
as the military hospital and the airbase, which made things even more
intimidating. Every man for himself was the general motto, and top-down
corruption – or the perception thereof – had translated into horizontal
rudeness and brutality.

No policeman ever came to organize traffic or remove private partitions. At time, a member of the armed forces, caught in the maelstrom, used his uniform, along with a menacing tone, to get out of the congestion. Observing the scene from my window on the second floor, I could not but think of Sa'b's rants about how Saudi urban society had transformed people into aggressive troublemakers. He called this mutation *istiklab*, brutalization or, almost literally, "dog-eat-dog." Urbanity was not synonymous with good manners; it was a wilderness that people wanted to flee.

4.2. The Urban Consequences of the Oil Boom

In 1973, during the third Israeli-Arab war, King Faisal reduced oil production, a decision that increased oil prices worldwide and multiplied the state's revenue by twenty times in less than ten years. This manna allowed the Saudi administration to "wrap itself around large parts of society," turning them into clients and "making brokerage of state resources a ubiquitous pastime" for powerful middlemen.[2] Doxiadis had designed Riyadh in 1971, two years before Saudi Arabia began experiencing the largest windfall in its history. Until the mid-1980s, the oil boom (*al-tafra al-naftiyya*) was accompanied by an urban boom (*al-tafra al-'umraniyya*), itself the occasion for a real estate boom (*al-tafra al-'aqariyya*) fueled by government loans, intense speculation, and the rise of huge development, construction, and import empires.

The first victims of the real estate boom were the shape, the structure, and the density of the city. Riyadh quickly expanded into the surrounding desert and became a gigantic suburb with single-family homes, low population densities, and a heavy dependence on cars. The master plan was calling for "higher, rather than lower, densities," which were "more in keeping with the climate and culture" than low-density neighborhoods with large roads, tract houses and open spaces. In Doxiadis's plan, the harsh climate would be smoothened by narrow, shaded alleys and lanes, while the social fabric of the neighborhood, woven around patterns of women's visits, men's sociability and children playing together, would be preserved by tightly packed community centers in each superblock. "Compact planning" wasn't only culturally and ecologically preferable. It would also "result in more economical solutions insofar as roads, water supply mains, sewerage networks and all other infrastructure works are concerned." Low-rise apartment buildings along narrow streets with "net residential densities of about 200 persons per hectare": this was the model Doxiadis had left to the municipality.[3]

This density would never be reached by the new extensions of Riyadh, whose sprawling development rapidly exceeded the plan's provisions. Community centers didn't develop: urban highways, at the superblock's periphery, were more attractive for commercial activities than superblock cores, less accessible by car.[4] Although the municipality was trying to keep the city within manageable boundaries, landowners and developers were of another opinion. Using Doxiadis's superblock as a model, they endlessly replicated it on the plateau and turned the flat and arid landscape into square subdivisions, with no reverence for the compactness envisioned by the planners. Superblocks were emptied of their meaning as pedestrian paths were turned into roads and individual villas built instead of apartment buildings. A few years after its publication, the master plan was rendered obsolete by both the economic boom and the poor regulation of construction activity.

Meanwhile, the new Riyadh, unlike other planned cities such as Brasília and Islamabad, turned immensely popular with middle-class Saudis. The extension of Riyadh took place at the eve of a dramatic influx of poorly paid laborers into the country and the city. In the oil boom years, the large number of rural and foreign migrant workers that poured into Saudi cities pushed the Saudi middle classes outside of their old neighborhoods, and in the arms of real estate brokers and investors. Triggered by oil, international labor mobility set Saudis in motion and led to sharp social and spatial distinctions.

The real estate sector became a powerful tool of oil revenue redistribution. Riyadh grew through a cascade of brokerages between the royal family and individual homeowners, and middlemen made fortunes receiving land grants from princes, creating real estate companies and exchanging lands on a skyrocketing market. Properties situated outside of the city proper belonged to the royal family and had been granted by the king to various princes and princesses. These lands were known under the term *iqta'*, which also meant fief or feudal estate and had earned the Al Sa'ud the nickname of *iqta'iyin*, feudal lords.

Here is how the land trade worked. Affluent princes would donate or sell their lands to brokers, individual buyers, or public administrations. The new owners would reach out to the Town Planning Office, whose agents would plan the new neighborhood, roughly following Doxiadis's design. Equipped with asphalted roads and basic services, divided into plots, the land was then sold at auction (*haraj*) to the public. The immense stretches of land in and around Riyadh were soon covered with billboards and hasty subdivisions (*mukhattatat*) as investors and agents cut through gravel and sand, planting their ubiquitous '*aqarat* (real estate) signs and setting up improvised sale offices. According to Paul Bonnenfant's observations:

After the '*asr* prayer..., perched on a truck, the auctioneer, *samsar*, shows on a map the plots that are being sold, details their advantages and shouts the bids in his megaphone. He begins with the most interesting plots, at the crossroads or along large avenues, and finishes with the plots located inside the subdivision, which where less in demand.... Around 1976, at the height of the real estate boom, well-situated properties attracted as many as 300 to 400 cars in the middle of nowhere.... Between 1974 and 1978, benefits were outstanding: 100 riyals for every riyal invested [10,000 percent] wasn't a rare thing.[5]

An urban middle class took shape and 'Abd Allah al-Ghazhzhami documented the emergence of the figure of the *biznisman*, with his ceremonial "*bisht*, sunglasses and attaché case," ready to invest his money in joint stock real estate companies (*musahamat*). Buying and selling land was the talk of the town, and al-Ghazhzhami was bewildered by the success of this nobody, this '*amm fulan* who was a misfit but "invested 10,000 that became 100,000, then a million and are still breeding more money." This success story was all the more striking, because he was "the old *fulan*, you know, this poor fellow who was starving, the school janitor who quit his job to open a real estate office."[6]

The chances of enrichment were not equally shared, and some were better positioned than others to enjoy the bonanza. Those happy enough to be in the right place at the right time amassed huge fortunes in a few years. After the 1973 oil boom, "mega-landowners realized that money could be made laying out roads and plots at the periphery" of the city.[7] The al-Jumayh, al-Rajhi, al-Rusayyis, Bin Kleib, al-Badr, Bin Sa'idan and al-Musa,[8] along with the family of Doxiadis's sponsor 'Abd al-Mon'em al-'Aqil, became known by the man in the street as those "few families that really own Riyadh."[9]

Brokers and developers tapped into public sector salaries and into the huge financial possibilities opened by the creation, a year after the 1973 oil embargo, of a well-endowed Real Estate Development Fund (*sunduq al-tanmiyya al-'aqariyya*).[10] Meanwhile, the influx of rural and foreign migrants intensified, and Saudi society was drastically modified by urbanization. Reliance on state subsidies, salaries, and loans increased. Economic and social distinction sharpened between urban Saudis and rural and foreign migrants. Urbanization, labor migrations and state

control went hand in hand. The royal family actively fostered the formation of vast networks of acquiescence and allegiance around the massive
resources generated by the oil boom. Each of these "fiefdoms" was linked
to a prince or a powerful commoner, who served as an intermediary or a
broker (*wasta*) between the interests of his constituency and the financial
sway of the state.[11]

Riyadh grew at a time when Western oil-consumer states were looking
for ways to balance their trade with Saudi Arabia and devised aggressive
commercial strategies in order to export consumer goods, in particular
cars and house appliances.[12] The circulation of people, oil, manufac-
tured products, and ideas between North America and Central Najd produced strikingly similar urban landscapes. "Not only did Middle Eastern
oil become indispensable to an automobile-centered, mass-consumption
society, but the sort of suburban landscape that flourished in the postwar U.S. shaped ideas about modernity that Americans then sought to
export to the Arab world."[13] Post–World War II suburbanization and
consumerism in the United States were triggered by abundant public
loans, stable wages, and cheap gasoline. It was now the turn of Saudi
Arabia to become addicted to gas-guzzlers, tract houses, and urban highways.

Subdivisions (*al-mukhattatat*) were soon out of control. In 1977, only
six years after the design of the master plan, spontaneous developments
more than doubled the area delimited by Doxiadis, adding an extra
100,000 acres (400 sq. km) to the plan's 75,000 acres (300 sq. km).
In the following years, the municipality implemented various strategies
to curb suburban growth. Sprawl "resulted partly from the privatization
of Saudi life and the increasing tendency to live in detached homes,"
but was also due to "the real estate mania" that had seized the city.[14]
Suburbanization was driven more by corporate interests and migrational
pressures in the inner city than by consumer desires.

DA's contract with the city of Riyadh was not renewed after Doxiadis
died in 1975. The following year, the Ministry of Municipal and Rural
Affairs entrusted the revision of the Doxiadis master plan to the Société
Centrale d'Equipement du Territoire (SCET) International. SCET International was a French public company created in 1959 to continue France's
involvement in its recently decolonized territories, in particular Tunisia,
Morocco, and Western Africa.[15] After Napoleon I sent Domingo Badia
y Leblich to explore Mecca and Napoleon III commissioned William
Gifford Palgrave to visit Riyadh,[16] Central Arabia had avoided encounters with French imperialism. But the 1970s oil boom triggered increasing

economic and military ties between Paris and Riyadh, and urban planning was a major security concern for King Faisal and his successors Khalid and Fahd.

SCET International delivered the second master plan of Riyadh in 1982. Unlike DA planners, whose "city of the future" had quickly been proved obsolete, the French experts limited their intervention to short-term implementation and action. They included informal developments in their design and produced a document that allowed the municipality to "not only react to specific private sector proposals," but also to "take the lead and initiate action."[17] Still working within Doxiadis's repertoire of axes and square superblocks, they added a second axis – the transarabian highway, or Mecca-Khurais Road – to the initial northwest-southeast spinal cord. The transarabian highway was already bustling with roadside commerce and surrounded by real estate speculation, which DA architects had refused to recognize. Less inflexible, the French integrated all existing projects into their plan, which was more an ex post facto legalization of informal activities than a high modernist gesture. With its cruciform shape, centered on Cairo Square's massive cloverleaf interchange, the new Riyadh was officially born.

The SCET International plan aimed at approving existing land subdivisions and didn't set a limit to real estate development. In the following years, subdivisions continued to leapfrog into even more remote areas in the north and the west of the city. The English translator of Abdelrahman Munif's *Cities of Salt*, Peter Theroux, who in the early 1980s was living in Sulaymaniyya, witnessed the rapid growth of the city:

Some form of manifest destiny – it was actually the unholy alliance of landowning princes and city planners – was pushing Riyadh west. The nicest neighborhoods were now those between Suleimaniya and the new airport; Suleimaniya itself, once a bumptious boondock in the distant northwest of walled Riyadh, was now midtown. As the city limits moved relentlessly in the direction of Los Angeles, successive city centers sprang up and were beaten down again by ever grander shopping malls, hotels, and villa parks to the west. My window – the half of it not occupied by a growling air conditioner – used to look out on a street bed and the naked horizon; now it was six lanes of al-Arouba [Arabism] Street, marble-clad apartment blocks, and the Sheraton one mile beyond.[18]

In the mid-1980s, when oil prices eventually stagnated and the state entered a severe financial crisis, the developers' growth strategies were still fuelled by accessible loans, long-term prospects of large profit, a steady demand, and the growing congestion of Riyadh's central areas.

Private investors were still afloat and more likely to invest in real estate than in a still underdeveloped industrial sector.

Meanwhile, the detached villa was presented by developers as the most desirable living space for the urban classes, who wanted to imitate the princes and isolate themselves from the perceived invasion of rural migrants. The *bayt sha'bi* (people's house) built in mud brick or cement and organized around a central open courtyard was replaced by the *filla* or tract house, which was its exact spatial and social opposite. Built in the middle of the courtyard, the villa was adorned with large windows and porches and equipped with western toilets and a bathtub. Needless to say that their residents spent a great deal of energy blocking the windows and erecting huge metal screens on top of the walls already surrounding the yard to block the neighbors' view.[19]

The Saudi state actively encouraged this quick adoption of Western symbols of progress and well being, even if it wasn't appropriate to the climate and triggered cultural unease. According to one interviewee, in order to be eligible for an interest-free loan in the 1970s, one had to present a blueprint including a balcony and a "French bathroom" (*hammam fransi*, that is, with a bathtub or baignoire, *banyu*). Fierce dust storms, water shortages, and the fear of being seen were less powerful than state loans and did not prevent members of the middle class from buying villas en masse. "Even the most modest households have a double bathroom, one in the women's part and one in the men's section, whose hallway presents two, three, sometimes five or six sinks side by side, a symbol of the host's notoriety, *makana*, and power, *'azhama*."[20]

The villa was the symbol of the social distinction between the middle classes and the rest of the population. The real estate boom had resulted in an increased degree of segregation by income, ethnicity, and national origin. The (mostly sedentary) burgeoning Saudi middle class lived in the north and the west; (mostly nomadic) rural migrants lived in the east and the south; international labor migrants lived in and around the old center. (See Figure 4.2.) Behind the shining image of a unified Saudi constituency, communing in dress, belief and consumption, behind magazines' and advertisements' glossy façade, the thoroughfare, the individual car and the tract house, far from bringing Saudis together, were in reality effective instruments of economic and social segregation.

Against Doxiadis's dream of an integrated urban society, middle-class Saudis settled down in single-family tract home developments, and were cut off from Bedouins, peasants, and foreigners, who were perceived as unstable and threatening. Rural migrants were relegated to outer

FIGURE 4.2. People's houses (left) and low-rise apartment buildings (right) in Al-Marqab, 2009. Copyright © Pascal Menoret.

suburbs, low-income projects, and slums. Foreign labor migrants occupied a deserted and dilapidated inner city. In the meantime, secured compounds and gated communities were built everywhere for Western expatriates, who lived in a state of quasi-isolation from mainstream society. According to Peter Theroux, compounds oddly reproduced the very urban forms that had been left behind by Saudi middle classes:

They were known by the company names: Alfa-Laval, Vinnell, Lockheed, Northrop. Each had a huge pool and a little row of shops, a rec center and tiny streets. Ironically, these American or British or Swedish enclaves had come to resemble medieval Arab towns, down to the tiny market square, guarded city gate, and deep sense of community, as the Arab city encircling them had demolished all its indigenous features to become a gigantic American-scale metropolis.[21]

The north-south divide, embodied by the transarabian highway, proved at least as strong as the distinction between urban middle classes, rural migrants, and foreign workers. The old center and the southwest of Riyadh, where I lived with Sa'b for six months, purportedly epitomized Najdi society: al-Sultana, al-Suwaydi, al-Badi'a were home to lower-middle-class families from Central Najd and the strongholds of esteemed religious scholars. In the south of the city, people criticized the northern neighborhoods of Sulaymaniyya and 'Ulayya for their lavish restaurants and promenades, and described the north of the city, with its grid and its shopping malls, as imports from the West.

"Us, we are the genuine Saudi society," young voters told me one day during an electoral meeting in al-Suwaydi. "Them, in al-'Ulayya, they are non-Saudi Arabs, Arabs whose traditions and customs have been altered by the colonization" of North Africa and the Levant. According to them, the more relaxed atmosphere of the northern neighborhoods, where women could go alone to shopping malls and youth would "lose their time" in cafés, was due to the influx of Arab migrants from Egypt, Lebanon, and Syria, countries where European colonialism had – in their view – emasculated the authentic Arab and Islamic spirit. People in the south of the city were proud that tobacco could not be bought in Suwaydi's corner shops and that Islamic bookstores were more numerous than anywhere else. Middle-class Saudis conversely nicknamed Suwaydi the "Sunni Triangle" (*al-muthallath al-sunni*). Deep cleavages crisscrossed a complex imaginary geography. Indigenous and foreign, sedentary and Bedouin, stable and unstable, and "Westernized" and "extremist" were the categories along which Saudis framed the fragmented space of Riyadh.

The distinction between rich and poor, although rarely mentioned, also structured the urban space. In order to keep slum dwellers and rural migrants away from the mainstream of urban society, the municipality planned several low-income housing schemes outside the city. In 1973, the Town Planning Office designed the community of Nasim (The Breeze) in the northeast of Riyadh, on a patch of steppe between the city proper and the eastern camp of the National Guard. Individual plots were auctioned in 1974 to Bedouin working for the state and the army.[22] Hayy al-Dakhl al-Mahdud (The Low Income Quarter) was planned in the southwest of the capital and was rapidly populated by rural migrants and Bedouin. Low-income Saudis who arrived in town in the 1980s and 1990s settled down in outer slums, such as Nazhim (The Canyon) under the ridge to the east of the city, which their inhabitants progressively turned into functioning neighborhoods.

Not all slums were cleared or modernized, however, and 'Adil once drove me to one of the last shantytowns in Riyadh. North of King 'Abd Allah Avenue, a dilapidated area was hidden behind rows of luxurious villas. Mud alleys wound between wooden huts, mud-brick shacks, and tin shanties. Children and youngsters roamed streets where garbage piled up and stray dogs wandered menacingly. Saudi rural migrants had built the place in the 1970s near a construction site belonging to a state-owned company. The place was called "the people's quarter" (*al-hara al-sha'biyya*). Ten years later, when the urban sprawl caught up with the area, a developer tried to evict the inhabitants, who refused the meager compensation he offered them and decided to stay in their homes in protest.

This put the municipality in an uncomfortable situation: it didn't want to alienate the residents or publicly rebuff the developer. In a Solomon's judgment, it froze all new developments in the area and denied electricity, water, telephone, sewage and asphalting to the inhabitants, who then stole power and water from surrounding neighborhoods. Developers relabeled the place "the violated quarter" (*al-hara al-mughtasiba*). In the late 2000s, the residents were still awaiting a reasonable compensation and the opportunity to find better housing.[23] The "violated quarter" was not unique. Several other slums were to be found in the shadow of the royal palace and in the vicinity of the industrial zones.

The biggest slum, however, was the city center. Excluded from the booming housing market, international migrants crowded into downtown Riyadh, which did not become the oasis of culture, history, and the arts the Greek planners dreamed it would. Dira, Umm Slem, Shumaysi and al-Marqab had plenty of landmarks: their small squares, winding streets and picturesque hills were lined with mud brick palaces, crowded souks and rows of old houses. Instead, the downtown areas became, according to the former deputy mayor of Riyadh, "a landscape of run-down slums, half populated neighborhoods of cheap architecture, housing low-income Saudi segments and a desperate Third World expatriate labor force."[24] According to 'Adil, Saudis were grateful that those he described as "dog-eating Koreans," who built the city's impressive road system in the 1970s, had rid Riyadh of its swarming and aggressive canine population. But their collective gratitude did not translate into the provision of labor rights, decent wages, and suitable housing.

Riyadh was no longer a city per se, but rather a monotonous and rapidly decaying system of ghettos, some for the rich and some for the poor, some for the indigenous population and some for the imported workforce. "A village of five million inhabitants" according to an interviewee, where rumors quickly spread and reputation was paramount, the city was suburbanized at the expense of its most vulnerable residents: foreign workers, Bedouin and rural migrants, lower-middle-class households. Huge real estate empires and commercial monopolies were created in the name of modernization and development, which only further deepened social and economic inequalities.

4.3. The Saudi Exception

In our first weeks in Sultana, Sa'b and I were driving around to shop for furniture and frequently stopped by corner shops (*baqalat*) to buy cold drinks and snacks. Sa'b pointed to the odd behavior of those customers who stopped their cars by the *baqala*, honked the horn and shouted their orders through the open car window, as if they were in a drive-in. If nobody came, they would eventually get off their car and step in the store, often making a row, sometimes insulting or threatening the store employee, who, often a foreign migrant, would lower his head in silence. Confronted with such rudeness, some courageous employees would turn the whole situation into a joke and, swallowing their pride, treat the obnoxious customer with an ironical joviality.

Seeing how startled I looked while witnessing these scenes, Sa'b had briefly explained that this uncivil behavior was one of the effects of what he called the "culture of the boom" (*thaqafa al-tafra*): no need to leave your car, because there were enough *baqalat* in town and enough space around them to stop right in front of the door; no need to go and shop yourself, because a pliable employee had been lured to your country by its riches and was bent into obeying you by an overall exploitative and violent system. Sa'b contrasted these attitudes to those of his relatives and friends in the steppe, where migrant workers were treated as equals and had picked up a Bedouin accent, and where people felt less entitled than in the city. There also were less *baqalat*, and everybody knew everybody, which limited the possibilities for anonymous humiliation. And even in the steppe, things were changing, anyway.

The oil boom was called *tafra* by ordinary Saudis, a word as opposed to the official notion of *tanmiya* (development) as a brusque leap is distinct from a progressive evolution. Although the state portrayed the modernization of society as a harmonious development following a well-engineered series of plans, the man in the street associated it with disorder, inflation, and a rupture with a well-established set of customs and traditions. The imported notion of development (*tanmiya* or *tatwir*), which implied the progressive germination of innate qualities, aligned well with the ideology of the state, according to which God had fixed His gaze on the Saudi people since time immemorial. State bureaucrats – in particular those in charge of education – didn't see modernization and development as an exogenous and threatening force. It was one more chapter of a sacred history that had started with Islam and had been revived by the Al Sa'ud's rule, more proof that theirs was indeed the chosen people.

When Aramco resumed its operations in the Eastern Province after World War II, modernization and development were thought of as goodwill policies intended to assess the oil company's concern for a local society that could easily have taken U.S. oilmen, imbued with racial arrogance and technical superiority, for a colonial vanguard. Yet building roads, airports, cities, irrigation networks and hospitals was not as disinterested a program as Aramco wanted Saudis to believe. As Robert Vitalis and Toby C. Jones have shown, developmental work was first and foremost destined to serve the company's operations and expand its bottom line. Its second intended use by the Saudi state was to better map and control society. Humanitarian aid, laid down in glossy magazines that the company published for the Saudis – and the Americans – to see, were not development's primary goal.[25]

During the 1960s, King Faisal's administration adopted development as the main ideology of the Saudi state. American, Italian, German, and Greek experts believed in the validity of technical answers to political and social issues, and their contribution was all the more welcome given that the Saudi state consciously avoided raising any topic that could lead to political tension. Tribal boundaries, class formation, and sectarian divisions were drowned in a technical discourse centered on the conquest and exploitation of natural resources. Development meant depoliticization. "The principles of science of expertise... lent themselves to the project of legitimizing Saudi political authority because of the claim that science and expertise were, in fact, apolitical." In other words, "while development continued to be mostly about strengthening [Al Sa'ud's] hold on the country, development discourse made an effort to mask this" by presenting their empire as the rule of science and reason.[26]

The main Al Sa'ud princes were not the only powerbrokers. A sizable clergy still dealt with religious, family, social and some educational issues, technocrats began to constitute a class on their own, and powerful merchant families were on the rise.[27] But senior princes were still the main decision makers in the country, and they collectively were the source of all power, especially financial and economic, and of all authority, even religious and moral. They promoted development as a state ideology by which enlightened and benevolent decision makers outsmarted their people (or flock, *ra'ia*, in the state's phraseology) through their collective achievements (*injazat*). The rule of experts made the legitimacy of the Al Sa'ud oligarchy.

Oil-driven modernization and Islamic principles were not thought to be contradictory: they both bore witness of the excellence of the Al Sa'ud, who had combined them to unite Arabia and bring prosperity to the people. According to former General Mufti Muhammad bin Ibrahim Al ash-Sheikh, "God opened the chests of the earth" in Saudi Arabia's oil province, to bestow His blessings upon the Muslim community.[28] A textbook version of this narrative was that God's plan manifested itself in the destiny of Arabia, from the creation of the universe to the revelation of Islam to the formation of Saudi Arabia to the discovery of oil and today's bonanza.[29] Shockingly overlooking chronology, official ideology presented Saudi Arabia as the birthplace of Islam and as the Prophet's homeland, and had developed a complex narrative of election under the rubric of the "Saudi exception" (*al-khususiyya al-su'udiyya*). Saudi Arabia was deemed unique because of its Islamic system of government, the presence on its soil of the two most sacred sites of Islam and the idea that – notwithstanding the 1915 Protectorate treaty and the 1927 friendship agreement signed with Britain – it had never been sullied by colonization. Almost entirely fictitious, the theme of Saudi exceptionalism was rehearsed by Saudi and U.S. opinion makers: Islam and development were supposed to legitimize Al Sa'ud's rule both internally and externally.[30]

During the 1990 Gulf War, Prince Khaled al-Faisal, one of King Faisal's sons, offered a flamboyant expression of the Saudi exception's narrative. While foreign troops were using the Saudi territory to march on Iraq, the official bard of the royal family chanted the supremacy of the Saudi nation:

> Raise your head, you are Saudi
> Your reputation crosses all borders
> You have no competitor in this world
> The others are deficient and you are superior
> Knight like your ancestors
> Of God's house [in Mecca] the custodian
> You received a glory that you bestow in turn...
> [King] Fahd our leader Fahd our torchbearer
> Fahd, free falcon who hunts
> And graced by God feasts with his people
> You elevate the Saudi nation.[31]

The poem later became the anthem of several Saudi soccer teams. In the early 2000s, a young Saudi answered the prince with a trenchant parody:

One of the senior buffoons once wrote a celebrated poem, in which he said: "Raise your head, you are Saudi, The others are deficient and you are superior." From this tribune, I wanted to make him swallow a stone – my excuses to the stone – and I wrote these verses:

> Lower your head, you are Saudi
> You are dominated, a slave, a dog
> Don't make any effort
> Be cool and stay in your bed
> Since you already have all you want . . .
> You only count in the world
> Don't pay attention to jealous people
> Who shamelessly criticize you . . .
> If they say you're a fat worm
> Don't cry, it's pure envy
> If they say you're an old perv
> Don't cry, it's pure envy
> If they say you're a donkey
> Don't cry, it's pure envy
> If they say you're a loser
> Don't cry, it's pure envy.

Interviewees would casually refer to Khaled's poem, most often with an ironic wink. They would mention it when it came to the huge discrepancy between the official, or "pompous" (*rasmi*), version of history, according to which benevolent princes harmoniously developed the country, and what had happened in reality. Nawwaf explained to me that the previous generations, these elders whom Sa'b's friends and cousins gently ridiculed, did indeed believe in a narrative of quasi-magical abundance brought about thanks to the royals' enlightened guidance. Born into prosperity and confronted with a bloated bureaucracy, arrogant civil servants and brutal police, the young generations did not feel the same gratitude.

NAWWAF – Elders are ignorant, I'm telling you, . . . people above fifty, when they were young, in their twenties, they worked very, very hard, they were doing hard jobs, working in construction. They worked from daybreak to sundown, then they came home and they slept. Again and again, daybreak to sundown and then sleep, to earn their daily crust of bread. Then came the economic boom [*al-tafra*], people became civil servants, they got cash and new homes. They thought that all these things were gifts from the government, and that they'd better consider themselves happy. That's how they saw things: I used to work, and then I stopped working. Life was harsh, and then it became easy. . . . (*He speaks more and more vehemently.*) For instance, when an elder buys a car with his own money, he bows to the royal family, he thanks them for the car, even though he bought it with his own money.... As if this money was the prince's property, as if the prince gave it away out of charity, not out of duty.... Look, now, in our society, the elders love the royal family. Those who came after them, a lot less so. A lot less so. To the extent that they began to hate the royal family. And their sons also inherit this revolt from their fathers. Today, young people my age or younger, you have to understand that they just curse the royals. It is something that we partly inherit now. Don't trust the newspapers, which repeat that things are getting better and that the spirit of revolt will fade away.

In his book on modernity in Saudi Arabia, 'Abd Allah al-Ghazhzhami recounts his version of the boom years in terms that echo Nawwaf's indignation. A young graduate coming home in 1976 from the United Kingdom, al-Ghazhzhami was flabbergasted by the rapid rate of social and economic change and by the deep moral crisis of Saudi society. "People no longer asked [him] about Britain and literature, thought or civilization. Everybody was talking deals, business, companies and speculation. They called each other sheikh and businessman; they had cars, checkbooks and attaché-cases. It's the boom, buddy! [*Innaha al-tafra, ia 'amm!*]." In the face of bonanza, the "modernist" ideals that the young graduate brought back with him sounded irrelevant. "We started doubting the value of the science we were carrying...; only millions and millionaires had any importance.... These millions didn't need competence or efforts or science, they popped up by pure chance."[32]

Coming home to his town of 'Unayza, in the Qasim, al-Ghazhzhami experienced a "moral shock." To him as to Sa'b, the "culture of the boom" (*thaqafa al-tafra*) was killing social and human values:

Change was not only about clothes, bottom lines and summering in London, but also about ways and customs. People's behavior changed: they were rushing through everything, generous of their words but stingy with their attention. They were bragging about their own merits, whereas before the boom they hated to talk about themselves. They started considering you as a colleague and no longer a friend, they were sitting down with you to talk about deals and look for business opportunities. They were no longer making conversation...In order to realize their commercial goals, people would cut the thread of conviviality (*ta'aruf*). In trade, you got to break human values and replace them with the values of acquisition (*takathur*). This is the most severe change that the boom (*al-tafra*) has provoked in this country.[33]

Al-Ghazhzhami's pages are reminiscent of a "Letter to the graduates of universities and higher education institutes" written in 1954 by 'Abd

Allah al-Turaiqi, the first Saudi oil minister and champion of the nationalization of the U.S. oil company Aramco:

I came back to my homeland imagining that... doors would spring wide open before me, that I would be given the place I imagined fitted my abilities and knowledge, which was, naturally, the first place.... I was full of naïveté, totally foreign to the reality of existence. An abyss so unfathomable that I dared not look into it was split open between my compatriots and myself.... All looked at me in pity and irony and saw a young delusional idiot whose body was physically here but whose mind and imagination roamed elsewhere.... I spoke of patriotism, devotion, and sacrifice. They spoke of So-and-so's success, of So-and-so's gains, of how So-and-so had become someone or had been granted a piece of meat, a new car or a yearly stipend.... The best ones told me to get rid of my naïveté and go see So-and-so, to toady to So-and-so, to hole up under So-and-so's armchair,... to kiss everybody's hand, to be humble and submissive with my boss, his servants and even his slaves.[34]

Beside the abolition of slavery, the difference between the 1970s and the 1950s was that princes no longer granted pieces of meat, new cars, or stipends, but huge real estate fiefdoms and import licenses, which would allow their owners to become kings in their own domain and to create their own commercial dynasty.

4.4. "The Inhumanity of the Place"

After 1973, massive profits were made by the happy few who, in the shadow of the royal family, had invested their riyals and their know-how in the right business. The bin Sa'idan family was one of those. In the 1940s and the 1950s, Muhammad bin Sa'idan, the father, was building mudbrick houses on the outskirts of the old Riyadh, in the palm groves that progressively gave way to streets and neighborhoods. His ancestors were caravan conductors, and he had also been a truck driver and a garment seller. Through his work as a homebuilder he got to know the main landowners of Riyadh and became a real estate agent in his own right. His reputation of honesty and shrewdness led General Mufti Muhammad bin Ibrahim to commission him to buy and manage properties for the Islamic endowment administration (*al-Awqaf*). He was thus introduced to the circles of power that would make his family's fortune.

In the late 1960s, as the price of land sharply increased and a housing crisis hit Riyadh, Muhammad's son Hamad opened a real estate agency with two friends, a religion teacher and a civil servant. Following his father's example, he created joint-stock companies (*musahamat*) with other agents to buy huge pieces of land and create subdivisions that they then sold to homebuilders and homeowners. Benefiting from his father's reputation, Hamad's elder brother 'Abd Allah created his own real estate office in 1974. The two brothers joined their efforts and, thanks to the oil boom, their venture became one of the first development companies in the country. Their patrons in the royal family granted them huge tracts of land all around Riyadh, especially in the new Central Business District – Doxiadis's central spine – and in the economically promising areas north of the city.

In the 1980s, in order to promote the interests of their profession, Hamad's younger brother Ibrahim created the developers' board at the Riyadh Chamber of Commerce. With their aggressive business practices, the bin Sa'idan brothers had both benefited from and contributed to the real estate boom that swept the capital in the 1970s and 1980s. Before the oil boom, their father was a self-made man and a well-respected homebuilder and broker; after 1974, his sons worked their way to a position of monopoly over many of the city's new planned and unplanned neighborhoods. Working with the royal family, they contributed to the dramatic explosion of housing prices that, during the last decades of the twentieth century, led to the city's sprawl. The bin Sa'idan were not princes, but they were not too far below the royal family either: the truck driver's sons were now called sheikhs by the capital's newspapers.[35]

The bin Sa'idan brothers' story was hardly unique. In al-Ghazhzhami's social circle, composed of well-to-do sedentary oasis dwellers from Najd, people were also intoxicated by easy money and started imitating princes in their manners, speech, clothes, rudeness, and demeaning attitudes. The old tribal ethics, based on honor, pride, and generosity, were replaced by ambition and greed. The real estate market became a "theater of adventure and gains," a public scene where people played the part of "individualistic and materialistic arrivistes." According to al-Ghazhzhami, the boom transformed independent and proud hard-workers into lazy and arrogant retainers. As a result of the rapid growth of the real estate market, the crowded towns of Najd became a suburban hell:

Spatial development cannot be mistaken for human development; the human dimension has been overlooked and one resents the inhumanity of the place. See our wide and asphalted streets, decorated with all sorts of advertisements, billboards, lamps, skyscrapers, and search for Man: you will only find roaring cars and squeaking tires. Whoever looks for a cozy place in this frozen splendor is shaken by his own solitude. Imagine a child, a woman or an old man strolling down our streets . . . how lonesome would they feel! People even frown upon walking in the street, not to mention the dangers that await women and children. . . . We abandoned to others the task of developing us. Had we decided to do it ourselves, we would have achieved a true development and avoided the leap into the unknown [*tafra*].[36]

Al-Ghazhzhami perhaps knew that Doxiadis had repeatedly denounced the "inhuman city," characterized in his eyes by the domination of machines over space. But the creation of large urban monopolies managed by private developers and construction companies and the drastic increase in cars had changed the city beyond its planner's intentions.

Saudi suburbia did not develop as a result of the demographic and economic growth of the middle class. Rather, it grew out of the oil boom and of the pyramidal power relationships between the royal family, the business class, the middle classes, and rural and foreign migrants. In the name of development and modernization, the royal family based the national economy of the kingdom almost exclusively on consumption. The state's massive oil revenues were not managed transparently and financed the royal family's opulent standard of living, huge military expenditures, colossal infrastructure projects, and public sector wages and pensions. These resources were tapped by the clients of the royal family. Real estate investors, developers, subcontractors, and importers benefited from state projects and built fortunes catering to a middle class that was eager to distinguish itself from peasants, Bedouin, and laborers.

The steep political and social hierarchy that grew out of the oil boom was not merely a matter of proximity to the royal family, but also of time and opportunity. Immediately after the 1973 boom, one's good fortune mostly depended on when important decisions were made and deals were struck:

The real estate market . . . expresses many aspects of Saudi society at a time of accelerated change: the royal family exerts a discreet but ubiquitous power; the bourgeoisie grows wealthier thanks to the patronage of the princes; the general population imitates the bourgeoisie but, coming too late, must rely on solidarity networks and extended families; all energies are invested in business deals; rural and Bedouin regions empty and their inhabitants flock to the cities; the odd foreigner tries to draw a maximum benefit from his sojourn in Arabia.[37]

After the first round of musical chairs, things solidified: there were only so many pieces of land to distribute around the city. The housing market boomed again in the 1990s, but latecomers had to be extremely shrewd if they wanted a place in the sun. In 2006, Nawwaf introduced me to a real estate developer, Abu Salih, who ran a small development agency in the north of Riyadh. Abu Salih had come to the capital in 1992, shortly after the Gulf War, because "Riyadh is like America . . . the city attracts people from all over the place." He claimed that his passion for real estate came from his family's reliance on land: his father was a peasant in the Qasim area, 300 kilometers north of Riyadh. A religion teacher in his hometown, Abu Salih became realtor on the side:

ABU SALIH – When I was a kid, I already loved real estate, the idea of buying lands. . . . I was an amateur and I became a professional. I opened a real estate agency in the Qasim but, really, my town was . . . limited. I was working well, thank God, but it was below my ambitions. I had several options: I could move either to Riyadh or to Jeddah or to Dammam. I preferred Riyadh because it was the capital. If I had been to Jeddah I would have been stuck there, with no possibility to invest anywhere else. Riyadh on the other hand is like the sun: you can travel along the rays it projects in all directions. That's why I came to Riyadh. . . . And the local culture is close to my own. If I had moved to Jeddah, I would perhaps have been in a different culture, I wouldn't have known how they build, how they live inside their habitations, what orientation they prefer. . . . Before I left the Qasim, I sold my house there to be unable to come back. I had made an irreversible decision.

Influential and wealthy agents already worked the real estate market in the capital and Abu Salih had to build his network from scratch. Unlike powerful merchants like Salih al-Rajhi, for instance, he could not benefit from close ties to the princes. Unlike brokers and developers like the bin Sa'idan brothers or 'Abd al-'Aziz al-Musa, he did not have the financial means to trade large properties. He built his business piece by piece, cultivating his networks among construction subcontractors to reduce his costs and investing time and energy in building relationships with his clients. He went back to school and earned degrees in real estate, finance, and personal management.

Regulations were significantly more restrictive than in the 1970s. A few years before Abu Salih moved to Riyadh, in 1989, the municipality had adopted a more rigorous approach toward suburban sprawl, which it dubbed "Urban Growth Boundary Policy." In order to discourage developers from investing in faraway projects, the Ministry of Municipal Affairs drew a line on the map of Riyadh outside of which the state stopped providing basic infrastructure and loans. Yet the new measure was accompanied by clauses that made it in large part ineffective: outside the boundary, land could still be eligible for government loans and services, provided that developers built roads and supplied electricity to the new neighborhoods. Instead of stopping the sprawl, the regulation put more power in the hands of the major developers, and transformed the landscape of the capital. Investors kept planning new neighborhoods and using their financial sway and connections to regularize their projects ex post facto. "The land was initially given by the King to powerful members of the society," which "contributed to the [developers'] sense of immunity from progressive legislative reforms and enforcement of controls.... The Ministry of Municipal Affairs and its surrogate Riyadh municipality . . . encouraged the dumping of valuable financial resources into vacant lands."[38]

This new policy favored the real estate barons. Small actors, who did not have enough influence and capital to assume the extra cost of development and shoulder their way through the local administration, were forced into subordinate positions as local brokers, homebuilders, and realtors. Abu Salih was not turned off, however, and soon focused his attention on the north of the city where, outside of the 1989 boundaries, the informal market was in full swing. His project was to team with big developers to fine-tune their offer, to build houses, and to sell a finished product to families. As the lowest link in the food chain, he was still determined to make some profit.

ABU SALIH – [In the north of Riyadh,] real estate investment started off in 1974 with the sale of bare land, big chunks of land. For instance, you bought a piece of land for two, three or four millions, you kept it two, four, eight or ten years and you sold it at a huge profit to somebody who would also speculate on it. And so on, until somebody decided to develop. The whole area was planned in 1974 . . . Actual development started only in 1994. . . . Lobbies of businessmen joined their forces to buy lands. They were subdividing, cutting off 2km by 2km blocks that they sold one by one. And the area in the north was huge, about 100 sq. km. Others would buy one block each, develop it and sell it piece by piece to individuals or companies. Now, since about ten years ago, companies [like mine] buy 200,000 or 500,000 sq. m properties and build housing units.

Between the planning of the area in 1974 and its development twenty years later, investors and merchants speculated on properties sold or granted by princes. In the 1990s, the outskirts of Riyadh turned into a nightmarish landscape of wide and straight roads that, leading nowhere, demarcated subdivisions (*al-mukhattatat*) and were built as a prerequisite for legalization. Riyadh was now encased in a glacis of naked square plots above which streetlamps, built in compliance with the 1989 regulation, glowed in the void, and where young Saudis, attracted by miles of flawless asphalt, drifted stolen cars. Away from the bustle of the city and its police patrols, the empty roads offered privacy and tranquility. During the relatively cool Najdi nights, youngsters could reflect on the shimmering grid of the capital in the distance from the slowly rising terrain to the north. Streetlamps would at time cause ugly accidents: many skidding cars ended their squealing trajectories against poles of steel and glass.

After 1994, when investors began to develop the area, homebuyers flocked to real estate companies set up in scruffy offices built overnight. Working with large investors, small developers like Abu Salih were building individual houses in the wilderness. Even with the added cost of infrastructure and utilities, investing in these scattered developments was still profitable for him: buying a house in a distant community proved far cheaper for homebuyers than one in the neighborhoods already planned by the Greeks and the French. The city was now a square 50 miles on a side and still growing. Real estate moguls kept buying new barren properties on the edge of existing neighborhoods, paving roads and erecting streetlamps. Young people kept drifting cars, their engines screaming and their tires screeching, under the eyes of terrified suburbanites.

Farther away, in the desert surrounding Riyadh, the royal family still held on to properties they had not yet granted to their clients and retained as future tokens of appreciation or compensation. It is in these remote zones that the king granted a huge stretch of land to his brother, triggering the disbelief, anger and despair of Thamer and his friends, in the rest house battered by a winter storm discussed at the opening of last chapter. Behind the façade bestowed upon the growth of Riyadh by expertise and urban planning, beyond sparkly notions of modernity and development, the mechanism through which the capital was expanding in all directions was truly feudal.

4.5. "You Don't Need to Innovate"

We don't risk, we don't play, we don't innovate.

– A civil servant[39]

The royal family did not only offer pieces of land; they also granted import licenses to their closest clients. Since the beginnings of oil exploitation, foreign companies could invest in Saudi Arabia only through the services of a local agent or *wakil*, who represented one or several companies in the country, smoothed relations with the state, and reaped a significant share of the benefits as a reward. This mechanism was officially dismantled in 2005 when Saudi Arabia entered the World Trade Organization. In practice, many foreign companies still stick to agents, whose services often prove less costly than direct investment.⁴⁰

Between foreign businesses and Saudi consumers, this system of proxy ensured the existence of a class of middlemen and facilitators who soon built immense riches representing carmakers, manufacturers, and banks in the most dynamic market of the Middle East. The intervention of the royal family was a key element of the system as it ensured a quasi-monopoly of the dealer for his products. Powerful agents were major political actors and companies were forced to pass through them in order to gain access to the Saudi market.

King 'Abd al-'Aziz granted one of the first car dealerships of the country to his advisor Harry St John 'Abd Allah Philby, an ex-British colonial agent who converted to Islam and started importing Ford cars and trucks in the 1930s. The oil company Aramco similarly granted licenses to its most successful employees, who created import and manufacturing businesses to serve the U.S. trust. One of the most representative members of this new class of entrepreneurs was probably 'Abd al-Latif Jamil, who started his career in the 1950s as a small subcontractor of Aramco. He ran a gas station near Jeddah, on the road leading to Riyadh some seven hundred miles to the East. In an odd vignette written in 1957, *Aramco World*, the oil company's magazine, likened Jamil's commercial skills to piracy. One of his employees warned drivers with a microphone that his station was the last one on the road. It was not, but this piece of false advertising perhaps contributed to Jamil's success.⁴¹ He soon became the head of a business empire that included the Toyota dealership in Arabia, real estate agencies and financial corporations. In the decade following the oil boom, the bold serviceman of Jeddah became one of the wealthiest commoners in the country.

After the 1973 oil boom, business opportunities were sprouting everywhere and the state liberally distributed commercial licenses. The dealership system facilitated the creation of business empires as the sales of American cars, German appliances and Japanese products soared in the 1970s and 1980s. Between 1970 and 1984, the length of asphalted roads was multiplied threefold, from 5,000 miles to 15,000 miles, while the number of registered vehicles was multiplied by 65, from 60,000 to 3.9 million. In 1984, there was approximately one motor vehicle for three inhabitants and one car for five inhabitants. Between 1969 and 1992, cars were "the largest or second largest import category" in the country.⁴²

Framed by the state and religious scholars as a godsend to the chosen people, oil wealth slowed innovation and risk taking and participated in what was called the resource curse of the country.[43] I observed Saudi businessmen's behavior during a lecture at the Riyadh Chamber of Commerce and Industry, to which I was invited in March 2007. Sheikh 'Abd al-Ilah had introduced me to a member of the chamber who had promised to record an interview about his economic and social projects. The businessman was congenial and talkative, and I thought that I could establish with him a relationship of trust. Yet after this first introduction, he began to regularly take rain checks, canceling meetings at the last minute, and putting off our appointments. After a few months of this treatment, he sent me an invitation to a lecture at the chamber, as if to show me his goodwill and apologize for his unpredictable agenda.

The lecturer was Ghassan al-Sulayman, who ran the local franchise of an international chain of furniture stores. He was the grandson of King 'Abd al-'Aziz's finance minister, 'Abd Allah Sulayman, who in 1933 had signed the oil concession agreement with the U.S. consortium that later became Aramco (and who had given his name to my neighborhood, al-Sulaymaniyya, built on land he once owned). After being introduced by the president of the Chamber, al-Sulayman addressed a crowd of deferential and attentive businesspeople. He was expected to talk about his experience and to give away the tricks of his trade. Many aspiring entrepreneurs, dressed to the nines, crowded the huge room. Saudis donned the national garb, consisting of an immaculate white robe and a red-and-white-checkered headdress. Some elders were draped in the thin gold-embroidered black wool coat (*bisht*) favored by princes. The rare Syrian or Egyptian had on sleek suits and ties. Businesswomen filled a second lecture room, in another part of the building, which was linked to our room by a closed circuit TV. As if at a debutants' soiree, pretenders were sizing each other up and glancing at each other with a guarded expression. Eager to benefit from al-Sulayman's experience, they seemed equally annoyed and angered to have to share it with others.

Al-Sulayman first recounted his modest start as a call center manager and insisted on the fact that his first business experiences were failures. "Entrepreneurs must not fear failure, for there is no shame in failure," he said against what he perceived was a received wisdom in Saudi society. His career was not that of a self-made man, however, and the wealth and reputation of his family proved at least as decisive as his own merits. Lured by his grandfather's sway, British investors soon approached him and sought his services to establish a furniture business in the country. A few years later, he became the representative of an international furniture company and opened their biggest store in the Middle East.

Al-Sulayman then mentioned the trajectory of his grandfather who, "after he retired and left the governmental service, wished to also become an entrepreneurial pioneer, not only for the sake of profit, but to develop our nation and . . . serve society." According to his grandson, 'Abd Allah Sulayman was determined to be first in many things. After he had been the first finance minister of the country, he created the first five-star palace in Saudi Arabia, the first cement factory, the first joint-stock company, and the first private college on a piece of land that he later donated to the state.

"Businessmen must serve society," he hammered at various times during the lecture. As we soon discovered, the real goal of his talk was not to explain the secrets of his success (inheritance seemed more crucial than entrepreneurship). It was to defend the reputation of the business community against accusations of selfishness. The Saudi printed press increasingly broached commercial "scandals." In 2006, during the Riyadh financial crash, big investors or *hawamir* (big fish) had been publicly held responsible for the losses of millions of small shareholders. Several financial and real estate scams, exposed by emboldened journalists, had also tainted the community's standing. Businespeople and investors were repeatedly accused of preying on gullible citizens.

GHASSAN AL-SULAYMAN – In 2000, with a bunch of Saudi businessmen, we got together to change the image of the Saudi entrepreneur, who was portrayed by the media as a greedy individual who is interested in his own profit and doesn't care about serving his society, developing his nation or solving the problems we have in our country. . . . We set up a tool to improve our image, the Businessmen's Association. . . . Existing businessmen associations had only two goals: human resources development and networking. We added two other goals: one, team up against individualism and the authoritarianism of most businessmen, who don't implement the [Islamic notion of consultation or] *shura*. And two, work on morality, on how we can serve society. . . . We want to develop the model of a Muslim businessman, of a businessman who serves society, to fight the wrong image exposed in the media and who gives a true idea of what moral businessmen actually do. The Prophet was a merchant and Islam propagated in Southeastern Asia and Eastern Africa through commerce, which means that the Islamic experience is successful in this regard. We need to look at this experience if we want to succeed.[44]

During the question and answer session, Al-Sulayman agreed to share some advice with the audience. The atmosphere was a bit friendlier after the President of the Chamber left the room, explaining in a paternalistic fashion to his "sons and daughters the attending businessmen and businesswomen" that, because "80% of our work is to serve the common good," [*sic*] he was to join Interior Minister Prince Nayef for a fund-raising party. After his departure, al-Sulayman lowered his guard and became less pompous. His answers painted a fascinating picture of what it really meant to create and operate a business in the country. In response to questions about how to become successful when first starting out in business, he praised the Saudi model, which combined state-granted monopolies with a general lack of innovation:

GHASSAN AL-SULAYMAN – The system of trade monopoly (*imtiyazat*) offers the best business opportunity to young entrepreneurs. Getting a trade monopoly has become a means to grow a business quickly. For instance, I am the only one who represents my company in Saudi Arabia and Bahrain... A lot of companies in the world grew by holding trade monopolies.... Kamal Jamjum for instance holds a distribution monopoly for... a renowned cosmetic company.... The good thing about trade monopolies is that instead of trying to invent something new, you can benefit from an experience that has succeeded elsewhere.... You don't need to innovate; all you need to do is to adapt already successful products to the Saudi market.

Everything was for the best in the best of possible worlds, since innovation was actually harder to come by than franchise monopoly. Innovation and creativity were not key qualities in a national economy that was primarily based on real estate and import. The predatory habits of the ruling elite fostered the creation of a tailored business world, populated with opportunistic investors and ruthless entrepreneurs who favored quick profit over long-term investment. Massive unemployment was the most visible consequence of this shortsightedness, which the royal family ironically encouraged under the name of development. Al-Sulayman wrapped up the meeting on a cynical note. Before leaving the conference room, he said, "Success is in God's hands because the market is a huge mess. Many succeeded without deserving it, and many failed who deserved to succeed." Several businesspeople displayed the same self-confidence, couched in an Islamic vocabulary that was intended to win their consumers' hearts and minds. Yet when merchants tried to reinvest their economic capital in politics, voters often rebuffed them in favor of authentic Islamic activists.

4.6. Urban Space, Contentious Space

When the royal family organized municipal elections in February 2005 – the first ones since King Faisal's accession to the throne in 1964 – many real estate investors, developers, and merchants tried to get a foot in the country's new municipal councils. That the responsibilities of the municipal councils were limited to an advisory role with no budget power did not discourage them. Elections were seen as a first step toward a more transparent management of cities and developers had to be part of this evolution. Badr bin Saʿidan, grandson of pioneer developer Muhammad bin Saʿidan, son of Ibrahim bin Saʿidan, and a major player on the real estate market, threw himself into the race in the fourth ward, where 'Ulayya, the capital's Central Business District, was located. As a result of the intense speculation driven by his family and their competitors, land prices were so high in the area that a majority of plots, waiting for an appropriate buyer, were still patches of yellow dust between scrawny high-rises and humongous shopping malls.

Bin Saʿidan planted his electoral tent on one of these empty lots, in plain view of the drivers rushing up and down King Fahd Avenue. Every night during the ten days of campaigning he offered a lavish dinner to voters. Like a wedding pavilion, the tent was equipped with round tables and chairs draped in immaculate cloth, its floor covered with richly colored Persian carpets. Incense burners were placed in strategic spots and a wood fire was glowing in front of the entrance. A podium divided it into two halves: a conference room and a dining room behind a partition.

Young Bedouin working for a private security company guarded the tent. Some of them belonged to families that had migrated between Syria, Kuwait, Iraq, and Saudi Arabia and were stateless people (*bidun*). Although culturally and linguistically Saudi, they were deprived of the Saudi citizenship and of the benefits that come with it. Probably *bidun* as well, waiters served coffee and tea and skillfully managed a gargantuan buffet, while retainers and employees circulated among voters, registering names and phone numbers. They intended to remind them to go to the polls on election day and, once in the booth, to make the right decision. Pakistani immigrants were cleaning the premises and disposing of the garbage. Its access carefully filtered and its surroundings secured, the place was a miniature Saudi society, organized hierarchically around a self-admiring landed lord.

Dressed in a white robe and a beige suit jacket, a large commercial smile on his face, Badr bin Saʿidan was chairing a debate on environmental urban design. Along with "affordable housing" and the "right to vote," "environmental design" was one of the pillars of his campaign, which recycled the communication of the bin Saʿidan group: "affordable housing" (*al-maskan al-maysar*) was for instance the name of one of the group's companies.[45] But voters' questions eluded the night's topic and

broached instead urban delinquency and security, car robberies, dangerous crossroads, uncontrolled youngsters, and the necessity to build more
gated communities.

As if to give some substance to their fears, a black Suburban van slowed
right in front of the tent. Its driver, a youngster wearing a tight *thub* and
a baseball cap, shouted in direction of bin Sa'idan, making his loud and
piercing voice heard by the whole audience: "What do you want, you
loser? There are no elections!" (*Wesh tabi ia fashil? Ma fi intikhabat!*).
His passengers, three or four teens with long, disheveled hair, burst into a
high-pitched laughter while he stepped on the gas, sending his car forward
with a deafening noise.

Inside the tent, bin Sa'idan did not acknowledge the incident. He carefully tried to evade the voters' questions and sported the half-annoyed,
half-superior air that was often the hallmark of Saudi elites. When a
young man asked about high unemployment among youth, he replied in
a bureaucratic tone that many issues were under the responsibility of the
state and not of the municipality, dismissing the young man's concerns.
Because municipalities were part of the state and enjoyed no financial or
political autonomy, his answer did not make much sense, but his tone was
definitive and the young man did not raise his hand a second time. Right
outside the tent, in the cold Najdi evening, cars were still swishing by,
relentlessly, on the eight lanes of King Fahd Avenue. Behind the campaign
site, paters were driving from one empty plot to the other, apparently on
the lookout for a parking spot.

Apparently bored with himself, the candidate nonchalantly announced
that the next day's lecturer would examine housing and invited the participants to move to the second room and have some food. Voters got
up and slowly lined up along the buffet, loading their plates with camel
meat and flavored rice before they headed back in small groups to their
tables. In front of the buffet, conforming to the rules of Najdi etiquette,
bin Sa'idan was not eating but was gesturing toward the steaming trays,
inviting everybody to join the feast. Right behind where he stood, an
artist was exhibiting his paintings, the most visible of which was a huge
portrait of the candidate. With its self-satisfied smile, it was oddly reminiscent of King Fahd's picture on the one-riyal banknotes.

Little by little, a group of retainers and voters formed around bin
Sa'idan. A middle-aged man who looked like a university professor
addressed him and tried to resume the conversation on unemployment.
"You always refer to the state's responsibility, but it is not what we expect
from you," he said, speaking with the authority of somebody who was

used to expressing himself in public. "Responsibilities must be defined, no doubt about that. But at the same time we must try our best to enlarge the municipalities' responsibilities."

As more voters were coming out of the tent and swarmed around the two men to listen to the discussion, bin Sa'idan maintained an impeccable smile and let the man talk. At some point, he murmured an excuse and, still smiling, left the man right in the middle of one of his sentences. A few feet away, the candidate simply joined a crowd of well-dressed businessmen and journalists, and listened to the compliments of a famous TV sports commentator. Visibly annoyed, the questioner was facing a few people who asked him to tell them what had just happened. As he began to explain the situation, the man suddenly realized that he had been spurned. He stopped talking, pursed his lips, and disappeared into the crowd.

Despite his connections to the royal family, bin Sa'idan ultimately did not win the election. In his stead, voters in the fourth ward chose a small real estate developer and university professor who belonged to an Islamic coalition. As if to deflate the fears of the local press, which had predicted a sweeping victory of tribal candidates and of businessmen, Riyadh voters had given the municipal council to the Saudi branch of the Muslim Brotherhood. According to 'Adil, instead of vouching for the "six families that own Riyadh," voters had expressed a clear political opinion:

'ADIL – For instance, why did I vote for the Islamists? I didn't choose them because I've seen that, *wallah*, they have the abilities and the competence to realize the country's and citizen's interests, no!...The main thing is that I wanted to tell [the princes]: "Secularists don't belong here. We aren't a secularist people, we are a religious people, we are Muslims, and we don't believe that anything but Islam can be our religion." That was the idea.... 55 percent of people didn't vote. And only 10 percent of those who could have voted registered. Which means that only 6.5 percent of the Riyadh electorate went to the polls. I consider this as a strike, in all the meanings of the word. (*He laughs*.) True or not? As if they wanted to tell this: "Elections mean nothing! But we will show you who deserves to represent us." Even if there were no elections, even if they only asked:...who do you think is worth representing you? I think that only Islamists can.

Badr bin Sa'idan's campaign was particularly infuriating. That the son of the very person whose greed had excluded a majority of Saudis from the housing market would propose "affordable housing" was, according to a young engineer I met during the campaign, "a farce." Another major developer, who had run in the election to no avail, became the topic of endless jokes and parodies. The rumor had it that his campaign had been the most expensive in the capital. A few days after the results were published, 'Adil received a text message with this satirical poem:

> I showered rice on them but the Arabs didn't care
> I lost my money and my efforts, catastrophe!
> I wished that on Election Day they chose me
> If only to serve tea in a Ministry
> But alas! They did not elect me
> Neither councilman nor even doorkeeper.[46]

Within the cracks and splits of the urban landscape engineered by princes, investors, and developers, another space was produced by ordinary people, by those who were expected to passively consume their allotted share of space and mobility in the form of costly housing and imported cars. Many were not expressing themselves in Islamic circles, in a voting booth, or on the Internet. Those I followed took to the street – and took the streets of Riyadh to another level.

5

Street Terrorism

The rich bring cars to us and play with us.

— Bubu

5.1. Public Disorder

I first encountered joyriding during a night of January 2002, three years before I started fieldwork. As I was waiting behind the steering wheel at a traffic light on Takhassussi Avenue, in the Central Business District, I heard a horrifying shriek coming from behind my car. Looking into the rearview mirror, I saw a huge cloud of dust closing in on me at lightning speed. I barely had the time to put the car into first gear, release the clutch, and turn down a perpendicular street. The drifting car swerved at more than 140 mph in the exact spot where my car was seconds before, and continued its course on the avenue. Jumping out of my seat, I stood on the pavement, my limbs shaking and my forehead drenched in sweat. I needed a good fifteen minutes to recover my composure. A driver stopped next to my car to ask if everything was all right, only to pull out with a shrug after I'd told him what had happened.

Yet the scene wasn't over. The drifting car soon came back, its tires screaming, leaving behind a billowing cloud of dust and smoke. It fled across the asphalt as though suspended by invisible threads, like its body had been freed from the laws of motion. The noise was deafening. With a police patrol on its tail, the car made a right onto Thirty Avenue (*Share' Thalathin*)[1] and jumped above the traffic island onto the other side of the road. The police car clumsily passed over the island behind it, while the joyrider was crossing back again in an attempt to dodge the cops.

Its lights flashing and its siren howling, the patrol crashed against a streetlamp while trying to pass the island a second time. Two cops got out, apparently without a scratch, and looked at the drifting car turning onto King Fahd Road and disappearing from sight.

A few years after this first encounter, the Central Business District was too jammed with cars, even late at night, to allow for such performances anymore. As a result of the demonstrations and bombings that had taken place between 2002 and 2005, police had also become pervasive in the central areas of the city. Witness to a bygone era of relative freedom, an avenue parallel to Takhassussi had been nicknamed by joyriders Share' al-Gizaz, "Glass Street." It hadn't earned this label because of the proximity of the royal palaces, where alcohol consumption was reportedly endemic. "Al-Gizaz" was rather a reference to a famous drifting accident that had littered the asphalt with car parts and the broken glass of shop windows. After their attempt at invading downtown was thwarted, joyriders withdrew to their original turf, in the interstices created by the dynamics of real estate development between the city and the surrounding plateau. Drifters would go to the outskirts of Riyadh for the long, straight, unspoiled asphalt tracks that connected the projected neighborhoods to the existing city.

In the hours after midnight, the dull and disciplined city became a wild playground. According to joyriding fans, the craziest hours were at dawn, when the police ended their night shift and before morning patrols set off. For thirty to sixty minutes, joyriding was at its peak and road accidents were most frequent: the city was virtually out of control. My interest in car drifting originally stemmed from the extreme contrast it highlighted between the well-policed Riyadh I usually experienced and the unruly place the city became at night or far away from the state's gaze. (See Figure 5.1.) The presence of joyriders was pointing to another geography of power in the capital, one in which the police, ordinarily potent, were overwhelmed and where the functionalist space of the city was turned upside down. The most fascinating aspect of joyriding was probably its subversion of the stringent bodily norms promoted by the state, the police, the religious police, and the "suspicious eye" (*nazhra al-riba*) that members of society turned toward youth.

During the post–oil boom years, the suburbanization of the capital triggered new usages of the urban space and modified bodily practices and norms. Made wealthier by the oil boom and leaning toward a moralistic conservatism, the Saudi state enforced a tighter supervision of the usages of the body, creating youth guidance institutions (among which, in 1974,

FIGURE 5.1. During a drifting session in east Riyadh, 2009. Copyright © Pascal Menoret.

the General Presidency for Youth Patronage, *al-Ri'asa al-'Amma li-Ri'aya al-Shabab*), giving free rein to Islamic groups, enforcing a stricter gender segregation, promoting a uniform dress code, and more closely regulating sexuality. In 2012, the research unit of the religious police revealed that 59 percent of Saudi youth were engaging in "forbidden or reprehensible behaviors," including wearing clothes with reproductions of living beings (43 percent); wearing tight clothes, wearing necklaces and wristbands (26 percent); or sporting a *kadash* or afro (24 percent).[2] This policing was at once superficial and overwhelming in its petty regulations.

Firas, a seventeen-year-old joyrider with a Bedouin background, would regularly mock his teachers and members of the religious police. He explained the free time on his hands by the fact that he'd been expelled from school for insulting one of the teachers. His elder brother offered him a trip to Canada, and his father's reaction was apathetic. To him, this was both good news and the epitome of parental weakness. A few days after he was banned from school, while he was touring the women's market in his neighborhood, members of the religious police arrested him and brought him to their local station. They shaved his head and introduced him to a bare room, in which the only piece of furniture, set directly on the floor, was a casket. They opened it, had Firas lay inside before replacing the cover and playing a recorded recitation of the Koran, "to have him think about what it's like to be in the grave [*al-gabr*]." The ludicrousness of the whole thing still made him laugh. In conclusion to the story, he yelled: "*'Alleg!*" (Cut your crap!). Other victims of the religious police were less jolly. In 2002, fifteen girls died in the fire of their school because the policemen, obsessed with gender segregation, had prevented them from leaving the blazing building.[3] Firas told his story as we were hanging out in his car, following swarms of other vehicles and looking for the joyriders who, he had promised us, would be out soon – but never came. Meanwhile, he was swerving the car to kill time, make a spectacle of himself ("*Ana marjuj*"; I am a nutcase), and show us his own drifting skills. Gesticulating and honking at random times, he comically conjured the divine protection against his own misdeeds, incanting at intervals: "Lord, guard me from evil!" (*Ia dafe' al-bala'!*).

As even minor divergence was criminalized, all sorts of violations tended to be widespread. Henri Lefebvre wrote that "state-imposed normality makes permanent transgression inevitable,"[4] and Riyadh was no exception to this rule of thumb. Such overtly deviant acts – in the Saudi context – as public flirting, homosexuality, or the consumption of drugs and alcohol became sites of contention against the strict behavioral and spatial order promoted by the state. Boys and girls and boys and boys flirted from car to car on select avenues, throwing their phone number at each other on scraps of paper, texting each other or following the other's car. Night after night, on Musa ibn Nusair Street, nicknamed Share' 'Aqariyya (Real Estate Street), in the Central Business District, an automobile parade of sorts slowly revolved about the traffic island, and guys of all shapes and ages would check each other out from their cars. The surrounding side streets were turned into an impromptu red-light district, where boys hooked up with boys and drove away to more intimate locations: a parking lot, a hotel room, or an empty plot on the outskirts of the city. In 2010, visiting Riyadh a few years after having completed fieldwork, I drove down 'Aqariyya Street for the first time in years. The municipality had changed the traffic pattern and made it impossible to make U-turns on the avenue. It was equipped with closed-circuit TV cameras and was monitored through the "*Saher*" ("Vigilante") surveillance system, a centralized law-enforcement scheme introduced in 2010 and criticized for its defects and unintended consequences. By making state surveillance both more visible and more predictable, the system paradoxically created zones of increased "traffic anarchy" (*fawdha mururiya*) every-where it hadn't been installed.[5] Men in search of sexual partners had probably moved to less controlled areas.

Alcohol and drugs were almost as easy to find as a sexual partner and could be picked up in various places, provided that you had the right contact and a car to get there. Captagon, an illegal amphetamine produced in Eastern Europe and smuggled through Turkey, Syria, and Jordan, was the most common drug, but hashish, cocaine, and heroine, imported from the shores of the Gulf and the mountains of Yemen, were also in high demand.[6] A local alcohol made from dates, nicknamed *al-kuhul al-watani* or "National Alcohol," was stored and sold in plastic water bottles, its limpidity making it undetectable to visual inspection. You would drive to the east or the south of Riyadh, meet your dealer, and transfer a few bottles from his car to yours. Once back at home you would mix the alcohol with non-alcoholic beer or sodas and quickly reach inebriation. As Saudis would say, what's prohibited is highly desirable (*al-mamnu' maghrub*), and Riyadh was haloed with the lure of the forbidden.

'Ajib, the drifter Rakan and I followed until our accident, was satis-fied with Riyadh's pleasures and would shun those of Bahrain, to which middle-class Saudis flocked at weekends in search of alcohol and pros-titutes. He was happy "with what we got in Arabia" and didn't need "what's to be found in Manama." We inferred that he was more inter-ested in boys than in girls and in date alcohol than in imported beverages. A few minutes later, he confessed his infatuation with this "attractive" (*hlewe*) nineteen-year-old joyrider who had recently provoked a terrible accident, two videos of which he showed us on his mobile phone. In the first one, the joyrider was knocking down a kid with his car. The second video was even less bearable and showed a close-up of the vic-tim's injuries. Seeing our reactions, he quickly commented, "Of course, joyriding is bad. But what's around is really cool." A few days before, one of his friends, his face ravaged with rosacea and his right leg in a plaster cast, had also said, "We know that joyriding is bad, but it gives sensations, it gives the sense of time and place [*al-hess bi-l-zaman wa-l-makan*]." 'Ajib had replied, straight-faced, "And there are boys," a propo-sition apparently so obvious that the other just repeated: "And there are boys."

Joyriding was embedded in a series of well-known categories that joyriders had adopted, transformed and subverted. The colloquial terms *hajwala* and *tafhit* had not always referred to the dangerous pastime during which young men spin stolen cars at high speed. In Najdi dialects, both words were connected to the word *tufush* in interesting ways. All three colloquial verbs, *fahhata*, *hajja*, and *tafasha*, originally meant to fly, to run, to escape. A *mufahhat*, someone who drifts cars, is thus, literally, a fugitive, an escapee, or an escapist. *Tafhit* also refers to the scream of toddlers, and by extension to the sound of screeching tires. *Hajwala* is still used in local parlance as a synonym for disorder, confusion, and anarchy. For the generation of my informants' fathers or grandfathers, a *muhajwil* is a tramp. Young joyriders had converted this mark of blame into a badge of pride – a *muhajwil* is to them a tough guy, a street hero.

A new layer of meaning was added in the 2000s, after al-Qaeda militants began a campaign of targeted assassinations and bombings in the country. Both joyriders and the press started comparing *tafhit* to violent activism, either as a provocation or to stigmatize drifting and call for increased repression. While reporting on joyriding, Saudi media recycled the religious notion of *fitna* (secession within the Islamic community), which both the Saudi state and Western conservatives used to depoliticize armed militancy and reduce it to a religious pathology.[7] In early 2006 a Saudi journalist coined the expression *fitna al-tafhit* (joyriding secession).[8] Later the same year, the state news channel *al-Ikhbariyya* aired a documentary movie on joyriding entitled *al-Jarima al-Murakkaba* (the compounded crime), in which the director called joyriding a form of street terrorism (*irhab al-shawari'*).[9] In the time of al-Qaeda, being a "tramp," a "punk" or a "tough guy" was no longer desirable – or blamable – enough. Joyriders now had to be terrorists (*irhabiyin*).

Joyriding existed in other places, from Lebanon to Egypt and to Kuwait, and carried various names depending on the location. It was known in the Gulf as *takhmis* (doughnuts), *tashhit* (stranding), *tashbih* (ghosting), *tantana* (droning), *'iri* (looping), *maltasha* (striking), *taltish* (idem.), *masiha* (flowing), or *tahyys* (craziness).[10] But nowhere did it seem more daring than in Riyadh, where joyriders performed the boldest figures. Although speed was essential to their performances, they did not perceive drifting as a speed competition, and privileged style and grace. The anonymous author of the "History of Thugs" noted that young Saudis "were drifting to enlarge their souls (*li-wisa'at al-sadr*), it wasn't about winning – they actually always reached a tie."[11] Drifting was about producing the most elegant figures, and panache was reputed to attract the highest number of fans. Spectators and fans compared drifters' prowess and voted with their feet (or their tires), flocking to those sites were famous drivers were performing. (See Map 4.)

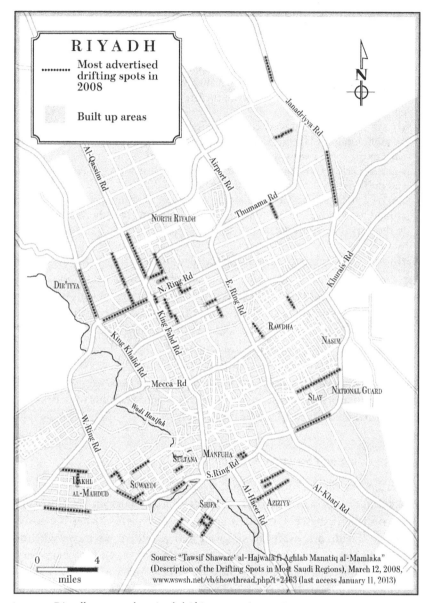

MAP 4. Riyadh: most advertised drifting spots in 2008.

Several websites proposed instructions and training under various title: "learning for a drifter's eyes is not a loss of time" (*al-tadris li-'uyun zahif ma hi khasara*), for instance, or "Joyriding is useless unless you break in the iron" (*al-hajwala ma tufid illa bi-ta'dib al-hadid*). The main figures

of drifting were the skid (*al-natla*), the knot (*al-'ugda*), and the opposite
(*al-'aksiya*):

SKID (*AL-NATLA*). Drive at more than 75 mph, shake the steering wheel a bit, turn
it strongly toward the left, then turn it slightly to the right twice before turning
strongly right, then turn it slightly to the left twice before turning strongly left,
and so on and so forth.

KNOT (*AL-'UGDA*). If you want to perform one single knot, drive at around 65–
75 mph in the left lane, turn right and handbrake neatly until the car turns its
back to the road, release the handbrake and turn all the way to the left. If you
want to perform two knots, repeat the above instructions for the first knot,
and don't use the handbrake for the second one.

OPPOSITE (*AL-'AKSIYA*). This is the most difficult joyriding figure. Drive at
around 75–85 mph, do two skids and at the third one turn the steering wheel
to the opposite and let the car go.[12]

Virtuosic drifters were combining them together, for instance, in the
"flashing light" (*al-sefti*), which was a combination of an opposite and
a knot. They would also combine them with less technical and more
daring figures: the game of chicken (*haraka al-mawt*), brushing against
another car (*al-tatwif*), various slaloms (*al-muruha*), or the "sparkle"
(*al-sharara*), a combination of skidding and brushing that aimed at producing sparkles (*shararat*) by scratching the car at high speed against the
traffic island. Riyadh's street grid was the equivalent of an arena where
several gladiators, each one in his own corner and with his own devices,
tried to attract a bigger share of the crowd.

5.2. Joyriding and Social Suffering

According to the interior ministry, 95.2 percent of all joyriders appre-
hended in the spring of 2003 were Saudis. In comparison, Saudi drivers
were only 63.2 percent of all road traffic offenders during the same
period.[13] Fieldwork evidence suggests that joyriders were overwhelmingly young men, aged between fifteen and thirty-five, and from the very
neighborhoods that had seen the most important influx of rural migrants,
Bedouin and Bidun. Bedouin families had settled down primarily in the
east and south of Riyadh, not far from the National Guard compound, in
the neighborhoods of Nasim, Nazhim, and Slay, and around the low-
income district. From Prince Salman's projected expulsion of 60,000
Bedouin in the late 1960s to the low-intensity and long-standing joyriding
rebellion of young Bedouin, there were some elements of continuity. Yet
it was difficult to say exactly who engages in joyriding.

Fieldwork evidence for this study is drawn from two groups of drifters, both of whom almost exclusively Bedouin. My two main informants, Sa'b and Rakan, have a Bedouin background, although they grew up in very different environments, Sa'b in the steppe and Rakan in Riyadh. But sedentary 'Adil, who never lost an opportunity to tell me how he hated and despised the Bedouin, was no stranger to the joyriding scene. A few weeks after we first met, in the fall of 2001, he had performed a few skids while driving me to a meeting of his Islamist friends, in the north of Riyadh. Figures published in 2006 by criminologist Salih al-Rumayh pointed to the widespread nature of the phenomenon – but they did not help determine the social origin of joyriders. According to al-Rumayh's 2004 survey of middle and high school students in Riyadh, Jeddah and Dammam, 45 percent of all students were involved in joyriding. Of them, 11 percent were "constantly" involved, 16 percent would participate in drifting "from time to time," and 18 percent of them would "rarely" engage in it. With one out of every five Saudis between fifteen and nineteen, these figures suggested that in the mid-2000s, right at the time I was conducting fieldwork, nearly 10 percent of the total Saudi population was in one way or another engaged in joyriding.[14]

To give an idea of who these 10 percent were, I focus on Rakan's background and on how he was drawn to joyriding while in high school. In his early twenties, Rakan belonged to a Bedouin tribe. He was born in the capital and spoke the colloquial Arabic of Riyadh's youth, characterized by its clipped expressions and its standardized intonations. I met him online before I started fieldwork. He was an open-minded, outspoken youth fascinated by his city and interested in learning more about youth groups. He had just lost his girlfriend in a car accident, and I thought his desire to help me conduct fieldwork was perhaps a way to busy himself. It was not the only personal tragedy that he'd gone through. A few years earlier, during a class trip to Mecca, he had seen a schoolmate die squashed between two buses. Rakan had lived in a world where traffic accidents were ubiquitous and lethal.

Rakan's father had migrated to Riyadh from the steppes of Central Arabia in the 1960s. He had found a job as a security guard, and settled in one of the informal areas that had sprang up around the palaces, to the northwest of the old city, and had been labeled "slums" by bureaucrats and urban planners. Unlike other informal areas, Rakan's neighborhood hadn't been cleared by new projects and was still standing, with its shabby buildings and its vast expanses of gravel and sand. During his childhood, Rakan had witnessed the greediness of slumlords, innumerous knife and club battles among local youth, alcohol and drug trafficking, and the violence of Saudi rural migrants toward the next wave of immigrants, who primarily came from South Asia. Once he saw teenagers from his neighborhood assaulting a South Asian immigrant, beating him up and kicking him in the face. They eventually set the man on fire, all "for fun," he wryly commented.[15]

At school, "there were only two categories of students, Bedouin Bedouin Bedouin [*bduwi bduwi bduwi*], and sedentary sedentary sedentary [*hdhari hdhari hdhari*] . . . Bedouin kept to themselves, and didn't mingle with anybody." Among them, Rakan was known as a hardworking student. He eventually obtained an accounting degree that allowed him to work for a private company, unlike a majority of his former schoolmates who were either unemployed or – more rarely – had a connection (*wasta*) and worked in the civil service. But being an A student hadn't prevented Rakan from developing a fascination with the drifters, traffickers, *sarabit* and *dishir* (toughs) who called the shots in the neighborhood.

Rakan was introduced to joyriding at 15 by his friend Khaled, "a drifter without an audience [*jumhur*]; he drifted in the neighborhood and only local kids were attending his joyriding." Khaled's father was notoriously in debt and had found an apartment in the neighborhood through a relative of his, who was well connected in one of the palaces' retinue of servants and guards. His relatives had also found him a low-paying job at a retail store (for a monthly salary of SAR 2,000, around $500). Yet Khaled's father's actual workday started after dusk:

RAKAN – Since they are little – but like: really little – [Khaled and his brothers] know that people come to their house to drink. His father organized a kind of nightclub at his place, all his pals would come to drink and when they'd get out we would make fun of them, because they were wasted, sometimes they'd fight, and you had always somebody who'd get in his car and crash into the wall, you know, the one in the curve.

Khaled was "good in school and calm," but his behavior radically changed one summer. After Rakan came back from his vacation in the steppe, he found his friend metamorphosed: he was now smoking cigarettes and hashish, drinking alcohol, and drifting his father's car:

RAKAN – He had met the joyriders of the school and started drifting outside [the neighborhood], attending joyriding sessions and all. He became big on that stuff. He started to know people. People who were not only drifters, people, hum . . . he became a dealer (*wasit*), an alcohol dealer. . . . Kids were coming to the neighborhood and they would call his cellphone and ask him to prepare alcohol for them. He didn't have any alcohol. But he would call the actual dealers, they would bring alcohol to him and he would sell it to the kids. And he would share the benefits with the dealers. That's how he started working. Not much, simple deals. He got more intimate with the other kids, he started going out, attending joyriding sessions outside [the neighborhood]; he would sometimes go all the way to Dammam to attend joyriding. He really got into it.

PASCAL – But he wasn't a real drifter...

RAKAN – No. He started drifting and attending sessions, but his problem is that he got into drinking more than drifting. Because he had a material advantage, he had connections.... His grandfather lived with them. After he died, his father put him in the grandfather's room. And it's a room with a door opening directly on the street, like a *diwaniyya* [a private reception area opening on the public space]. You see? So everybody is always in his room. And sometimes, depending on the weather, they hang out in front of the door.

In the first months of the following school year, Khaled had an accident with his dad's car, "and he lied to his father, he told him that another driver had run a red light," hit him, and run away, which is "what everybody says after a joyriding accident." In order to repay his father's car, he dropped out of school and became a full-time alcohol dealer, which was facilitated by his father's activities. Khaled tried to justify himself to Rakan by explaining that because the whole economy was based on connections, alcohol trafficking allowed him to meet more influential people, and was therefore more useful than school:

RAKAN – He told me that thanks to booze he gets to meet celebs and big shots in ministries or companies. But up until now nobody [among these contacts] hired him. So in the end he hooked up with this guy that everybody calls "the Factory" (*al-masna'*) and they drink all the time. They call him like that because he always has some alcohol at his place, and he never gets sober.

PASCAL – And what do they drink? "National Alcohol" (*kuhul watani*)?

RAKAN – Of course! They don't like anything but that stuff.... Since he was a kid, Khaled has an inferiority complex because of his father. He knows that his father is a bad man. He tried to change people's opinions about his father but there were always some kids coming and ... [insulting his father.] That's it. When he stopped joyriding, Khaled kept hanging out with the neighborhood's kids, the same ones. He wanted to quit drinking, but they were constantly asking him to get them alcohol. Now he found a job in a theme park, he works on a roller coaster.

PASCAL – How did he get hired?

RAKAN – Somebody introduced him (*fi wahid gaddam 'aleh*). But having a job didn't help him say goodbye to his previous life. The last thing was the day before yesterday, we went with him to al-Badi'a, and he didn't tell us where he was going. But in the end he told us that he was meeting "the Factory," who lives there.

Social suffering among Saudi rural migrants could be more intense than in Khaled's family, however. Rakan's next mentor in the joyriding world was another neighbor and schoolmate, Migrin, whose father lived on welfare but still managed to support four wives. Migrin's mother was "ignorant and weak" and his father, "a mountain," was a domestic tyrant who would often beat him in a grisly manner. He would tie him up with a chain in their backyard and hit him with an iron bar. Migrin's eldest brother was put in a mental institution. His second brother ran away from home. While in middle school, Migrin stabbed another student and was sentenced to three years in jail.[16] After he served his sentence, he again stabbed a local resident who had called him a "criminal" and a "liar" and was sent back to jail. In the meantime, his father had run away, spent more than a year in another city with another woman, and came back to Riyadh during the 2005 stock market boom. Each Saudi citizen was entitled to a limited number of shares, and he took this opportunity to invest in his children's names. He pulled out of the stock market right before the 2006 crash and ran away again with the money.

Rakan remembered that, while they were in primary school, Migrin's father once came all the way to the classroom to punish his son for having stolen "lunch money for himself and his brothers." The schoolteacher tried to stop him, but "the mountain" managed to beat his son in front of the class. Rakan was angered to read in the local media or hear in conversations that joyriding was a privilege of the idle rich. To him, joyriding was the tree that hid the forest of social despair and urban dereliction, the tip of an iceberg of poverty and violence that was rarely reported on. The joyriding world, with its princes and its parades, its accidents and its violence, was a macabre mirror image of Saudi society as a whole.

One scene in particular illustrates the social gap between drifters and the sedentary middle classes. Rakan and I hung out for a while with drag racers, young Saudi males racing cars at night on the outskirts of the city. They would meet regularly in a café a few blocks away from my apartment, and were very different from the joyriders with whom they shared the empty, straight roads of Riyadh's new suburbs. Most of them belonged to middle class, sedentary families and were either students or young professionals. My main contact in the group, 'Umar, had started an import business and used his free time turning a Chevrolet Lumina into a stock car. One night, he took us out for a race on the outskirts of Riyadh. We drove to the south of the city, surrounded by two dozen other cars and around sixty people. 'Umar drove very fast but with a steady hand. Unlike drifters, his driving style displayed a strong concern with safety. We arrived in Dhahyat Laban, a suburb built on a narrow plateau above the Wadi Laban, to the southwest of the city. In a sparsely built area not far from the towering structure of the al-Riyadh soccer club, drivers began racing on a large, empty, and freshly asphalted road. We followed the competition seated on a mound of gravel above the road.

The spectacle was very different from what we were accustomed to with joyriders. Drivers would race in a straight line, two at a time, over a relatively short distance. The racket of accelerating car engines would shatter the stillness of the neighborhood, whereas in joyriders' shows, it was the sound of tires that was overwhelming. I began to wonder how long it would take the police to catch on to them when I saw a familiar sight. A young guy driving a Camry with three friends stopped on the road's shoulder and started observing the scene, his head cocked in the direction of the racing cars. With cars lined up along the road and scores of young people hanging out on the curb, our group looked vaguely like a joyriding party. As soon as he realized his mistake, the Camry driver pulled out, accelerated out of sight, and came back drifting on the avenue in large skids that sent piercing shrieks around. He came back a second time at higher speed; on the third time, he contented himself with honking and waving bye-bye to the crowd of drag racers, oblivious to the cruel remarks his drifting had triggered among them.

'UMAR – Each time we go out, it's the same story: one of these fucking drifters comes turning around, they round up the cops, as soon as we see them we run off. . . . It is like this one day when a drifter came to stir up shit in our gathering, we chased him with stones. . . . Because . . . if you give them face time, that's all they can dream of, they'll come back even more numerous and ruin your party. . . . Them, they are lawless, they're fucked up, they have accidents and all. Us, our first goal is . . . safety. Which means that, 70 percent of the time, when you ride with us, it is *safe (in English)*. . . . Us, we have goals, we know what we're doing. Them, they're acting like fools, it is total confusion (*hamajia*). . . . Plus, they look like crap, as if they came out from under the earth, with their standing hair (*sha'rhum wagef*) and their moustaches. I may not be very handsome or attractive, but I wouldn't like to be alone with one of them.

In accusing joyriders of confusion and foolishness, describing them as untidy individuals, and implying that they were only interested in sex, drag racers were calmly displaying a fair degree of social and ethnic racism. The divide between Bedouin and sedentary/urban dwellers, which reflected the divide between lower and middle classes, ran along perceptible distinctions in driving, clothing, and grooming. The use of English

words, the reference to goals, and the mention of heterosexual normativity completed the picture: drag racers didn't want to be confused with
those whom they portrayed as lowlifes. Social racism notwithstanding,
their precautions against joyriders were consistent with what Rakan and
I knew about the latter. Drifters usually meant trouble:

RAKAN – One day, [Migrin's] brother told him: we're going to Dammam, you
come with us? And they all went. And they had a light accident (*sudma*) as
soon as they started drifting. Then they went strolling around, they visited
the famous drifting spots, and they didn't find joyriders. Instead they found
drag racers. And yet they wanted to drift. So his brother's friends told Migrin:
"C'mon, show them what drifting is!" And his brother: "No, don't do it,"
because they already had had an accident. Migrin said: "One or two shots
and then we stop." His brother said: "Okay." Migrin started drifting, and
his brother didn't ride with him.... First shot, second shot, third shot – and
an accident. There were two other kids with him I think. The car rolled over
several times. And they had rented it. And it crashed into somebody's car,
somebody who was following the drag racers.... Then Migrin told me that
they fled the scene, and that he immediately called the police to tell them that
the rental car had been stolen.... That's every drifter's trick: drift on rented
cars and file a report to the police if they have an accident or crash it. So they
can't be accused of joyriding.

Drag racers saw drifting as the final stage of a process that led from
consumption of tobacco and alcohol to car robbery, homosexuality, drug
addiction, drug trafficking and often to death in a car crash. Drifters were
homosexuals and "fools" whereas they, drag racers, were responsible
individuals with a purpose. Against this backdrop of moral and social
superiority, one of Rakan's obsessions was to reconstitute the logics of
joyriding and to explain that Saudi migrant youth were subjected to a
set of social pressures that pushed them into drifting: they were not fully
responsible for what was happening to them. As joyriding fans casually
said, they "fell into drifting" (*tiht fi-l-tafhit*) after a series of events that
often entailed dropping out of school, losing a parent, being jobless, or
having a car accident.

When asked about the context in which they got interested in drifting,
fans and drifters almost unanimously referred to *tufush* and mentioned
a feeling of emptiness and worthlessness, or the rage of young rural
émigrés who compare the opportunities offered by Riyadh to their own
condition. This malaise overwhelmingly affected lower-class youth, who
had a harder time getting a relevant education, finding decent housing,
and eking out a living.

This was the picture Rakan wanted to reconstitute: drifting as a symptom of extreme destitution. In his perspective, street violence was not only a Bedouin rebellion against an overwhelmingly sedentary state, but also an expression of suffering and angst. No amount of storytelling could romanticize the misery of the Riyadh underclass and the suffering that were both prompting joyriding and elicited by it. Rakan and 'Umar paradoxically shared a common perspective on joyriding, which they both saw as being the ominous sign of a general evolution toward social decline. Yet their assessments of drifters' roles were diametrically opposed. 'Umar saw drifters as responsible for what was happening to them, whereas Rakan thought that society as a whole was guilty of marginalizing a part of its youth and, by not offering them better opportunities, turning them into delinquents.

5.3. The Story of Joyriding

"Street terrorism" could as well have been called "car terrorism." Born after the 1973 oil boom, joyriding couldn't have developed without the gigantic road network and the massive importations of private vehicles fostered by oil wealth and free market ideas about urban planning and infrastructure provision. Sulayman al-Duwayri'at, a sociology professor at Riyadh's Islamic University, locates drifting's "real beginning" around 1979. This was the moment when it became "a sizeable practice on the streets and in the public spaces in various regions of the kingdom."[17] Joyriding developed at a striking pace in the very decades when thousands of miles of new roads were paved and a staggering number of cars were imported.

As a consequence of the decision to suburbanize Riyadh and to favor individual car ownership over public transportation, car use was pervasive. In 2001, 93 percent of daily trips in Riyadh – around 5 million trips every day – were done by individual car. Only 2 percent of all trips were made using collective transportation, while the remaining 5 percent were arguably made by taxi. Even school transportation, albeit representing more than a quarter of all trips, was overwhelmingly left to the responsibility of families. The state company SAPTCO (Saudi Public Transport Company) controlled only eight lines within the urban area of Riyadh, whereas small private companies operated minibuses – mainly crummy Toyota Coasters – on informal lines called *Khatt al-Balda* (city line).[18] Minibus drivers, proverbially known for being mustachioed, heavily-accented Bedouin, were the target of anti-nomadic stereotypes and of

FIGURE 5.2. Middlemen stop and inspect cars outside the Shifa' car market, 2007.
Copyright © Pascal Menoret.

the parsimony of the bus owners, who weren't too eager to renew their
fleets or to raise salaries.

Because public transportation was virtually nonexistent, cars had
flooded the city and were widely available. Cheap car rentals were to
be found in almost every neighborhood, and the city counted several
secondhand car auctions, where car owners (or their agent) would take
bets from potential buyers while driving their vehicle along a track until
a reasonable price was reached. Transactions could be conducted with
the help of a middleman (*shreti*), who would take a commission on the
final price. (See Figure 5.2.) As both car rentals and auctions were well
frequented but poorly regulated, cars were relatively easy to come by.
The domination of individual vehicles over a public space reduced to
hundreds of miles of paved roads accounted for the importance of the
drifting scene. One of my neighbors, another cousin of Sa'b's who lived
in a cramped apartment with his brothers, would often tell me, "Where
do you want us to go? All we have is streets and cars."

Cars were not mere commodities: they were also given a political and
geopolitical signification. During conversations with drifting fans, I heard

somebody jokingly say that drifting was part of "a Zionist-American conspiracy: they import cars to kill our youngsters." My neighbor summed up the whole business: "It is with our oil that you [in industrial countries] make cars. And you sell them back to us at top prices. And us, we take 'em and trash 'em, period." If cars were the "almost exact equivalent of the great Gothic cathedrals" that Roland Barthes celebrated in the 1950s, then joyriders were automobile iconoclasts. "Conceived with passion by unknown artists," cars were "consumed in image if not in usage by a whole population, which appropriates them as a purely magical object."[19] Yet joyriders consumed cars in usage, not in image only. They swerved them until exhaustion. They didn't succumb to the car's magic, to this appropriation or "prostitution" of the object that Barthes defined as the "very essence of petit-bourgeois advancement." They weren't interested in the exchange value of cars. To them, only their use value was relevant. The speed they submitted their vehicles and their bodies to wasn't metaphorical or spiritualized, but meant to epitomize car consumption in both an economic and a metabolic sense.

Drifting was a daily reminder of the lethal nature of cars. In 2002, approximately 1,180,000 persons were killed by cars worldwide – or one person every thirty seconds.[20] Cars were deadly inasmuch as they were vital to urban and suburban life. Cars and drivers could be seen as composing a hybrid, the car being the mechanical continuation of the driver's body and the driver training his body in turn to be a biological extension of the car. *Tafhit* was an instance of extreme hybridization. Their bodies had grown so well attuned to swerving that, even when not in front of a steering wheel, some of my informants kept executing steering movements, opening their mouth wide to reproduce the sound of screeching tires, and mimicking veering cars with their whole body.

How did that extreme hybridization happen? Like the history of skateboarding, the history of joyriding is "shrouded in mystery"[21] and its origins are unknown. This obscurity gave way to all sorts of myths. Some presented drifting as the product of U.S. movies, as a threatening foreign influence, and as an "imitation of the West" (*taqlid al-gharb*).[22] Others saw in *tafhit* a continuation through other means of the Bedouin culture of competitive masculinity and chivalry. It was widely admitted that in the 1970s, joyriding was a limited hobby, practiced in alleys and side streets, and generally perceived as inoffensive. When a youngster drifted in a neighborhood, people would go out, watch, and casually gossip about the event.

According to the famous drifter Bubu, the age of innocence ended in the early 1980s. When he was in high school, Rakan had belonged to Bubu's circle of admirers and had managed to reconnect with him. We interviewed him in a café in the spring of 2006. Seated with us around a table, next to a French window overlooking the crossroads of Tahliya and 'Ulayya Avenues, Bubu unfolded a genealogy of joyriding that could have rivaled tribal or royal genealogical trees. He told us that the first *tafhit* star, Husain al-Harbi, was jailed in 1985 during a police crackdown. Al-Harbi used to drift at relatively moderate speeds (around 90 mph) on his own car, a Datsun 200L.[23] In the 1980s, Japanese carmakers were the "unquestioned market leaders in Saudi Arabia," controlling 50 to 75 percent of car sales thanks to aggressive commercial strategies, including the introduction in the country of car credit and installment plans.[24] Imported on a massive scale, Japanese cars were popular among drifters for their lightweight, powerful engine, and wide availability. In a celebration of imported vehicles – especially the particularly appreciated Toyota Cressida – young Shaharin, members of a southern Bedouin tribe, would proudly say, "The iron comes from Japan, the pilot is from Shahran" (*al-hadid min al-Yaban wa-l-tara min Shahran*).

According to Bubu, the police crackdown didn't alter the enthusiasm of the *tafhit* crowd, and a new star soon rose to the joyriding sky. Known for drifting Toyota Cressidas, Sa'd Marzuq increased the speed and developed a series of new techniques, including the "American Style" (*tafhit amriki*). This technique was adapted to the automatic gear and to large U.S. sedans, which constituted around one third of all Saudi car sales in the 1980s.[25] The "American Style" consisted, at 125 mph, of putting the gear on neutral, which immediately provoked perfectly shaped doughnuts that the driver would control by using the steering wheel. The main difference with classic joyriding was that "American" drifters didn't have to use the handbrake to swerve the car: the automatic gear was doing that part of the job. This apparent simplicity was misleading, however. "American cars, not everybody can drift them," 'Ajib told me one day, before adding, somewhat cryptically, "Because when American cars fuck up, they fuck up big time. When they go, they go. And when you can't master them, you can't master them."

Sa'd Marzuq was arrested in the early 1990s. He was succeeded at the pinnacle of joyriding by two new heroes, Su'ud al-'Ubaid aka "The Carrot" (*al-Jazura*), and Badr 'Awadh aka "al-King," who for a few years was a contender for the honor of being recognized as "Riyadh's best drifter." After his release from prison, Marzuq retired in the northwest of Saudi Arabia near the Jordanian border, and kept his distance from a *tafhit* scene that was evolving rapidly. In the 1990s, cars were lighter and more powerful, which allowed for more figures, more speed, more noise, and more danger. At more than 140 mph, the slightest mistake was fatal and accidents were more frequent than ever. "The Carrot" Su'ud al-'Ubaid died in a car accident in 2001. As for "al-King" Badr 'Awadh, who was born in 1970 and continued joyriding well into his thirties, he provoked a few accidents and was repeatedly thrown in jail. In the early 2000s, he was challenged on the streets of the capital by Bubu, who was younger, more reckless, and more inventive:

RAKAN – Bubu took joyriding to another level (*akhazhzh al-tafhit ila bu'd akhar*).... He put a lot of creativity (*ibda'*) into his drifting... and sometimes, especially when he drank, he would get to a level of craziness that nobody... I mean, he would challenge the devil himself!... He would drift everywhere. He would discover new spots all the time. Al-'Ammariya [Road], for instance, in the north of Riyadh, he was the first drifter to go there, as soon as a real estate project was planned there. And in the south of Riyadh, al-Ghurub [Road]. And al-Breksat [Road], he's the one who made it famous. He drifted in Dammam. He drifted in Jidda. I heard he also went joyriding in the Qassim [region], but I don't know if it's true.

PASCAL – He was a genius in a way...

RAKAN – Big time.... He would drift on Camrys, and sometimes on [Hyundai] Accents. Accents were not real joyriding cars; they were cars you use to escape, emergency cars, in case you crash your Camry, so that nobody gets caught. And around that period, Bubu started joyriding on Accents.

In 2005, according to a survey conducted by the joyriding website Rahhal (Nomad), the "best joyrider" (*ahsan mufahhat*) was still al-King (33.7 percent of votes), followed by Bubu (21 percent), "the Councilor" (*al-mustashar*, 6.1 percent), "the Sufi" (*al-sufi*, 5.5 percent), and Abu Zegem (3.3%).[26] Rakan couldn't agree more: although Bubu repeatedly tried to dethrone him during expertly orchestrated and well-publicized drifting sessions, "al-King" remained unchallenged:

RAKAN – Bubu never got to Badr 'Awadh's level. They both threw many challenges at each other. Not in the same spot, but: who's gonna attract more people? Badr, or Bubu?... For instance, Bubu would drift in the north of Riyadh, Badr in the east, and they would compare the number of fans.

PASCAL – And how would they count them?

RAKAN – Fans would take pictures, they would look at who had the biggest audience. Or they counted cars.... It was the fans' business to guesstimate... or the supporters'.

PASCAL – And did they publish the results somewhere?

RAKAN – They would spread rumors among themselves. And on the internet, when they started using forums (*muntadayat*), they would announce that Bubu was gonna drift (*yekhesh*). And when he or Badr drifted, there were always two or three other drifters with them, there were no "*one-star-shows*" (*in English*), there were always a few drifters. The first to go was usually the youngest, then a more senior, and so on and so forth until Bubu who would drift until the end.

PASCAL – Like an opening act at a concert?

RAKAN – Yes! And they would have a break, sometimes Bubu needed a rest... because he would drift for around four hours at a time... and junior drifters would run the show when he stopped, to keep the audience interested, otherwise people would leave.... Until Bubu comes back and drifts until 8 or 9am. That was the summer schedule (*al-dawam al-saifi*). But Bubu was no match for Badr 'Awadh. Badr 'Awadh would drift but [unlike Bubu] he wouldn't provoke the cops, he wouldn't waste his time in dare-devilries (*jari'at*). Badr 'Awadh's system was pure technical challenge more than anything else, he would drift only for pleasure. And he never drank, contrary to Bubu, who would drink and drift all the time.

Both Badr 'Awadh and Bubu repented from joyriding around the beginning of my fieldwork, after a terrible accident ended one of their competitions and reportedly caused the death of seven people in the audience. A young joyrider in a tight *thawb*, his locks impeccably maintained by a shiny layer of hair gel, narrated to me the accident a few weeks before we met Bubu. I had met him through yet another cousin of Sa'b's, whose crew (*shilla*) was regularly gathering in a rest house (*istiraha*) next to the King Fahd Stadium. Called by one of Sa'b's friends, the joyrider arrived with an older guy in tow, who had powdered his face and reminded me of the old roué on the vaporetto, at the beginning of Visconti's *Death in Venice*. His younger companion provided a wealth of details about the circumstances of Bubu's and Badr's accident. Both drifters were competing for the attention of a beautiful boy and were particularly reckless. It wasn't clear whose car, Bubu's or Badr's, had mowed down the seven boys. Neither Bubu nor al-King had been brought to justice, but the shock had been strong enough to lead them to repent and retire from the joyriding scene altogether.

5.4. "If You Have a Lexus, You Are a Lexus"

One of the most important events of the 1990s in the joyriding world was the import of the new Toyota Camry in 1995, which could be swerved at speeds of more than 140 mph. The second development in the 1990s was an unprecedented police crackdown on drifters in the second half of the decade. The success of Badr 'Awadh and, to a lesser extent, Bubu was linked to both events. Their driving prowess and the technical possibilities offered by the new Camry allowed them to challenge the police on a regular basis. Badr 'Awadh stayed on top of the game for many years, and his career as a drifter elicited many commendations. For instance, the anonymous author of the famed "Book of Joyriding" wrote:

> This generation distinguished itself by the variety of figures and the crazy speed. They were using any long road and even the Ring Road. Their leader was naturally Badr 'Awadh, whom I consider to be the successor of Sa'd Marzuq because of his self-confidence and his coping with the consequences of drifting: accidents, prison, and other social problems. The spirit of sacrifice was their characteristic, and they presented their art on a black rectangle. We won't forget how, before he repented, "al-King" was drifting on a weekly basis, despite the strong concentration of police patrols and the fact that many joyriders quit drifting.[27]

Others were less positive. Baffled by his ability to dodge patrols and, when arrested, to get away with minor sentences, rivals accused the "King" of being a snitch, or of pulling strings and having a *wasta* (connection).[28] Meanwhile, partly thanks to his aura, the Camry almost instantly became a legendary car. "Gimme my C. [cap], get in the C. [Camry], where is the T. [*tafhit*]?" (*hat at-ta* [*tarbush*], *irkib al-ka* [*Kamri*], *wayn at-ta* [*tafhit*]?)[29] was the motto of the "Camryists," this new generation of joyriding fans that emerged after the "Cressidists," the Toyota Cressida admirers, faded. In Riyadh's suburbs, cars were a second skin, the iron clothes in which people introduced themselves to others, and the foundation of collective and individual identities. In rural areas, youngsters even erected roadside statues of Toyotas or Hondas by mounting cars on stone pedestals, an operation known as *tahjir* or "petrification." "If you have a Lexus, you *are* a Lexus; if you have a piece of shit, you *are* a piece of shit," young Saudis would casually say. Joyriders were both embracing and breaking this logic of appropriation.

The Camry plays a starring role in many short poems that joyriders and their fans memorized, sprayed on walls, exchanged through the Internet or by mobile phone, or wrote on huge stickers that they would glue to the rear window of their cars. These brief pieces glorified not only individuals like Badr 'Awadh or Bubu, but also cars like the Nissan XL, the Chevrolet Lumina, the Honda Accord or the Toyota Camry.

When I see blinkers on the Ring Road	*La shift bi-l-da'iri takbis*
And a Camry drifting at 130 mph	*Wa-l-Kamri tantell 'al-meyten*
I know that it's Bubu, joyriding master	*Hazhak Bubu abu al-tajrih*
Woe to whom he drives crazy	*Miskin ia mjannenah miskin*

O Bubu be quicker than I	*Ia Bubu 'ajjel 'aleyy bi-l-shawt*
The Camry rears and swerves at 140 mph	*Al-Kamri gamat tatlafat 220*
I'm happy that her back	*Wana mabsut saddam-ha*
Competes with her front	*Yisabeg al-rafruf*
Your passion is to honk, swerve, disturb	*Sharbek bawari nutal wa iz'aj*
The neighborhood of your beloved o Bubu	*Harat al-zain ia Bubu*
Wreak havoc among the cops	*Khalli al-hakayem tlagi iz'aj*
So that they give up the chase	*Wa yitubu min tardek yitubu*
O Bubu drift on the Ring Road	*Ia Bubu entell 'ala-l-biban fi-l-da'iri*
We call you "Driver of 'Utaiba"	*Ismek tara tara al-'Utban*
And "The One who Broke in the Camry"	*Iahmel al-Kamry tahlil*

Bubu's tribal identity ("driver of 'Utaiba")[30] was as relevant as his way to "break in" cars. Yet above all, joyriding was both a way to seduce one's beloved and to challenge the police.

I want to drift today	*Abgha ahajwel al-yum*
And see a navy-blue Camry	*Wa ashuf Kamri bahriyya*
Driven by a hero – a madman	*Yisug-ha tara wa majnun*
Who doesn't fear the cops	*Ma hammatah tardat al-dawriya*
A Camry licensed in Arabia	*Kamri khususi su'udiyya*
A Camry scaring the police	*Kamri tatuf al-dawriya*
Speeding at sixty plus sixty	*Sur'at-ha meya 'ala meya*
On Abu Hadriyya Road	*Maska khatt Abu Hadriyya*
In full dawn	*Fi 'ezz al-fajriyya*
A Camry color of kohl	*Kamri kuhliyya*
Western songs	*Aghani gharbiyya*
Iraqi anthems	*Lutam 'iragiyya*
Terrorist skids	*Natlat irhabiyya*

The Camry was often the "color of kohl" – a Bedouin eye cosmetic – or sometimes "navy-blue." It was tamed early in the morning at the sound of Iraqi resistance songs and cheap Western electro:

How can we leave joyriding behind?	*Al-hajwala kef natruk-ha*
And who will break in the Camry?	*Wa-l-Kamri min yi'addeb-ha*
Who will execute four doughnuts?	*Arba' 'ugad min yittabeg-ha*
And the sidewalks, who'll brush past'em?	*Wa-l-arsifa min yishtef-ha*

Through joyriding, man had to become, as it were, master and possessor of the urban environment, of this second nature manifested in roads, overpasses, and sidewalks. At the same time, cars were being attributed human emotions, expressions and desires, or personalized like mounts or mares. Hybridization was a confusing operation, and joyriders at times didn't know if they were driving their cars or being operated by them:

His cap back to front	*'Akes al-tagiyya*
In a Camry color of kohl	*Bi-l-Kamri al-kuhliyya*
Hesitating: will I swerve, or spin?	*Muhtar bein natla wa 'aksiyya*
Fly o Camry fly	*Tiri ia Kamri tiri*
Fly for Sultan's beautiful eyes	*Tiri li-'uyun Sultan*
Fly with your companions	*Tiri wa ma'ts s-habets*
Fly, Sultan is with us!	*Tiri wa ma'na Sultan*
Drift o Camry drift	*Ia Kamri entali ia Kamri*
Swerve o Camry swerve	*Ia Kamri 'ugadi ia Kamri*
Don't cry o Camry don't	*La taz'ali ia Kamri la taz'ali*
O Camry his love	*Ia Kamri hubbah*
Made me forget about my folks	*Nassani ahli*
O Camry, by God, my own folks!	*Ia Kamri wallah nassani ahli*[31]

Joyriders were not fascinated by luxury or sport cars in the way that most car fans worldwide are. They were content with out of the factory, unattractive sedans. They transformed them only marginally by adding stickers here and there and by removing the license plates. There was a striking difference between joyriders' minimal intervention on cars and drag racers' attention to transforming their machines. Drag racers would patiently and lovingly customize their cars, adding rims, fins, and stills; swapping or boosting engines; and modifying the suspension. Drag racers also added various safety features to their cars, whereas joyriders could care less about safety: "Only faggots buckle up." They were in the business of destroying cars, not pampering them. Drag racers were enhancing the value of their cars, which they took an amorous care of. Joyriders were stripping cars of their exchange value and were focusing on using – and abusing – them. Drag racers contributed to the production of their cars by transforming them and making them faster and safer. Joyriders' attention focused on the performance itself rather than on the object-car.

As a performance, drifting wasn't producing anything other than itself and the surrounding space. The road became a stage, and this element of spectacle was accordingly what made *tafhit* fun, whereas the focus on car customization made drag racing tedious. "The Camry was made in Japan and remade in Saudi on the side doors" (*al-Kamri suni'at fi-l-Yaban wa fi-l-Su'udiyya 'ala-l-biban*) was a famous motto. The expression "on the side doors" (*'ala-l-biban*) referred to the sideways movement of a swerving car, which actually presented its side doors to the road. If cars were produced in Japan, it is only in Saudi Arabia that they were re-created as swerving devices, transfigured by a use for which they hadn't been engineered. Joyriding epitomized the failure of a system of "automobility" that "includes cars, car-drivers, roads, petroleum supplies and many novel objects, technologies and signs," and "generates the preconditions for its own self-expansion."[32] It was the breakdown of the patterns of mobility that had been put in place since the planning of the Saudi cities. It was the glitch in the car-city-driver machine.

As though to drive home the point that they were less interested in the exchange value than in the use value of cars, joyriders either stole or rented the cars they drifted on. Senior joyriders usually had helpers and admirers provide them with cars and wouldn't take the pain to find them themselves. Drifting sessions would be organized by Bubu's closest supporters, his "posse" (*ta'ziz*), made of those who "support him" (*yi'azzizun lah*). One of them would find a car, often asking rank and file to go out and "borrow" one. Another one would organize the group of "auxiliaries" (*musanidin*), five or six drivers who would remove their license plates and drive around Bubu, blinking and honking at regular interval to inform other drivers that a joyriding session was happening. In case of an accident, auxiliaries could turn their cars into makeshift ambulances. If Bubu's car crashed or became unusable, they could lend him their vehicle. In case of an encounter with the police, they would disperse to confuse the patrols and allow Bubu to escape the scene. An auxiliary was thus expected to be "a scapegoat" (*kebsh fida'*).

A third supporter would map out the session's route. He would be assisted by two important characters: "the radar" (*al-radar*) who would keep an eye, through his friends and networks, on the police patrols, and "the scout" (*al-muwajjeh*), who knew the best spots, helped design several possible trajectories, and reached out to the fans who, driving either their own vehicles or rented and stolen cars, would make out "the procession" (*al-mawkeb*).

It was extremely easy to join joyriders. There were no other organizations than the ones created, on the spot and ad hoc, each time a drifter wanted to make a show of his skills. *Tafhit* groups had no fixed boundaries. They developed out of circles of friends and relatives that hung out on a sidewalk or an empty plot, waiting for a show to be organized or – if they counted drifters in their ranks – throwing a party on their own and advertising it through cell phones or the Internet. Drifters generally welcomed newcomers, as they needed the assistance of many little hands to manage the material aspects of a show. As a way to test their commitment, novices were given master keys and asked to steal cars on parking lots and empty streets in remote neighborhoods. Should they decline the offer, they would remain confined to a subordinate position in the group. Were they to accept it, they would soon be given other challenges and be granted the opportunity to work their way up to the drifters and their "posse" (*ta'ziz*).

I recorded several panel interviews with four of Thamer's students, all of them high school seniors. They lived in one of Riyadh's peripheral neighborhoods, where Bedouin and Bidun had found cheap housing. They explained the ease with which local kids were drawn into joyriding, which they contrasted with the general unattractiveness of the high school's religious awareness group (*jama'a taw'iya islamiyya*). Undisturbed by the fact that Thamer, who was heading the religious group, attended the interview, they bravely explained how a majority of students joined drifting groups:

SU'UD – In junior high, we started this joyriding thing and all.... And I stayed two years with them, until high school. [...] I liked... (*Silence. Everybody listens attentively whereas a minute ago, before Su'ud mentioned joyriding, the other students were all speaking at the same time. Su'ud looks embarrassed.*)...

SALMAN – No, tell him, the day you stole a car! (*Laughter.*)...

SU'UD – I would pick up a car in another neighborhood and bring it to our neighborhood. Joyriding!...

TALAL – You know the Forty Street (*Share' Arba'in*)? It's the best spot for joyriding in the neighborhood, behind our house. We need to take you there.

SU'UD – It is *the* spot. During Ramadan, that's where there is the most joyriding. As they say: Ramadan is joyriding season....

TALAL – Up until breakfast, you see people joyriding in the streets, stuff like that. And the police come all the time, like up to twenty cars some days ... and even police buses. But nobody can stop [joyriders].... Because if you catch one of them, the others will just destroy everything....

SU'UD – I was in the street all the time. I didn't think about accidents, stuff like that. It was an addiction (*idman*), like when you start taking something, you *have to* take it. There was even this one time, when I was thrown in jail, they arrested me and my brother took me out of there, my brother who became a civil servant. I wasn't thinking about anything! I would go out by mid-afternoon (*ba'd al-'asr*) and come back late at night. And [my parents] would shout at me....

PASCAL – Do you remember how you began joyriding?

SU'UD – This kid came to me, one of the neighbors. He liked to steal, stuff like that. And from that day on, I went with him. We would take cars and I was scared. On the second day, he took a car. On the third day, I took a car, alone. I found it exciting.... Islamic groups? I feel like... only one percent of the people are destined for Islamic groups. Islamic groups attract a few people and keep them in a narrow circle. As for drifting groups, they are larger, they give you master keys in junior high, the keys we use to rob cars, they distribute them among students. And I remember this one day, I was walking home and I saw two kids, young'uns. They said they wanted to rob a car, they had a key. So [drifters] distribute keys, that's their way of recruiting people. And they gather huge groups.

TALAL – And also, belonging to joyriding is easier than joining an Islamic group. I mean, you watch them from your window, maybe you're gonna go down in the street and there, by your door, there is this guy, you chat, and the guy, maybe, he's game! He's gonna let you in his car on the second day. It's way easier! ...

THAMER, THEIR TEACHER – (*Dubious.*) So joyriding groups are more appealing than Islamic groups? ... But like, how much? Compared to the members of our group (*shababna*), how much? ...

SUʿUD – They are a lot more numerous. You start as a spectator...

TALAL – Before the state cracked down on joyriding, before that, everybody had only one obsession: becoming a joyrider.

Master keys were easy to come by. Suʿud and Talal told me that the key to their Nissan pickup (one of the most popular vehicles among young Bedouin) would open and operate all other Nissans, including the much-coveted Nissan Maxima. If joining joyriding was much easier than joining Islamic groups, it was partly because Islamic groups were deemed too elitist to be really inclusive. Islamic leaders also had the reputation to be intrusive, pushy, and to expect too much from group members. For a short period before he became interested in drifting, Rakan had belonged to a religious awareness group. When he was in eighth grade, "the bigots" (*al-mtawiʿa*) started infringing on his study time, and he decided to leave the group. This was easier said than done. He was enmeshed in day-to-day community activities such as organizing picnics, dinners, and lectures and ended up cutting his ties to the group all at once.

As a result of his experience with both drifters and religious activists, Rakan was able to draw interesting comparisons between them. Islamic groups were proselyte but paradoxically failed to attract much of a following, whereas joyriding groups, although closed and paranoiac, drew huge crowds of fans, sympathizers, and apprentice drifters. The main reason for their success was probably the fact that the city itself was the biggest joyriding terrain. As Talal remarked during the interview, you would watch joyriders "from your window" and, once "down in the street," find them "by your door." Although they tried hard to occupy as many spaces as possible, Islamists just couldn't be as ubiquitous. If everybody wanted to become a joyrider, it is simply because unlike Islamic activism, drifting was omnipresent in the city.

5.5. Reclaiming Urban Interstices

The space of Riyadh was speckled with vacant plots, sometimes as small as a house, often as big as a neighborhood. These interstices had been left aside by real estate investors for future development and were not accidental but essential to maintain the market in a state of scarcity. Shortage was not a glitch, but one of the engines of the real estate market growth.[33] These vacant plots, called "white lands" (*aradhi baydha'*), were often used by entrepreneurs to support temporary commercial activities such as theme parks or sport facilities. In the east of Riyadh, Rakan and I often hung out on a series of vacant plots turned into soccer fields. A few "soccer entrepreneurs," one of the players told us, had graded the ground, installed goal posts, drew marks, hired referees, and organized soccer tournaments for the local youths, who would form teams and pay a participation fee. As there were no other places to play soccer, youths were forced to pay to play and formed a captive market.

In the Central Business District of al-'Ulayya, a businessman had opened an amusement park on a "white land." Simply called Fun Park (*hadiqa al-farah*), the theme park was being torn down when I started fieldwork, creating a striking contrast between the colorful but shabby wooden planks and the sleek pyramid of the Faysaliyya Tower, designed in the 1990s by British architect Norman Foster. A skyscraper would soon be built where roller coasters once stood. On the outskirts of the city, people would rent out the cheapest "white lands" to serve as pens for sheep and goats or corrals for dromedaries. Joyriders and their fans also targeted these interstitial urban spaces, and acted like yet another category of entrepreneur. Joyriders usually used vacant plots at a critical juncture, when real estate developers were ready to go public and, to comply with municipal regulations, had the plots subdivided, lined with asphalted roads, and connected to the electricity network.

Vacant plots were often those "subdivisions" (*al-mukhattatat*) that municipal regulations compelled developers to outfit with freshly asphalted roads and streetlights. With their impeccable streets, their lamps, and their emptiness, subdivisions were pieces of outfitted desert, a cozy wasteland, a furnished wilderness at everyone's disposal. The space of joyriding was the geometrically designed frontier of the ever-expanding

FIGURE 5.3. Drifting on a fresh strip of asphalt under newly laid streetlamps. On the horizon, a real estate office advertises a new development. Copyright © THE BEST.

city. Its timeframe was squeezed between the creation of scarcity (the plots, artificially left vacant) and the extraction of rent (the new housing developments). Joyriders were overrunning these gray areas where land grabbing and speculation were inflating the real estate bubble, drastically restricting access to home ownership.[34]

Joyriders would point to land grabs with a mix of anger and irony. In the mid-2000s, the anonymous author of an online "History of Thugs" in Saudi Arabia wrote that joyriders "don't want to hear of the boom of the [Saudi] stock market. Why? Because when stocks go up, real estate goes down or stops. And if real estate goes down, new subdivisions are frozen, and new avenues aren't built. You know how the story ends."[35] New subdivisions, designed on the plateau along the grid of Doxiadis's superblocks, were a drifter's paradise. (See Figure 5.3.)

The peculiar ecology of joyriding was thus composed of long stretches of fresh asphalt, lined with streetlamps and adorned with billboards advertising future suburban developments. Some drifters dubbed the *mukhattatat* "killers of youth," as streetlamps were the cause of many drifting accidents, but their presence didn't discourage joyriders from using the smooth roads. When the first villas were built, joyriders and their fans started looking for new territory, because residents often called the police on them and had the municipality install speed bumps (*matab-bat*). Yet drifters would keep using the area until the new neighborhood was definitively controlled by the police, which sometimes simply never happened. Even speed bumps were not a real deterrent: many joyriders incorporated them into their drifting routines, using them as springboards or simply driving around them. The creation of a police station wasn't always effective either. Informants recounted a story of how one precinct had been robbed of its computers and air conditioning units a few days before its official inauguration. To the embarrassment of the police chief, the thieves were never found.

Joyriding was a by-product of the real estate market after developers and builders overpowered Doxiadis's plan and built settlements in the desert, far away from the control of the planners or of the police. The growth of Riyadh, and the automobile riot that it triggered, followed patterns that could also be observed in the suburbs of Los Angeles. In Southern California, skaters imitated surfers and "found, adapted and reconceived . . . the modernist space of suburbia . . . as another kind of space, as a concrete wave." By doing so, they radically transformed the meaning of urban spaces. "New hillside housing tracts lost their hideous urban negativity and emerged from the metamorphosis as smooth uncrowded ribbons of winding joy."[36] Joyriders similarly transfigured Riyadh's modernist superblocks by turning the freshly asphalted tracks from signs of capitalist accumulation into expressions of escapism and defiance. New thoroughfares and vacant plots were the tangible sign of the "failure of urban modernism,"[37] the symptom of the master plan's powerlessness in the face of the investors', developers', and builders' accumulation strategies.

It is on one of these vacant plots in the north of the city that I started hanging out with a group of drifters to whom Sa'b's brother Dhaifallah introduced me. Dhaifallah's friends couldn't afford to rent a rest house (*istiraha*) and instead converged on a huge vacant lot between a residential neighborhood and an empty superblock, where they would chat and drink soda until the first light of dawn. They had set up a large rug on the narrow path that linked the main avenue to a mosque under construction in the middle of the "white land." It was an isolated place, on a hill overlooking the northern districts of Riyadh. Mostly born in the steppe, drifters and fans had recently moved to Riyadh to study, work in the army, or look for a job. They would complete their daytime commute, from house to college or barracks, with a nocturnal journey, from house to rug with a view. They occasionally "threw the iron" on the neighboring six-lane highway, but tried not to attract the attention of the neighbors. They loved their

spot and the panoramic view it afforded and feared their exploits would
be a magnet for police patrols. They tried to keep it a haven from which
they could launch drifting expeditions in the new developments to the
north of the city.

Although he presented his friends to me as a bunch of "losers" and
"lowlifes," Dhaifallah confessed that he had also been a regular member of the group a few years earlier, after he moved to Riyadh from
the steppe to attend college. Mike Davis analyzes low-riding groups in
Los Angeles as a "cool space of socialization for poor youth arrived
from rural regions."[38] Between Dhaifallah's installation in Riyadh and
his college years, the joyriding group had similarly been a judgment-free,
action-packed space of socialization. Like skateboarding, joyriding was
"an attempt to know others in a city of unknowns, without resorting
to the institutions of family, school and team sports."[39] Vacant plots
were the spatial translation of the vast amounts of free time that unemployed youths were desperate to kill. Between emigration and unemployment, failed studies and grim prospects, their time was eaten away by
tufush, social despair, and spatial confusion. Drifting from vacant plot
to vacant plot was not just turning the asphalt into "concrete waves." It
also helped them to get along with the city and transformed the "ruthless
and unknowable metropolis" into a "city that [provided] opportunities
for survival and getting by."[40]

Joyriding was a way to learn the city with its geography, its itineraries,
its various social atmospheres, its resources, and its dangers. It gave a
direction to the empty time and the abstract space that overwhelmed
young migrants. Joyriding "gives sensations," 'Ajib's friend had told me
and Rakan, "it gives the sense of time and place" in a city where time
and place were difficult to get a sense of. Borne out of *tufush*, it was a
way to fight *tufush* by reclaiming and re-creating the space of the city.
Suburbanization had depoliticized the city and subjugated Saudis by way
of real estate loans and spatial dispersion. Joyriders re-injected some
degree of confrontation into that artificially tamed space. By their unruly
practices, their crashes, and their chases with police patrols, they were
calling everybody's attention to the forgotten yet obvious spaces where
the city was produced and where real estate capital was reproduced.

Renaming the streets was part of that process. Joyriders had invented
a parallel geography, with coded names for the main drifting spots.
Al-Janadriyya Road, which passed through dromedary corrals before
heading to Janadriyya and, further north, to Kuwait, was renamed al-
Ba'arin (dromedaries) in its southern section, around the corrals, and

al-Furusiyya (chivalry) in its northern section, near the Janadriyya horserace track. Names were linked to joyriding events, like Share' al-Gizaz in the Central Business District. Streets could also be renamed after physical or geographical characteristics. Share' al-Breksat (Barracks Street) owed its nickname to the prefabs that lined it during the construction of the Kingdom Hospital. Other streets bore their usual nickname. Thalathin al-Rabwa was named in reference to its width (30 m, *thalathin meter*) and to the neighborhood in which it was located (al-Rabwa). Several online guides helped apprentice drifters find their way in the maze of directives published on the Internet or by text messages. Share' al-Baramil (Barrels Street) could be reached by keeping to the following instructions:

BARRELS STREET. Its location: take the Northern Ring Road and leave behind you Exit 7 (the Islamic University), Exit 6, and Exit 5 (the Kingdom Schools). You'll see a sign "Al-Qassim Road," follow it by making a right. You'll find yourself on a flyover; this is the road to al-Qassim. You'll see a first exit, Defense Road: don't take it and continue until the second exit. Make a right and go forward, forward, forward, forward, until you see an overturned Camry on the side of the road: this is the street. It is not lit up by lamps; it is in the Press District (*hayy al-sahafa*); it is better to drift on it during daytime.[41]

These descriptions were not peculiar to joyriding. The geometric space of Riyadh was so confusing that all businesses in town provided detailed location instructions to their customers. One of 'Ajib's friends remembered how, back in the 1990s, drifters used to plan sessions by pager, using one star to symbolize al-Furusiyya, two stars for al-Ba'arin, and so on. The next generation of drifters used text messages to organize sessions and tended to avoid Internet forums, which were monitored by the police. Riyadh's geography was no longer centered on visible monuments, such as the old Masmak fort or the iconic Mamlaka and Faisaliyya towers. It had become a series of asphalted tracks, al-Bahri, al-Breksat, or al-'Ammariyya. The city was taken away from the princes' pompous vision. Its most forlorn locations and vacant plots, on the edge of the city, in new developments and ex-slums, became as central in joyriders' representations as they were to the real estate market. Around the city, drifters were occupying the Saudi equivalent of Wall Street.

5.6. "Sexy Boys Compete for You"

Drifters created an entire subculture, complete with bodily techniques, mechanical procedures, arts (music, songs, poetry, prose, graffiti, and video), and a complex celebration of same-sex love. The core of the drifting subculture was the driving performance itself, whose completion required a set of techniques and moral attitudes, and triggered a peculiar aesthetic, strongly influenced by risk taking and death. Spinning cars were the center of the joyriders' world, and their movement, by producing a novel and exhilarating urban spectacle, redefined urban spaces. Cars were at the center of the new city princes and developers had built around Riyadh. For joyriders, they were the alpha and omega of individual valor and courage, of new notions of space and society. In the drifting subculture, masculinity was linked to territory, and Riyadh, the capital of Najd and of Arabia, was the most exciting joyriding ground, the place where true virility, virtuosity, and courage were leading the drifting game. "Joyriding is nowhere bigger than in Riyadh; in Dammam and Jeddah they're just a bunch of faggots," would say Dhaifallah's friends. In an odd reproduction of the exceptionalist and racist phraseology of the Saudi state, joyriders would celebrate the "true drifting" (*al-tafhit al-sahih*) that was only to be found in Saudi Arabia. Other Gulf States were simply excluded from the picture: "They don't drift; they just do doughnuts" (*ma yifahhitun, bas yikhammisun*)," was a common and scornful statement.

Regions were ranked depending on the bravery of their drifters and the variety of the figures they would perform. Chutzpah and craziness were key elements of a drifting career. Along with drag racers, middle class society judged joyriding as being "temerity and nonsense" (*tahawwur wa 'abath*). Yet drifters were not necessarily as out of control as hinted at by their public persona. Beginners and advanced drivers became disciplined through the acquisition of bodily techniques, vital in an environment characterized by ubiquitous dangers and intense competition. As joyriders used to say, their "madness [was] manifold" (*al-junun funun*), it had many varieties and required the development of various skills.

Just like dancing, joyriding was an art and a discipline: a good joyrider didn't drink or smoke and was dedicated to his excellence as an extreme driver. (See Figure 5.4.) Private virtues were turned into public disorder by the skillful management of dexterous drivers. This ethics of self-control was, according to Bubu, the reason why his nemesis, Badr 'Awadh, remained at the pinnacle of joyriding for sixteen years, while other less dedicated drifters were wounded or died. Migrin, whom Rakan befriended in high school, was also committed to a certain discipline. After his two stays in prison, he was now hoping to find a "quiet job" that would allow him to "go to work at 8 AM, like everybody else, finish at 2 PM and come home to take a nap," but joyriding was all he knew. He

FIGURE 5.4. Bedouin youth dance an acrobatic *dabka* during a wedding, 2007. Copyright © Pascal Menoret.

had a managerial conception of drifting and of the relationships between joyriders and their young male admirers, as he told Rakan one day:

MIGRIN – If you work in a company, and there is an outstanding employee, of course, you will wish to become better than him. It is the same thing with joyriding. There is the love of younger boys (*al-wir'anjiyya*). But it is a kind of extra reward (*imtiyaz*) you get only if you become the best employee. If you get into joyriding for younger boys' eyes, you will be a bad drifter and lose the boys (*al-wir'an*). You gotta get into joyriding for the sake of it, and become excellent as a joyrider. Because boys love excellence and dedication.

There was an ethics of joyriding, and drifters skillfully managed themselves to reap the full benefits of what could be called their bodily capital.[42] Watching hands whirling around the steering wheel and the handbrake in a wild dance, grasping or releasing them in a brisk manner, could only give a very approximate idea of the dexterity that was needed to swerve a ton and a half of metal and plastic on the road. But dexterity was not all there was. The whole idea behind joyriding was, in order to prove one's mastery, to give up the idea of mastery itself and to let the car, its accumulated speed, and its kinetic energy, progressively take over. Drifting was contained in this dialectical movement: "throwing one's self out of control to pull it back in,"[43] driving to the edge to prove one's freedom and courage, losing control to regain control. The same went with the relationship to beautiful boys. You had to give up power in order to gain power, to focus on your driving prowess and, in order to attract boys' attention, forget about the boys.

Drifters displayed aggressive bodies through their self-presentation, their driving practices, and their celebration of macho male-to-male sexual practices. 'Ajib described how most drifters actively sought attractive boys (*wir'* pl. *wir'an*), and organized shows in front of middle and high schools to convince teenagers to join in and ride shotgun with them. The mention of the love of boys (*wir'anjiyya*) sent a shiver of delight among his friends, and he dryly commented, "We barely see girls. Therefore, we use boys." Another drifter facetiously exclaimed, "Glory to God! Our boys look like girls . . . " while 'Ajib took my notebook and traced the following verses:

Put the speed at 125 (mph)	*Shidd al-'izz taht al-meyten*
Push the engine at 6,000 (rpm)	*Dhught al-makina 'ala sitta*
Sexy boys compete for you	*'Alek yisabeg al-helwen*
Tell the one you're into.	*Kil ta'nak 'allamtah*

Homosocial romance was common among Riyadh's youth, both male and female.[44] Some Saudis linked this situation to the system of overly well-enforced gender segregation, whereas others attributed it to moral decadence and the "imitation of the West."[45] Speaking of homosexuality would be a stretch, as sexual identities were relative to social class as well as to the adoption of various roles during romantic and sexual encounters. Upper-middle-class Saudis could claim to be gay, but were quite isolated in this regard, as a majority of young men who engaged in same-sex relations did not necessarily perceive themselves as homosexuals. Sexual practices weren't predicated on preexisting gender identities, but produced the very attitudes adopted by the various partners during the act itself.

Rather than being seen as homosexual or heterosexual, sexual partners were perceived as either active or passive. Active partners (*mujib* pl. *mujibin*, literally "obligating," or *wir'anji*, literally "boy chaser") epitomized masculinity and were "polysexual" rather than hetero- or homosexual, as they were potentially interested in the other sex as well as their own. By their ability to sexually dominate other males, they perceived themselves and were often perceived as even more virile than those men who weren't interested in boys. "*Al-hamdulillah, ana rajjal*" (Grace be to God, I'm a man), boasted a friend who claimed to go out with several boys every night.

Passive partners (*salib* pl. *sawalib*, literally "negative," or *wir'* pl. *wir'an*, literally "boy") were usually younger, and were sought after for the pleasures they could offer with no risks of pregnancy or of family dishonor. They were not as despised and frowned on as one could expect and could wield enormous power. They were in high demand in a society where, as a result of labor migrations, men largely outnumbered women and where women remained mostly out of men's reach. Roles were not cast in stone, and sexual identities were relatively fluid. Passive partners were expected to become active with time and to seek the favors of younger boys. Active partners, however, were less likely to become passive. Cross-dressing was common enough to be explicitly banned and repressed.[46] Girls dressing as boys were nicknamed *boyat*, whereas boys dressing as girls were called – and disparaged – as *mukhannathin* (hermaphrodites or effeminates), *wir'an* or, sometimes, *ladyboys*. Whatever their biological gender, active partners were viewed as masculine, whereas passive partners were identified – and sometimes identified themselves – as feminine.

Joyriding was part of this homosocial culture, and its celebration of unfettered masculinity accordingly accentuated the level of sexual violence between joyriders and their fans. Gender segregation probably increased the frequency of same-sex practices and arguably played a role in the high level of sexual violence that the city witnessed. But it didn't seem to be the main reason why same-sex practices were common. As in the Arab provinces of the Ottoman Empire before the imposition of Victorian categories on sexual practices (including the notions of homosexuality and heterosexuality),[47] the Saudi sexual *Weltanschauung* expressed an unapologetic masculine domination. Even after their marriage, active partners would often seek the company of other males, some of them hanging out with the joyriding crowd in search of sensations and, probably too, sexual adventures.

Within the joyriding world, there were two sides to the love of boys (*wir'anjiyya*). The first one was the celebration of beauty and the romantic relation between a joyrider and his favorite fan, who was allowed to ride with him and share a fragment of his glory. Joyriders would perform "for the beautiful eyes" (*li-'uyun*) of their beloved, whose name they'd often write on stickers that they glued to their car. Known for his asceticism and his dedication to joyriding, Badr 'Awadh was also reputed for his love of younger boys:

RAKAN – Badr 'Awadh had a whole procession (*mawkeb*) follow him. They thought he was gonna drift, but he drove all the way to al-Badi'a, in the old Riyadh, and he had them drive around his lover's house. He'd told the boy: I'll bring you a procession of cars, and they'll drive around your house. And he had them turn for a long time, do you imagine? Seventy cars in an old neighborhood, around one single house? Badr 'Awadh was a first class boy chaser (*wir'anji*).

The joyrider-boy relation was often of an educational nature. One would learn joyriding "for the beautiful eyes of" another drifter. With its celebration of beauty, *wir'anjiiya* was, according to Rakan, closer to Platonic love than to lasciviousness and desire. Same-sex relationships were a narrative commonly and jokingly used around drifting sessions, a trope that epitomized the joyrider's mastery. This gestures to the second side of boy-loving (*wir'anjiyya*): the celebration of an aggressive masculinity, of violence against boys, against society, and against the self. For criminologist Muhammad al-Saif, sexual violence and sodomy were among the most visible "deviances" (*inhirafat*) accompanying joyriding. Al-Saif quoted several interviews he realized with jailed joyriders about their sexual practices. Although he claimed to have been faithful to "the language they use in daily life," all excerpts were reworked and translated into classical Arabic:

With my friends, we drift near middle and high schools for boys and sometimes inside neighborhoods to attract those youths who watch joyriding, witness our acrobatics and our amazing skills. Some are bedazzled by our art and we ask one of them to accompany us during the show, we tell him that we are ready to teach him joyriding, and we agree on training him in the desert (*fi-l-barr*) outside of the city, for security reasons. He comes several times and we seek his consent before we practice sodomy with him. Some accept from the beginning, while others accept only if we give them an opportunity to sodomize other boys their age who agree on doing it, which leads them to accept to be sodomized.

While this first interviewee seemed eager to show that sodomy was practiced with the consent of the passive partner, al-Saif's second interviewee described more violent scenes:

When I drift, I get to know beautiful adolescents and boys. I ask one of them to ride with me a few times, and I show off with him in front of the audience. We do that several times, until our relationship becomes stronger, and I introduce him to other joyriders, I show him the place where we meet, and we begin to think about sodomizing him. We invite him for dinner in the desert, outside of the city, and we ask him to sing and dance, and my friends start sexual jokes with him. If he welcomes these jokes with good humor, we start having sexual desires and we sodomize him. But if he doesn't show any satisfaction or consent, we resort to violence, we threaten to expose him publicly, and sometimes we threaten him with weapons.[48]

Joyriders' violence was directed at younger boys, at cars, at urban spaces, and at themselves. The body of the joyrider was not only adjusted and attuned to the car, but also refined, sharpened, fashioned as a weapon. Drifting was comparable to boxing, this "scientifically savage practice" that is "a series of strategic exchanges in which one pays for one's hermeneutical mistakes immediately, the force and frequency of the blows taken . . . providing an instantaneous assessment of the performance: action and its evaluation are fused."[49] Like al-Qaeda's supporters, joyriders emphasized the importance of being fit and lean in a society where obesity was rampant.[50] "Drift, and you'll lose weight!" (*Ezhef, tanhaf!*) was another joyriding motto.

The drifter's body had to be adjusted to the machine through various exercises in order to confront the risk and the possibility of death. The care of the body began with clothing practices. Like Najdi women and armed militants, joyriders veiled their faces, not only in order not to be recognized but also as a display of coquetry and – paradoxically – masculinity. Other clothing practices distinguished young drifters, in particular the long dress (*thawb*) with short sleeves, as well as recognizable ways of wrapping their headdresses (called *shakhsiyat*, "personalities"). (See Figure 5.5.) The body of the drifter was glorified through its ability to confront death and to reject dominant corporeal codes. If there was any heroism in drifting, then it was in this sublimation of ordinary bodies into will-o'-the-wisps that animated masses of steel and made them dance on the asphalt. With its processions of swerving cars, its expressions of homosocial sentimentality and its demonstration of public disorder, drifting was a rebellion of the body against the spatial, moral, and political normativity of mainstream Saudi society. The reinterpretations of the common dress code, the proclaimed deviant sexual behavior, and the ability to put one's physical integrity at stake were the most visible symptoms of this aggressive masculinity.

Yet the joyriders' masculinity was as vulnerable and fragile as it was violent. This ambiguity was celebrated in *kasrat*, popular songs originating in the rural Hejaz that in the 1960s and 1970s had followed nomadic migrations into Najd.[51] *Kasrat* had been adapted to express the urban experience, the hopes and despair of marginalized youth. They were

FIGURE 5.5. Joyriders veil their faces for security reasons and out of coquetry, 2007. Copyright © Pascal Menoret.

sung along with a lute, drums, and often a keyboard accompaniment, and were performed during sessions (*jalsat*) held in private, in houses or on vacant plots across the city. *Kasrat* sessions couldn't be advertised publicly, given the risqué nature of the songs, which often broached joyriding, unemployment, police brutality, and same-sex love. Their very name, derived from the root *ka-sa-ra*, which means "to break," reflected that underground nature. *Kasrat* were reportedly elaborated during oral contests in which rival poets or tribesmen were attempting to "break" their challengers with their wit and their eloquence. Another possible meaning of the word was connected to the very language and subject of the *kasrat*, broken songs written in broken verses by damaged youth dreaming of a better life, far away from restrictive norms, police surveillance, and political and social repression.

Kasrat were recorded with homemade means and sold under the counter in most music stores across the country. Older Saudis spurned them as mere teenagers' song, and urged me, instead of digging into what to them were the garbage bins of Arabia, to study nobler sources. I would regularly listen to classic Saudi singers Talal Maddah and Muhammad

'Abduh and sometimes to ex-*kasra* singer Faris Mahdi, who had bowd-
lerized his production to enter the formal music market. But in their
exposition of the underground car culture and of the chivalry that young
joyriders were inventing, made of gallantry towards beautiful boys and
boldness behind the wheel, *kasrat* said more about life in Riyadh than
censored and defanged mainstream songs did.

A *kasra* by a famous singer, Abu Faisal, describes the aimless life
of a joyrider under the title "I Went Once to Tahliya" ("Al-Tahliya
jit-ha marra"). Tahliya Avenue in the 'Ulayya district was nicknamed
after the Higher Desalination Authority (*al-mu'assasa al-'uliya li-tahliya
al-miya al-maliha*) whose headquarters were located at the corner of King
Fahd Avenue. Lined with luxury boutiques, cafés, and Second Empire
replica streetlights, it was nicknamed the "Champs-Elysées of Riyadh"
and became, night after night, a runway on which Saudi youth paraded
and sought romantic adventures.

> I came to Tahliya once and had my heart stolen
> I wrote a tune about it for the loverless
> I came with my Lexus, the 2004 model
> And saw a boy staring at me, who took my heart and set it on fire
> He'd dabbed his eyes with kohl, his hair was soft and blond
> He had this kind of swagger, and man, his body was tight!
> He wore jeans and a skullcap, and had a Panda-phone[52] in hand
> Everyone was sweating him and his ride, a Honda I think
> I stopped at the light, he rolled down his window and said:
> "Come to the side street." "Why?" I asked. "You tell me," he replied,
> "But just so you know, my brothers are here. I told them we're
>   classmates"
> He said: "Take my number, I want you to free me"
> Praise God, that was a relief! Now I go every afternoon
> And my worries disappear. It sucks to be without a lover![53]

In the following strophes of the song, Abu Faisal sings about how he
became a bad student, dropped out of school, and ultimately engaged in
joyriding. "I wasted my life with thugs, and now I regret it. . . . Everyone
around me has a future, but all I see is ruin."

Songs were not the most visible artistic production in the joyriding
world. Videos, posted on YouTube and watched on computers and
mobile phones, seemed to be the most present. In them joyriding identities
were created, collectively enjoyed, and communicated to new users and
viewers. Joyriding video directors were often retired or aspiring drifters,
and were admired and celebrated almost as much as joyriders themselves.
Rakan and I met a filming crew that, under the ominous pseudonym of

"Gangsta," was known for following processions onboard an old Nissan XL, a mythical vehicle from the top of which they shot their movies. Other movie crews called themselves "Irhabi" (Terrorist), "Borran" (deleted in Spanish), or "Taxi." Videos were widely distributed and viewed; they were a way for the joyriding underworld to acquire visibility and legitimacy. Although repression and surveillance confined joyriders to the peripheries of the urban space, videos were visible in the transnational space of YouTube.

There were roughly three sorts of videos: those showing drifting shows from outside the car, those filmed from inside the car, where the driving performance was accompanied by the comments of the joyrider, and those showing joyriding accidents. This last category of videos, which were often brutally grisly, was broadcasted either by joyriding fans or by anti-joyriding activists. Videos would be widely exchanged, and joyriders would casually watch terrifying accident scenes. Videos were the result of a compulsion to make joyriding visible even outside of Saudi Arabia, where a few drifting clips had remarkable careers. One of them was sent by young Saudis to the BBC show *Top Gear* and broadcasted in 2003 while Jeremy Clarkson, "doyen of laddish commentary on motor matters,"[54] commented,

[Beginning of the video: a Toyota Camry is swerving on a road at high speed.] This is a Toyota Carina [*sic*], front-wheel drive . . . So he must be using the hand brake to make it do this (*laughter*). Into the oil tanker . . . ? No, he just misses that, well done! Oh! That's just madness! He's in the street, and people and . . . this man is insane! This is the problem . . . you see, this is what happens when you don't let people drink . . . (*Laughter.*) When you . . . (*The Camry is going into a wall.*) Oh, what's happening there? He's going into the wall! You see, a new castle, you go out, you convert your kebab into a pavement pizza . . . (*The Camry rolls over.*) That's big trouble! . . . Then you have a fight, then you go home! (*End of the video, camera on the audience.*) Saudi Arabia looks to me like a lot more fun! (*Laughter.*)[55]

The authors of the video probably didn't expect Clarkson's racist comments, but certainly appreciated to be taken as representatives of Saudi Arabia. They were those who made the country look "like a lot more fun." Another famous video was featuring Bubu drifting a BMW 7 Series, nicknamed "Ben Laden" in Riyadh, "because it looks mean." The story happened at the time when Bubu was trying to quit joyriding:

RAKAN – [Bubu] stopped drifting for a while, but people were making him offers, people were going to his place and were proposing to give him a car, to give him cash, Bubu was making loads of cash with his drifting. Sometimes, it was not money but, for instance, they'd lend him a car, an apartment, they'd bring him food, pay for a trip for him, he wasn't taking a wage as if he was working for them. And you remember that story I told you, about this one time when somebody challenged him, and offered him 15,000 riyals [about $4,000] to drift the new BMW 7 Series, the very first one that arrived from Germany to Saudi Arabia? That guy, everybody was treating him like a sheikh or a prince – no, wait, he said sheikh, not prince? On that day, Bubu organized three drifting processions (*mawakib*) [to mislead the police]. The first one was in the south of Riyadh, the second in the east of Riyadh, and the third in the north of Riyadh, on al-'Ammariya [Road]. That's where he drifted the BMW. In the beginning, he couldn't spin it, but he eventually made it. He had to push it at 170 mph to be able to spin it.... And the other guy [the sheikh] was filming the scene and he sent the tape to BMW Germany. Because [engineers] were claiming that the car would hold the road no matter what, and this guy sent a letter saying: "Look at what our kids do to your cars!"

Joyriding videos contributed to turn "Saudi drifting" into an internationally known phenomenon. Through videos, Saudi dare-devilry was flaunted in front of massive numbers of online spectators, who were probably more interested in crash pornography than in the joyriders' driving skills. Videos were sent to producers of cars (in the case of BMW) or of worldwide images (in the case of the BBC). Similar to graffiti, clips were quickly produced and placed in full visibility, for the world to watch and the Saudi state to ruminate on a response. Joyriding videos didn't only create an imagined community of drifters, fans, apprentices, and admirers. They also openly challenged the state's claimed monopoly over the representation of Saudi society. They upset the accepted image of the country as a deeply religious nation, where crime was minimal, and dissent unheard of. Drifting videos didn't just promote joyriders. They also posed a counterimage to official propaganda. In brief, they showed to the world that in great Saudi cities – and even in the capital itself – the state was not in control of public spaces.

6

Street Politics

6.1. The Death of Sharari

My last meeting with 'Ajib was exactly two weeks after the famous joyrider Mish'al al-Sharari died in a drifting accident. This meeting was supposed to be our first face-to-face encounter. Until then 'Ajib and I had met only with other drifters, supporters, and Rakan. I wished to negotiate a recorded interview, and I thought it more appropriate to see him alone. A few hours before our meeting, however, I inexplicably changed my mind and decided to go with a European colleague of mine who was visiting for a week. 'Ajib also came with a silent youth in tow, whom he introduced as his cousin.

This was a serious blunder. As a result of my willingness to show that I was not alone in studying the Arabian Peninsula, we never recorded the interview. Probably scared off by the presence of not one but two awkward foreigners saying they were scientists, 'Ajib evaporated after this last conversation. However hard I tried to find him, calling him and his friends or begging Rakan for help, I didn't succeed: he had definitely cut all ties. I met him by chance a last time, as I was leaving the country – and never saw him again after that.

I never recorded any conversation with joyriders, apart from a long biographical interview with Rakan and an embarrassed dialogue with a drifter while driving aimlessly in eastern Riyadh. In most cases, it was impossible to even chat with drifters. They generally spoke with an extreme circumspection and tended to answer questions, tongue in cheek, with a mixture of half-truths, allegories, and moralistic clichés ("drifting is a sin") before clamming up and trying to escape by any means possible.

Islamic activists were relatively easy to interview and almost impossible to observe. Joyriders were both difficult to observe and impossible to interview. They were as elusive as guerrilla, as secretive as conspirators, as cunning as political activists. Caught in what appeared to be a perfect anthropological storm, I was deprived of the usual tools of fieldwork. I supplemented my scarce firsthand information by reading press articles, listening to *kasrat*, watching YouTube videos, and analyzing online literature produced by joyriders and their fans. This slow acculturation helped me better understand the few conversations I had with them.

During this last encounter, 'Ajib narrated in detail the death of Mish'al al-Sharari before announcing his own intention to quit drifting. He had had two accidents himself, the first one two months and the second barely a week before we met. One of his friends had filmed his first accident, which he showed me on his smartphone. After a well-executed lateral skid (*natla*) at 140 mph, the Honda Accord he was driving unexpectedly jumped in the air without rolling over. The head of one of the rear passengers hit the ceiling; the guy was still hospitalized. Nobody was hurt in the second accident, but the rented car was wrecked. 'Ajib said he now owed SAR 5,000 (about $1,300) to the rental company. He just wanted to quit. When I called Rakan that evening, he said in a blasé tone that most joyriders were just divas. 'Ajib didn't exactly look like he was about to quit, what with his multicolor Yemeni headdress folded in an artistic and sloppy bunch, his invitation to join his next drifting session, and his cajoling insistence on drifting "for [my] beautiful eyes" if I rode with him.

The story he narrated, however, could make you want to take public transportation for the rest of your life. On the day of his death, Mish'al al-Sharari had first refused to drift for his group of admirers. He preferred instead to cruise around in his car with another joyrider, Shaytani (Diabolic). Disappointed, his fans organized a procession (*mawkeb*) of several dozen cars and drove at top speed across Riyadh until they caught up with him and urged him to entertain them. Won over by their enthusiasm, Sharari started drifting and took the procession of cars to the Low Income District (*Hayy al-Dakhl al-Mahdud*). To the south of the district, new real estate developments were projected along Najm al-Din al-Ayyubi Avenue, a wide road cutting through large swathes of sand and lined up with sheep pens and isolated villas. Joyriders had renamed it "al-Ghurub" (Sundown), which was the name of the new development. It was now mid-afternoon, and spectators had turned up in the hundreds to follow Sharari's performance. At the end of a *natla*, his Camry crashed at full speed into a small pickup truck that was exiting one of the sheep corrals. Folded in two by the violence of the impact, the car mowed down a group of fans in attendance. The Camry was barely slowed down by this encounter. It crashed into several cars while spectators were running away in all directions. After it stopped its deadly course, spectators rushed toward the carcass to pull out the joyrider and his crew. The car suddenly burst into flames, its four occupants burning alive and – 'Ajib reported – screaming in terror and agony.

Beside the four occupants of the car, at least five other people also died, including four spectators and the passenger of the pickup that had caused the collision.[1] In the following months, poems and texts were published online to celebrate the memory of Sharari while aficionados exchanged gory videos of the accident. Some videos endlessly replayed the moment of the collision and reproduced the terrible soundtrack of the accident, made of shrieks and screams. Others, including the one 'Ajib showed me, alternated images of the accident with religious advice given in a soft voice over a musical background of Islamic hymns (*anshuda*, pl. *anashid*).

The accident sped up repression. A few days after I saw 'Ajib, the Riyadh police department announced the arrest of two "leaders of the joyriding sedition" (*ru'us fitna al-tafhit*).[2] The first had killed a spectator on the infamous al-Ghurub Avenue, and the second was drifting in a posh neighborhood. Other drifters were arrested in the following days, including "al-Mutahawwir" (the impudent), twenty-one, who was picked up by the police in a restaurant after killing a spectator.[3] This crackdown was neither the first nor the most important, but it made my job more difficult: most drifters, including 'Ajib, would now keep a low profile. Before the death of Sharari, connecting with joyriders was a precarious operation; it was now nearly impossible.

Between its emergence in the 1970s and the first massive crackdown in the 1990s, joyriding was constructed as a public issue by entrepreneurs in morality, who denounced it as a symptom of moral decay and political carelessness. Sociologists, criminologists, and religious preachers worked on youth crime and road safety in general, and joyriding in particular. Article after article and lecture after lecture, they drew the contours of an anthropology of youth that could be used by the police, the schools, and the penitentiaries. Repressed by the state and their behavior constructed as a political problem, joyriders in turn politicized their activities, and transformed a suburban pastime into an open challenge to the police and the preachers.

The joyriding subculture didn't develop in a vacuum, but in reaction to the state's spatial politics and to the strategies of princes, urban planners, developers, policemen, religious preachers, sociologists, and criminologists. Joyriding became political in three distinct ways. First, it was politicized from the outside: constructed by sociologists, criminologists, and preachers as a public issue and turned into an object of science and debate, joyriding slowly became synonymous, in the public's eyes, with the young generation's collective suicide. Second, as a response to repression, joyriders also identified the political value of their driving practices. From an innocent hobby and a hazardous game, from a grassroots reaction to social and bodily norms, joyriding became a wider revolt against state surveillance. Their encounters with the police, religious preachers, and state experts conferred onto joyriders an aura of political rebellion. Drifting became a way to physically escape police repression, a violent sport whose forms, figures and techniques were also antipolice maneuvers. With its complex pyramidal organization, its large crowds, its processions and parades, its cultural and artistic production, its legends and its martyrs, joyriding mimicked the operations of the state. In the words of one interviewee, it was "a state within a state" (*dawla fi-l-dawla*).

Third, joyriders were not only politicized from the outside and not merely reacting to state repression. They also had an agency in their own right, and they actively criticized the production of space in Riyadh. Many joyriders were aware of the intrinsically contentious dimensions of their driving prowess and pointed to the overwhelming importance of real estate and car import in the making of the city. The networks of power continuously engineering Riyadh's car-based suburbia were on their minds, and they often formulated sharp critiques of Al Saud's nepotism. This chapter reconstitutes the story of the criminalization of joyriding and of its complex politicization. It follows the encounters between joyriders and several state actors and shows how their relations evolved toward more police organization and more joyriding temerity.

6.2. "Either Death or Repentance"

The religious repertoire was central in the criminalization of joyriding by the state, and joyriders sometimes internalized the accusatory finger pointed at their activities. The first night I spent on the rug-with-a-view with Dhaifallah and his friends, one of them stepped forward and introduced himself as an intermediary between the group and myself. At twenty-two years old, 'Atiya was the only college student among school dropouts, jobseekers, and soldiers of the National Guard. He was both distinguished and marginalized by this status, and he made it very clear that he had only contempt for drifting and drifters. He said aloud a few times how "retarded" (*mutakhallifin*) they were in his eyes, which struck me as insulting and inelegant. 'Atiya also insinuated that my interest in joyriding was a way of accessing the underworld of drugs, alcohol, and homosexual sex. As I vehemently protested, he explained to the others that I surely wanted to explore the dregs of Riyadh to publish in the West a denigrating account of Saudis and Muslims. He displayed a very protective attitude toward "Saudi society" (*al-mujtama' al-su'udi*) and wanted to preserve its "80 percent Islamic" reputation from the stain of drifting and from any suspicion of amorality or lewdness.

Posing as an intermediary, he was also determined to keep me at arm's length: this self-proclaimed ally was in fact a saboteur. I grew more and more uncomfortable as he explored aloud his friends' "motivations" (*dawafi'*) to drift cars. He said they were the innocent victims of their lust, and their thirst for fame came from their passion for younger boys, which he had no words to condemn. To bypass his mediation, I tried to speak directly to the other youths, but they tended to respond with a smile about how 'Atiya was better than they at analyzing joyriding. 'Atiya's victims seemed to adhere to his analyses, and each party apparently played his role. 'Atiya was the good kid who sincerely wondered why his friends had fallen so low, and they accepted his scolding, possibly knowing that he too was seeking what they'd found in the street: the warmth of a group, the thrill of adventure, perhaps ephemeral love.

The conversation stalled, and we went for a ride. Joyriders were expected to perform in the north of the city, on "Share' al-Breksat" (Barracks Street), next to the Kingdom Schools, and we started off in three cars. Five excited guys in a small Korean sedan sped down the highway while Dhaifallah tried to keep up with them and with the third car, a small pickup. Crammed in with two soldiers and myself in Dhaifallah's car, 'Atiya continued his diatribe, now explaining that joyriding was an invention of "the devil." The two soldiers nodded distractedly. They were busy comparing drifters and marveling at how joyriding figures were "evolving all the time." One of them growled from the corner of his mouth, "yeah, drifting is bad; it is the work of Satan." The Korean sedan overtook our car, one of its passengers waving at us from the back seat and trying to attract the attention of one of the soldiers with an explicitly sexual gesture. We arrived on "al-Breksat." Soon a police patrol showed up, its lights and sirens blazing, and Dhaifallah sped away through back streets, panicking at the idea that the cops could track him down with his license plate number.

Back on the rug, 'Atiya continued his moralistic diatribe, which now was echoed by an older joyrider, Muhammad, who had punctuated his arrival with a few well-applauded swerves on the avenue. In his mid-thirties, his face ravaged by chickenpox and with a mischievous air about him, Muhammad cracked joke after joke. As I showed interest in nicely executed figures and the technical aspects of drifting, they both learnedly explained that I shouldn't get too excited, because "the end of drifting [was] either death or religious commitment and repentance" (*ia-l-mawt ia-l-iltizam wa-t-tawba*).

Muhammad was now leading the conversation, and forced 'Atiya into the role of silent onlooker. He said that since drifters wanted to attract young students, their next goal was to reach celebrity (*shuhra*) and become "great joyriders" (*kibar al-mufahhatin*). Some made it in a few months while others needed years. Most importantly, joyriders were expected to be reckless (*mutahawwerin*), the ideal among drifters being to "speed like crazy," "chain-drift," and "fear nothing," neither death nor the cops. He explained that drifters were "experimenters" who had tried everything – boys, alcohol, and drugs – had looked death in the eyes, and were surrounded by the memories of departed friends. He added that becoming born again Muslims was the only adventure most joyriders hadn't yet tried. The greatest drifters were more likely to dabble in religion and become religious zealots (*mtawi'a*). After their repentance, some joyriders-turned-preachers would set up tents near famous drifting spots, where they called young men to repent and quit joyriding, cigarettes, drugs, and alcohol.

Muhammad wasn't interested in drifting only. He wanted to raise Saudi Arabia's position in a world dominated, in his view, by industrial economies and what he called "Western moral values": individualism, materialism, and hedonism. He had very strong words about Saudi Arabia being the "garbage bin of civilized countries" (*zbala al-buldan al-mutahadhdhira*) and sketched a theory of car consumption, describing how cars were engineered in such a way as to force you to buy spare parts after a few years and how Saudi car dealerships were organized in a series of monopolies (*ihtikakat*) granted by princes to key individuals. His conclusion was that in order to protect your dignity in a world dominated by ruthless economic interests, you had to stick to your religious values, even if you were a lowlife and a thug (*sarbut*). Otherwise, you were just a "retarded Bedouin" who was still "branding his camels."

After Muhammad's self-deprecating remark, a young aficionado got up and started dancing around the rug. His slender body wrapped in tight robes and his straight, jet-black hair enshrined in a white skullcap, he began teasing everybody, wriggling, writhing, and lasciviously rubbing himself against his friends. Nicknamed al-Gamla (head louse), he interrupted Muhammad's ethno-religious pontifications with a scream: "I hate Saudi Arabia!" A bit later, as Muhammad was demeaning those who engage in joyriding for the love of boys, al-Gamla came closer to me, grinning, and shouted in my ear: "Don't listen to him! He only drifts to get laid! Look at the videos of boys he has on his phone!" Everyone laughed except straight-faced 'Atiya, whose scolding sent al-Gamla on another screaming and dancing binge. Al-Gamla was the truth of Muhammad's polished and defensive discourse. He was screaming that the emperor was naked, that Muhammad sounded too patriotic to be honest, that his motivations as a drifter were obviously to gain the favor of slim, cheeky boys like himself. As the call to the dawn prayer resonated from a mosque across the avenue, al-Gamla rushed into the closest car and furiously hit the horn, yelling: "Prayer time! Prayer time!"

Al-Gamla's behavior revealed that the language joyriders used to communicate with me was a form of doublespeak disconnected from their actual personas. 'Atiya and Muhammad systematically reframed my inquiry in a set of questions about drifters' motivations: they asked the other drifters *why* they engaged in joyriding, *why* they joined a joyriding group, *why* they dropped out of school, or what *motivations* lead to joyriding (*wesh al-dawafi' elle tu'addi li-l-tafhit*). As expected, members of the group laughed in discomfort and either stayed silent or gave short answers to shift the attention back to 'Atiya and Muhammad, who would look at me, trying to assess if my curiosity had been quenched. At one point, 'Atiya asked me if I had "enough stuff now to write my book." Everybody looked at me, expecting a relieving "yes." Embarrassed, I tried to explain that I wished to spend more time with the group and learn more about joyriding.

Ridiculed by al-Gamla, 'Atiya's and Muhammad's speech was oddly reminiscent of how Saudi psychologists and sociologists analyzed joyriding. A 2004 study of "joyriding's motivations" by Sulaiman ad-Duwayri'at, professor of psychology at Riyadh's Imam Muhammad bin Saud Islamic University (or "Imam University"), pointed to nine reasons why youths drift cars: a weak religious faith (*dhu'f al-iman*), the thirst for celebrity, the love of adventure, idleness (*al-faragh*), the imitation of a clique (*muhakat rufqa al-su'*), weak familial oversight, the influence of media and computer games, a nonrecognition of the value of things, and homosexuality.[4] Muhammad wittingly or unwittingly reproduced the normative academic discourse elaborated by Saudi joyriding experts. He spoke from a very filtered position, as if he wanted to represent the whole of Saudi society in the face of the foreign fieldworker.

It was now six in the morning, and a guy in his fifties, chain-smoking and dressed like an unruly teenager, his headgear piled up above his head in a studied disorder, was chatting with Muhammad in a deep, coarse voice. He got up heavily and drove away while doing a few clumsy skids on the avenue. 'Atiya gave me another appointment a few days later, but never showed up or answered his phone. Despite a promising beginning, I felt stranded on an unwelcoming shore. Dhaifallah asked me not to multiply my visits to the rug, and obviously felt uncomfortable at the idea, suggested by 'Atiya, that I was seeking sexual adventures. He saw my interactions with al-Gamla and the other joyriders as potentially tarnishing his reputation as a dependable, God-fearing, and old-fashioned youth.

Dhaifallah also told me that many drifters thought I was working with the infamous secret police (*mabahith*). Everybody knew U.S., British, and French experts had participated in recent antiterrorist operations. Jailed joyriders were sometimes questioned by criminologists and sociologists about the very "motivations" 'Atiya and Muhammad were eager to explore in my presence, and several studies on drifting were based on observations and interviews collected in the jails of the capital.[5] Members of Muhammad's group were no strangers to security operations. One of them, aged eighteen, was serving a three-year sentence for having stolen thirty Nissan Maximas. I must have looked concerned, for 'Atiya said, "Don't worry, he already acclimated to it."

The "criminology of joyriding" that was developed to make crackdown more efficient certainly played a role in the group's desire to keep me at bay. The link between scholarship and repression was so obvious that, after a few misadventures, I resorted to presenting myself as somebody who wanted to "write a book about joyriding." That sounded more acceptable to drifters than being a "*bahith*" or showing an interest for such characters as al-Gamla. As 'Ajib cheerfully told me, "That's right, you would make a lot of money if you wrote a book about us."

6.3. A State Sociology of Joyriding

In 1982, fifteen years after crafting his Bedouin removal project, the governor of the Riyadh's province, Prince Salman, signed a ruling stating that drifting was a misdemeanor (*mukhalafa*). First offenders could be jailed for up to a week, pay a fine, and receive ten lashes. They would be released only on their father's or tutor's warranty (*kafala*), and provided that they sign a written statement (*ta'ahhud*) by which they promised not to engage in joyriding again. Recidivists could be jailed for up to a month, sentenced to fifty lashes "administered" – the text viciously added – "in one single spell," and their car could be confiscated. If caught drifting, civil servants could be subjected to disciplinary sanctions and students could see their grades lowered. The punishment could extend to the father or the tutor, who could be jailed and fined for having let his son or pupil engage in drifting again, although it wasn't clear if this measure was limited to minors or applied to state employees as well.[6]

A week or so later, the Riyadh police department (*Murur al-Riyadh*) followed the governor's lead and defined joyriding as "high-speed driving whereby the driver plays with the steering wheel in order to shift the car laterally while producing a powerful and disturbing shriek with the car's tires, endangering the life of other road users and the life of those who indulge in this reckless activity themselves."[7] This definition pointed to speed, noise, and danger as phenomena that were at once undesirable, quantifiable, and avoidable. The police ordinance was probably needed to implement Prince Salman's ruling.

The same year, Egyptian psychologist 'Abd al-Meguid Mansur published what was perhaps the first scientific article on joyriding. Mansur had probably emigrated from Egypt after the oil boom. He taught psychology at Riyadh's Imam University and other schools and stayed in Saudi Arabia until his death in 2005. He was one of many Egyptians who joined the Saudi education system, along with Muslim Brothers Manna' al-Qattan, Tawfiq al-Shawi and Sayyid Sabiq. Mansur worked in particular on the "Islamization of psychology," an attempt at finding precedents in the Koran and the Sunna to the scientific exploration of the human mind. He was also one of the first experts to articulate a coherent discourse about Saudi youth, delinquency, deviance, the crisis of the family, and the need to build alternative models of education.

The title of his 1982 piece is "Al-Tafhit min Mazhahir al-'Unf 'ind al-Shabab," which could be translated either as "Joyriding, an Expression of Youth Violence" or as "Joyriding, an Expression of Violence on Youth."

This ambiguity was at the heart of Mansur's analysis of joyriding: to him "dependence, violence, and aggressiveness emerged only in specific social situations."[8] Unlike Prince Salman and the Riyadh police department, he didn't blame youth for the accidents provoked by drifting; to him, this peculiar form of street violence was the symptom of a more general crisis:

The social environment and the processes of socialization (*al-tatbi' al-ijtima'i*) during childhood and adolescence are generally responsible for the development of aggressiveness and violence, when the relationship between adults and youths doesn't follow its natural course.... Severity is a form of parental excess in the affirmation of the traditional ways and customs; it may be counterproductive and incline children toward aggressiveness and violence.... These days, we see adolescents and young adults using cars in a way that violates public order and road regulations, and caring neither for their responsibilities nor for the consequences of their acts. All this perhaps shows that this disorderly phenomenon of our modern society [joyriding] stemmed from the prime socialization of children at the hands of fathers and teachers. Add to this the global growth in car production, the reduction of their price relatively to the production's added value, and the many temptations to buy cars for one's children to celebrate their success or the first signs of masculinity...: *youth... may use this commodity to harm themselves.*[9]

Mansur's argument was bold. Despite the claims of the religious institution, conservatism and severity did not bring about a more Islamic society, but helped create a more authoritarian, more violent (and probably less Islamic) environment. The emergence of joyriding was thus an argument against "severity" and "excess in the affirmation of the traditional ways and customs," which "may be counterproductive and incline children toward aggressiveness and violence."

For Mansur, drifting was related to a general crisis of patriarchal values. Five factors accounted for youth violence: (1) hierarchical family structures produced humiliation and violence; (2) fathers and elder brothers humiliated younger children, who responded violently; (3) failing to assert their authority, fathers tended to become even more violent, which increased their children's recklessness; (4) fathers with a numerous progeny couldn't be equally fair to all their children, who were brought up in injustice and grew unaware of the distinction between good and evil; and (5) most children were born undesired, as wives who didn't necessarily want to give birth submitted to their husband's wishes. Patriarchal disorders resulted in a widespread disorientation of the younger generation. "Childhood is the age of the system," wrote Mansur, and those fathers who couldn't organize family life along clear and stable lines were responsible for their children's mistakes.

A tyrannical society produced tyrannical families, which in turn produced tyrannical children, who knew only how to either submit or revolt. This was in Mansur's eyes the original sin of Saudi society: public disorder was rooted in a dysfunctional private sphere which itself was embedded in a problematic public space:

Adolescents and young adults seek to voice their frustrations through acts that distinguish them as heroes in the eyes of their peers; they might become bossy with them at school, or disobey their family's orders, or drive their car at mad speed to attract attention, or revolt at the slightest pretext. All these phenomena are evidence of this age's instability.

Volatility, instead of being innate or strictly age related, was the outcome of a conflict-ridden family and social life. Mansur tried to cast an optimistic gaze at these "revolts of the soul" (*thawrat al-nafs*) that agitated young Saudis. He believed that society could and must reform itself, provided that institutions invested youth's free time to help them and others benefit from their energy:

Another aspect accounts for the generalization of this phenomenon [joyriding] that society refuses: it is the lack of material facilities to exploit the energy deployed by adolescents and young adults during their free time (*awqat al-faragh*). There are no clubs, no sports fields, no cultural centers that expose youth to religious, cultural, and social activities they might benefit from.

Mansur believed that police repression, although indispensable, was a "temporary solution" and that it was urgent to bring about "positive solutions" to youth violence, such as the creation of libraries, sports clubs, swimming pools, shooting clubs (*sic*), aviation clubs, and naturally car racing clubs. Cheap cars and wide roads, parents' inexperience, authoritarianism, and social violence were the institutional factors that accounted for youth's automobile revolt. Joyriding was not an individual deviance, but a public disorder that was produced by social and economic dynamics, and could only be solved by an institutional answer.

Mansur believed youth was a resource to be harnessed by society, a naturally positive force turned by its artificial idleness into a danger to both society and itself. His theory of youth would be embraced by religious activists. The notion of free time (*awqat al-faragh*) emerged with oil abundance and the generalization of education and waged labor, and was used by psychologists, sociologists, and preachers to characterize youth as the age of idleness. This free time was not a void however, but an energy (*taqa*) that could be used efficiently to combat despair (*tufush*) and public disorder (*fawdha*).[10] Yet Mansur's reformist focus on social violence would disappear from Saudi academia's radar. Later studies pointed an accusatory finger at individuals, and generally tended to absolve society.

According to Saudi sociologist Salih al-Rumayh, who in 2006 revived some of Mansur's insights, the second important study of joyriding was also conducted in 1982. Sociology students and future social workers were intrigued by the presence of numerous drifters in jail, and designed an opinion poll on the motives (*al-dawafi'*) that lead to joyriding.[11] The anonymous authors of the study interviewed hundreds of jailed drifters as well as psychologists, educators, social workers, policemen, and judges. They identified four main reasons why youths engaged in drifting: (1) to fill their free time, (2) to have fun, (3) to submit to their followers' desires, or (4) to imitate others. They thought that joyriding was "expressing a challenge to the various authorities dealing with social control: the family, the school, road regulations, and social traditions."[12]

In 1983, the King 'Abd al-'Aziz City for Sciences and Technology (the state body in charge of censorship), created a National Traffic Safety Committee (*al-Lajna al-Wataniyya li-Salama al-Murur*), whose mission was to "contribute to the study of the issues and obstacles that impede the implementation of the development plans."[13] Road accidents and joyriding were thought of as mere interferences on a linear path toward progress, and the King 'Abd al-'Aziz City's bureaucrats thought appropriate procedures would eliminate these glitches. In the 1980s, the King Saud University, the Imam University, the King Fahd Security College, and the Prince Nayif Academy for Security Sciences designed anti-delinquency policies with the King 'Abd al-'Aziz City and the Riyadh police department. Joyriding took a back seat in the literature on delinquency; although several publications explored road safety, only a handful mentioned drifting.[14]

A doctoral thesis on sex crimes, defended by Muhammad al-Saif at the Imam University in 1993, was clearly an exception. From his position in one of the most prestigious Islamic institutions of the capital, al-Saif attempted to break the public image of Saudi Arabia as a crimeless country. He published his findings in a book that analyzed joyriding along with erotic literature, sentimental music, pornographic videos, telephone flirting, and sex tourism. Al-Saif was more interested in the sexual dimensions of joyriding than in its relations with road infrastructure and youth socialization. Based on an ethnographic enquiry and numerous interviews in jail, the study was destined to reflect as faithfully as possible the everyday life of sex offenders. Al-Saif's work coincided with a nationwide moral panic orchestrated by religious activists.[15]

6.4. Moral Panic

In the 1990s, several ex-joyriders reinvented themselves as religious activists and started preaching repentance to their former supporters. The early 1990s witnessed an important wave of Islamic activism, which responded to the 1990 Gulf War in a series of protests. Rallies were organized in universities and mosques, and grievances were articulated by such figures as Salman al-'Auda, Safar al-Hawali, and Muhammad al-Mas'ari.[16] The repression of political protest from 1993 on did not put an end to religious activism, whose widespread presence was a sign of general dissatisfaction with the royal family and a way, for new political generations, to re-enchant the discourse of the state, monopolized since the 1950s by princes, bureaucrats, and development experts.[17]

The propagation of Islamic activism did not leave untouched the joyriding subculture. Central to the functioning of society and to people's value systems, cars were not foreign to the Islamic movements. Driving materialized gender segregation and discrimination, proclaimed the highest value of masculinity (*rujula, marjala*), and demonstrated Saudi exceptionalism. Automobiles were also political tools: young religious activists navigated Riyadh's sprawl only if driven to the mosque, the school, or their mentor's house. In Egypt, the smallest unit in the Muslim Brotherhood was called "the family" (*al-usra*), in a reference to the patriarchal structure of power that the Brotherhood was attempting to emulate and subvert. In Saudi Arabia, too, Islamic groups were composed of "families," but there was a smaller unit, which was called "the car" (*al-sayara*). A "family" was made of several "cars," each comprising four young men and a driver who shared a ride to their group's gathering. On their commute, young activists would organize "car activities" (*anshitat sayara*), designed to make use of the time lost in transportation. Following an idea of productivity that was perhaps inspired by 'Abd al-Meguid Mansur, loss of time (*madhi'a waqt*) was seen as a moral shortcoming, and every bit of idle time (*waqt al-faragh*) had to be utilized. One of the passengers would read to the others, the driver would play a taped sermon, or students would launch a conversation about a point of religion or morality. Suburban commuting was so pervasive that members of a "car group" would regularly gather in "car meetings" (*liqa'at sayara*) held in roadside cafés or rest houses.

In the mid-1990s, during the crackdown on Islamic movements, religious activists started focusing on subjects that were under the state's radar, including such social issues as joyriding and drug consumption.

During the same period, several senior joyriders repented and became Islamic preachers. Bubu was one of them, although he operated his conversion (*al-tawba*) later, in the mid-2000s. Rakan's mother, who was friends with Bubu's mother, had witnessed his conversion:

RAKAN – The story of how he repented... I didn't hang out with him at the time, but my mom told me that, all of a sudden, after he killed another kid [in an accident], he started drifting much less than before, ... he changed, and Abu Zegem and the other religious guys (*al-multazimin*) of the neighborhood started hanging out with him all the time. Because when Bubu started to calm down, all his joyriding buddies abandoned him. They didn't want him to stop, they would tell him, "Let's go, Bubu, drift for us!" And he didn't wanna hear that anymore. And one day, that's what his mom says and what my mom told me, he got back home, he took the television set, and he threw it in the garbage. All of a sudden. And from then on, we knew he'd become religious (*multazim*).

Bubu's conversion to religious activism was midwifed by one of the most popular preachers at the time, Sultan al-Dughailibi, alias Abu Zegem, himself a repented ex-drifter. Abu Zegem had been a famous drifter in the 1980s, in the heydays of Sa'd Marzuq. In the mid-1990s, he joined the Jama'a al-Tabligh, a proselyte organization that was created in 1926 in India, became influential in Saudi Arabia in the 1960s, and was relatively spared by the crackdown on Islamic groups. Members of Tabligh groups were active as social workers and religious proselytizers. They shunned political activities and organized missionary expeditions (*khuruj*) into the steppes, the countryside, and such marginalized parts of society as rural migrants' neighborhoods.[18] Abu Zegem's charismatic persona soon allowed him to reach out to a vast public and to call other drifters to repent and join his anti-joyriding crusade. While still in school, Rakan had witnessed Abu Zegem's debut speeches:

RAKAN – He's the one who started this type of lectures [on joyriding], which are now widespread in the schools. When I was in school, they had these lectures in the east of Riyadh, ... that's where he became super famous... Because Abu Zegem is the one who started using jokes while preaching. In the beginning, all those who were preaching in primary and middle school, they were super serious, their lectures were no joke. Abu Zegem became famous, but not because he was preaching to joyriders. No, he became famous because people started to say: "There is a drifter, he is a preacher!" (*Fi wahid zahif da'iya.*) "There is a drifter, he is a zealot!" (*Fi wahid zahif mtawwa'.*) By God, that was it. "There is a thug who is a preacher, what's his name again? Abu Zegem!" "Wait, Abu Zegem the drifter?" "Yeah! Abu Zegem the drifter!" "No way!" And that's how he became famous. Because he was making a lot of jokes, people rushed for his tapes, because he was funny, because he wasn't stern and a bore like the others, who talk about death, hell, the afterworld, creepy stuff (*ashia' tudhayyiq al-sadr*) as they say. By God, seriously! That's what they say: that other religious sheikhs are just creepy. But Abu Zegem, he came up with something new, with jokes and all. . . . Abu Zegem, he talks to people in their own language.

Thanks to his preaching style and to his hybrid identity as a thug turned zealot, Abu Zegem was invited to share his experience in schools and mosques. His taped lectures sold well, but his eloquence was not the only reason for this. He also had a sophisticated approach to joyriding, which, like 'Abd al-Meguid Mansur before him, he analyzed as a grass-roots revolt against institutional violence. In one of his taped lectures, he introduced his preaching buddy Abu Hasan, "ex-thug and drug fiend," who narrated how he started joyriding. One day, as he was ten years old, he was subjected to the bastinado (*falaqa*) for stealing a sandwich and was later kicked out of school. Abu Hasan declared to his audience that "schools were the beginning of perdition,"[19] and therefore needed to be thoroughly reformed. Abu Zegem thought that repressive institutions pushed young Saudis to be either apathetic or violent, and that schools did not encourage them to engage in society. Thamer, who experienced school authoritarianism on a daily basis, couldn't agree more:

THAMER – The family is repressive, it's like that everywhere. In universities, too, there is repression. Wherever you go, you must get used to the fact that the one above imposes himself on the one below, by force if necessary, and [forces him to admit] that he is better than him, that he runs things in an appropriate manner, that he is better – by force! He doesn't let anybody go right or left, he doesn't consult anybody's opinion. That's the situation in the entire society.

In his preaching, Abu Zegem wasn't looking down at joyriding or berating its aficionados. In describing the drifting scene, he had replaced the term "deviance" (*inhiraf*) by the more positive notion of "energy" (*taqa*). Deviances could only be repressed, while energies could be redirected and channeled toward righteous outcomes. To convert joyriders to this optimistic religiosity, Abu Zegem created a network of preachers and activists. They aimed at reaching out to senior joyriders in the hope that their followers would also repent. Young people would come to public events he organized under huge tents; encouraged by both the preachers and the audience, they would publicly repent from their sins, burn their music tapes, and tear their cigarette packs to pieces. Abu Zegem midwifed the conversion of several famous drifters, including Bubu, Badr 'Awadh,

Wewe, and al-Mustashar. Bubu's conversion was a good example of the group's methods:

RAKAN – Abu Zegem didn't come directly to Bubu. Hum... young religious guys (*al-multazimin*) who preach in Bubu's neighborhood were connected to Abu Zegem. Thanks to his networks all over Riyadh, [Abu Zegem] knows where the main drifters live, their names, their story. He has a full network of activists... and knows every single drifter, even the new ones, even the total beginners, the nobodies.... Abu Zegem would talk to people in their own language, that's how he worked his way to them. [Local religious activists] also started talking to Bubu in his own terms, they were dealing with him like his followers used to do, and one day they called Abu Zegem to assist him in his repentance. That's how he met Abu Zegem.

Bubu was already religious before his repentance: "even when he was drifting, he'd stop by a mosque at dawn, pray, and then resume drifting." After his conversion, he devoted himself to preaching. Once an expert at dodging repression, Bubu now proposed to put his know-how at the service of the police:

RAKAN – After he repented, [Bubu] started working with the traffic police. He put the project of a fight against drifting (*mukafaha al-tafhit*) on the table, with the collaboration of religious activists (*al-multazimin*). Abu Zegem heads a very powerful network, a network more extensive than the traffic police or even the secret police... his network is everywhere, he knows everybody, he knows what's going on, who drifts, who is a beginner, who attends drifting sessions, who films drifting... And they snitch... I heard that they don't give away the drifter's name, only his nickname, they don't give his address either. They just tell the police where he drifts.... Preachers proposed their help to the police, [but] nothing is written between them. They just volunteered their help... I heard that they had difficulties communicating with the police. But after a while, the police understood that they were useful, and they used Abu Zegem's and Bubu's experience, they used several young drifters who began to repent (*bada'u yaltazimun*). For instance, on a street like al-Breksat, where do they need to put speed bumps to stop joyriding, to spoil everybody's pleasure? When does drifting begin, and when do you need to send in patrols?... If joyriding decreased lately, I think that it's because of Abu Zegem's networks. (*Tires shrieking in the street, outside my building.*) And I also think that they helped redefine the sentences.... They know that it's not enough to jail a drifter for one night. But if you know that on your third arrest, you go to criminal court and you can get six months, if you know that just having a nickname gets you six months... Six months, that's scary.

Drifting accidents, which multiplied after the import of the new Camry in the mid-1990s, often helped the preachers get their message across. But Abu Zegem's strategy was not entirely successful: the rank and file were not easily convinced. After Bubu repented, instead of emulating him, many of his fans became drifters, while others followed new joyriders. To Rakan, instead of gaining the aficionados' hearts and minds by converting senior drifters to its call, the anti-joyriding moral panic had opened the way to a whole new generation of drivers, who were younger and even more reckless than their elders. Preachers had ironically helped bring new blood to joyriding, making it even more chaotic and dangerous. An open competition now opposed the repented and the unrepentant. Joyriders swerved cars next to preaching tents to attract the preachers' audience to their drifting sessions. Religious tents also offered a convenient excuse to drifters and fans. Were the police to come to the area, drifters would argue that they had nothing to do with sinful behaviors:

RAKAN – After [preachers] announce that they will set up a religious tent in a place, [drifters] advertise the location, gather drivers and fans, and exploit the whole preaching business. They use it in two ways. Because usually, if they come for drifting and get arrested by the police, they can't find any excuse. "Why did you come ova'ere?" Of course, they're gonna get caught. But now, they can always say that they came to hear the sheikh.

Some repented drifters put all their energy in working with institutions fighting joyriding, such as the police, Islamic charities, and even psychiatric hospitals and prisons. Abu Zegem, for instance, worked as a religious consultant at the al-Amal psychiatric hospital in Riyadh, where he was involved in a drug rehabilitation program.

Following 'Abd al-Meguid Mansur and Abu Zegem's examples, other preachers took drifting as a symptom of larger political issues. Muhammad al-Duwaish, who taught at the Imam University's school of education, supervised a vast network of Islamic awareness groups in the capital's high schools. (See Figure 6.1.) He was also known for his reformist opinions and his conviction that Islamic activism needed to be more social.[20] In his religious lectures, drifting was a recurring example of how delinquency was not an individual disorder, but the product of a repressive society. During the 2005 electoral campaign, al-Duwaish supported several Islamist candidates and lectured at their campaign headquarters about youth, education, and the necessity of a nationwide dialogue.

Joyriding, in al-Duwaish's words, was a "truncated way of expressing oneself, which youth wouldn't resort to had they had a chance to express themselves freely." Instead of calling for more repression, he called for a more open public sphere: if "deviance" was the outcome of authoritarianism, the only way to build a more moral society was to call for

FIGURE 6.1. A summer camp in south Riyadh, 2006. Copyright © Pascal Menoret.

more freedom. For al-Duwaish, far from being a curse and a lost cause, drifters and delinquents were actually a blessing in disguise for the Islamic movement and Saudi society:

MUHAMMAD AL-DUWAISH – There are several trends among youths. You have religious people, whom we need to deal with so that they don't fall into religious extremism and know how to invest their religious energy in a peaceful and useful way. And then you have deviant people, sex-addicts, and drifters, with whom we need to keep in touch. Islamic activities are inadequate because we tend to preach to the choir and to aim at some youth, not all youth. The center of our interest and efforts should precisely be those problematic youths, because their energy is not utilized.... We need to care about those youths who aren't religious at all, because religion is the business of everybody, not of a minority to the exclusion of the others. We need to get closer to those who don't behave like we would like them to. Why are they drawn to the other [side], and not to ours? Their energy is lost on us. That's why we should design programs and activities that fit them, while keeping in mind the final goal of our religious call (*da'wa*).[21]

State institutions were reluctant to adopt this comprehensive view of youth delinquency, and enrolled the moral panic launched by religious preachers at the service of police crackdown. Activists also tried to turn joyriders' "energy" into a resource, either to fuel the career of individual preachers (such as Abu Zegem) or to reinforce the Islamic movement (as Muhammad al-Duwaish proposed). Their self-serving project was probably doomed to fail.

Almost by definition, joyriders resisted any discipline that didn't stem from the driving practice itself and the untamed mobility it afforded them. Joyriding couldn't be recycled into classic political and religious activism: it generated its own politicization. Drifting politicized the act of driving, the spaces of the city, and the consumption of such widespread commodities as cars and roads. It had turned into tools of public disorder the very devices that princes and developers had thought would tame society. More than the moral panic orchestrated by religious preachers, this oppositional stance was probably the reason why, in the course of the 1990s, joyriders became public enemy number one.

6.5. Criminologists and Policemen

The number of reported drifting cases exploded in the late 1990s, even if it wasn't clear whether it was joyriding itself that became more widespread or whether the police was looking more closely at joyriding. From 1413 AH through 1424 AH (July 1992 CE through January 2004 CE), the interior ministry counted an average 11,000 drifting cases per year nationally (or an average of 30 per day). There were two peaks in this curve. In 1997–1998, the police gave 44,000 drifting fines; an average of 122 drifting tickets were issued daily, the equivalent of a new joyriding case every eleven minutes. In 1999–2000, the number of drifting fines burst again at almost 35,000, or a new case every fifteen minutes. Since then, joyriding stagnated at an average of 8,500 reported cases a year (or 23 a day). (See Figure 6.2.) Drifting was still marginal compared to other road infractions: between 1420 AH and 1424 AH (April 1999 CE-January 2004 CE), it represented only 0.06 percent to 1.08 percent of all traffic violations. This proportion rapidly shrunk in the following years. (See Figure 6.3.)

Even at the height of repression, joyriding was probably still under-reported. The interior ministry's figures were uncertain and said more about police repression than about the reality of drifting. Sulayman al-Duwayri'at writes, "in certain years, the traffic police allocated units specialized in the repression of drifting,"[22] which probably boosted the numbers in 1997–1998 and 1999–2000, and testified to the state's

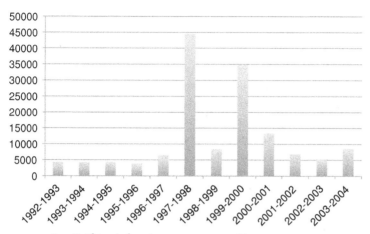

FIGURE 6.2. Drifting infractions, 1992–2004.[23]

concern with joyriding. The Riyadh police department even created a working group dedicated to the war on joyriding, which gathered officers with a background in social sciences and criminology. It is only after the crackdown hit its maximum that the Interior Ministry issued, in 2001, the first nationwide anti-drifting regulation (the 1982 regulation was limited to the Riyadh province). The 2001 regulation distinguished between first, second, and third offenses. First offenders could be condemned to a fine, five days in jail, and a one-month car confiscation. Second-time offenders could be jailed for up to ten days, and sentenced to a two-month car confiscation. Third-time offenders could be transferred to the provincial

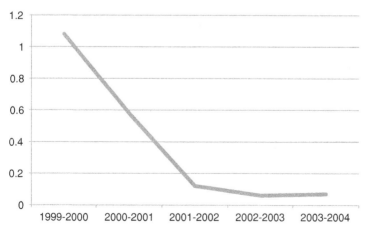

FIGURE 6.3. Drifting infractions as a percentage of all road infractions, 1999–2004.[24]

governor, who would then decide "what he must do with them in accordance with Islamic regulations (*ma yajibu bi-haqqihi shar'an*)."[25] These sentences were lighter than those entailed in the 1982 regulations, but purportedly more severe than common police practices.

Despite these efforts at codifying the state's response, the juridical framework of repression remained murky. The 2001 regulations didn't specify whether drifting was a misdemeanor or a felony; the interior ministry had actually mixed both notions, leaving the implementation of the sentence to the judgment of both the policeman and the judge. Al-Rumayh explained in 2006 that there had been a "debate" about this point, some arguing that joyriding was a felony because of its "psychological, social, economic, and security consequences."[26] The debate was cut short a few months later by the Permanent Committee for Religious Research and Fatwas (*al-Lajna al-Da'ima li-l-Buhuth al-'Ilmiyya wa-l-Ifta'*). The leading religious body in the country issued an unambiguous religious ruling (fatwa) stating that joyriding was a sin against human life, private property, and public order:

Joyriding is an evil phenomenon...perpetrated by a handful of depraved youth...as a consequence of failures in their education and in their moral guidance, and because of the negligence of their parents. [Drifting] is religiously prohibited (*muharram shar'an*) because of the deaths that it provokes as well as the destruction of property, the trouble to public order and the obstacle to traffic that it entails.[27]

The fatwa had no force of law, but merely echoed the 2001 regulations. It held a middle ground between reform and repression: it both justified the repressive stance adopted by the state, and confirmed the relevance of Mansur's description of joyriding as a social deviance.

Why did the state wait so long before extending the 1982 regulations to the entire national territory? Moreover, why was repression uneven, and its results difficult to assess? Why, after nearly ten years of crackdown, was drifting still pervasive in the capital? Why, unlike joyriding, was dune bashing (*tat'is*) considered an innocent pastime? (See Figure 6.4.) In the 2000s, scholars and journalists still complained about the police's indulgence, receptiveness to "connections" (*wasta*), and corruption.[28] Several publications analyzed drifting's resilience in this context of uneven crackdown. A 2001 study of the influence of joyriding on the students of 109 middle and high schools in Riyadh mapped out once again opinions about drifting and drifters' "motivations."[29] In 2004, the National

FIGURE 6.4. Unlike drifting, dune bashing (*tat'is*) is considered an innocent pastime, 2005. Copyright © Pascal Menoret.

Traffic Safety Committee organized a conference on road safety in the country – the second of its kind in more than twenty years – whose debates were partly dedicated to drifting, underage driving, the undying question of joyriders' motivations, and the study of road violations.[30] This flat body of literature treated joyriders as pathological cases to be interned or jailed. Mansur's insight seemed to have been lost, and the sociology of joyriding now studied the psychological factors leading to crime. Did joyriding necessitate an individualized treatment more than a public policy? Would joyriders be abandoned to psychiatrists, preachers, educators, and prison wards?

Two years after the 2004 conference, al-Rumayh's study of joyriding's "influencing factors" (*al-'awamil al-mu'aththira*) broke with his colleagues' obsession with psychological "motivations" (*al-dawafi'*). Al-Rumayh doubted that any serious solution would – and could – be brought to joyriding. In his view, part of the responsibility should be borne by the academic community itself: by reducing joyriding to an individual deviance, scholars had failed to understand its social and political roots. Not merely a road traffic violation, drifting showed that the socialization of youth in the family, the school, and the job market – all three heavily subsidized and controlled by the state – was a failure. In response to the institutional violence that targeted youths, joyriding poked holes in the official discourse about Saudi exceptionalism and the so-called harmonious development of society from above. The joyriders' crime was to act as if the mighty Saudi state had nothing to offer them. Joyriding was not a pathology: it was the opium of the downtrodden.

Al-Rumayh was no anarchist, and called for an increased control of youth's activities: "Youths who practice drifting mirror to a large extent the weakness of the socialization operations and the need for a greater attention to social control, since their behavior contradicts the Islamic values that undergird Saudi society."[31] Control, but not violence: the more violently students were targeted by disciplinary institutions such as the family, the school, or the police, the more likely it would be that they would start joyriding. "Experiences of violence accumulate and are subsequently reflected in the student's behavior."[32]

Al-Rumayh's study covered 1 percent of all students registered in 2003–2004 in Riyadh, Jeddah, and Dammam's private and public schools and reformatories (*dur al-mulahazha*). One couldn't understand drifting outside of a study of delinquent socialization, as the most repressive schools seemed to be more conducive to joyriding: 64 percent of reformatory students declared participating in joyriding against 43 percent and 45 percent for public and private school students, respectively.[33] Unlike most of his colleagues, al-Rumayh didn't ask respondents for their opinion about the subjective "motives" of drifting, but rather tried to measure the objective "factors that influenced" their decisions. By shifting from the joyriders' discourse to students' social conditions (academic level, economic level, family and school violence, etc.), from the consciousness of joyriders to quantifiable variables, al-Rumayh renewed the sociology of joyriding.

"Weak" and "average" students were under-represented in his survey (5 percent and 4 percent, respectively), whereas "good," "very good," and "excellent students" were overrepresented (28 percent, 41 percent, and 22 percent, respectively, of his sample). Weaker students were probably less responsive than were better students, for reasons ranging from defiance to self-denigration and class tensions. Using a questionnaire led al-Rumayh to focus on better students, even though they were less likely to be involved in joyriding. There was a very strong correlation between academic level and the declared participation in joyriding events. Of the

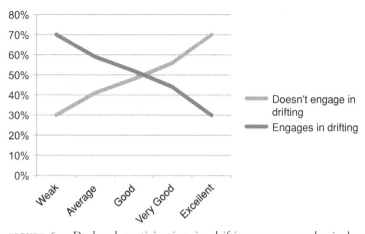

FIGURE 6.5. Declared participation in drifting versus academic level, 2003–2004.[34]

"weak" students, 70 percent declared participating in joyriding compared with only 30 percent of the "excellent" students. (See Figure 6.5.)

Just like stronger students, those engaged in religious activities were less likely to participate in joyriding. Al-Rumayh tested more or less the very variables mentioned by Mansur in 1982, and quantitatively showed that parental violence, the physical violence of teachers, and the symbolic violence of schools and institutions were the strongest factors influencing the practice of joyriding. These findings were rendered more powerful by the fact that the population he measured, overwhelmingly composed of good students, was admittedly less involved in road violence than was the youth population as a whole.

The practice of joyriding was inversely proportional to the respect enjoyed by youths in their family, at school, and in state institutions; it also ran opposite to participation in extracurricular religious activities. It was proportional to family, school, and police violence, to frequenting of public spaces and listening to "noisy music." To strengthen his points, al-Rumayh also tested the "motives" mentioned by other studies, the media, and religious preachers, who thought joyriding was "caused" by the lack of religious practice, youth disorientation, the influence of foreign movies, and the dissolution of families. On these points, interestingly, al-Rumayh collected as many positive as negative responses among students. This indifference probably showed the irrelevance of foreign movies and religious practice to a conversation about drifting. Teachers had another take on this, as 95 percent of them thought that the lack of religious practice was one of the causes of joyriding. Not surprisingly, teachers defended the institution, its discourse, and their own professional ideology.[35]

Other joyriding experts called for awareness campaigns (*hamlat taw'iya*) to incline students and youth toward a greater respect of public order and state institutions. Al-Rumayh turned the table and proposed that parents, educators, and bureaucrats be trained to better deal with adolescents. Such harsh sentences as flogging were in his view useless: they were "punitive" (*ta'dibiyya*), not "curative" (*'ilajiyya*), and would "contribute to the persistence or growth" of the very phenomenon they were meant to combat. There was no need for an exceptional legislation, such as the 1982 and 2001 anti-joyriding regulations: existing "road regulations are sufficient, and the true challenge is their implementation in such a way as to be uninfluenced by favoritism and connections, the occurrence of which could cause a multiplication of joyriding cases and an augmentation of the number of road violations."[36] Excess was counterproductive, and it was the implementation of the rules, not the rules themselves, that had to be improved.

The dialectic of repression and joyriding seemed to give reason to al-Rumayh. Harsher sentences for the few drifters who were caught didn't deter others from challenging law and order. At the same time, police patrols were not numerous enough to cover the vast urban spaces created during the real estate boom, and the letter and spirit of the 1982 and 2001 regulations were violated every weekend and every holiday in the new developments of Riyadh, Jeddah, Dammam, Burayda, Medina, Ta'if, and Abha. To understand repression's failure, it is necessary to look at the joyriders' counter-crackdown techniques. Far from being defeated by the interior ministry, joyriders waged a war on the state and turned the streets of Riyadh, Jeddah, and Dammam into their battlefield.

6.6. "Camry Plays, Police Puke"

What were the consequences of police repression on the drifting scene? How did the increased surveillance of streets and aggressive law enforcement weigh on the strategies of joyriders? My encounter with 'Ajib and his group, my participation with Rakan in a few drifting sessions, and the long hours we spent exploring various low-income, peripheral neighborhoods with some of their young residents helped me better understand the many challenges posed by drifting to law enforcement. Just like joyriding, our study of drifters was no picnic, and we experienced defections,

sudden disappearances, and purposeful avoidance. Rakan would sometimes be torn between his aversion to the joyriders' "dirty ways" and his
fear of "falling back into drifting."

RAKAN – The problem with drifters is that they behave in a dirty way.... And
all these stories weigh on me. I am scared of falling back into drifting. I don't
know how I was able to get out of it last time. Joyriding is like a spell, it is
hypnotic, I am really afraid I won't be able to get out of it this time. I am
afraid to ruin everything.... I am disgusted (*tafshan*), I wanna commit suicide
(*jokingly*)...
PASCAL – (*In the same tone.*) That's easy, man: here is the street. Throw yourself
under a car.
RAKAN – Nooo, I wanna do it in a respectable way (*zayy al-nass*). Got a gun?

What Rakan dubbed "dirty ways" were not consubstantial to drifters,
but tactics devised in reaction to state surveillance and repression. On
our first meeting, 'Ajib was supposed to be somewhere on Khurais Road,
in the east of the city, around midnight. He texted us en route that he
would actually wait for us somewhere else, on an empty lot along Salman
al-Farsi Avenue. 'Ajib and his two acolytes waited for us in a pickup
truck. After a quick round of introductions, we got back into our car and
followed them around the traffic island to 'Ajib's favorite café, located
across the avenue from the vacant plot. Seated behind the glass window
overlooking the avenue, 'Ajib's friends protected their positions until the
very last minute. Seeing us without being seen, they had perhaps given a
last green light to 'Ajib.

The group split up as a result of our visit. 'Ajib was involved in the
conversation but the others seemed to seethe in their corner. A tall guy
came in and, hearing that we wanted to talk about drifting, said in a loud
voice: "Here I am!" When he saw me and Rakan, he turned on his heels
without a word and rushed outside. He later called 'Ajib, asking him
straight out, "What do these guys want?" The same scenario happened
each time we met new groups of drifters. Repression set everybody on
edge.

The police crackdown also influenced the organization of joyriding
groups and drifting sessions. Drifters were not cornered into a passive
position, and did more than merely react to police strategies. For one
of 'Ajib's friends, the goal of joyriding was "to jump traffic lights, to
speed like crazy, to dodge the cops, and to slalom between cars." Bubu
went a step further. Not only did he "dodge the cops"; he also organized his group like a guerrilla movement. In high school, Rakan started
attending drifting sessions "during summer," when "there was nothing

to do," everything was "pure boredom," and "there was nowhere else to go." Rakan had no car and rapidly grew tired of the technical aspects of joyriding; he was more interested in the organization of the drifting underworld. It took him six months to climb the joyriding hierarchy from the rank and file to Bubu, a period during which he interviewed nearly two dozen people and overcame the drifters' suspicions.

He learned to analyze the tensions between the joyrider's assistant and his fans, who competed for the big guy's attention. When he started meeting with Bubu, Rakan himself was the target of the fans' envy and of the joyrider's defiance. "What do you want from us? What brings you to the group?" was Bubu's first reaction. Rakan was a good student, which increased everybody's suspicion:

RAKAN – I started hanging out with his group. Little by little he got to know me, he knew my name and, by chance, what happened is . . . his mother started taking classes at the institute for illiterate people, and (*he lowers his voice*) my mom studies there too. And they became friends. And, by chance . . . I didn't know where his house was, but this one day I drove my mum to her friend's house, and then I rang the bell and Bubu opened the door. And he got to know me better . . . I mean, we had a link besides drifting. He started coming to our place, I was going to his house, we knew each other better. Not much but in the end, he would tell me a lot about his plans, his projects, we were talking about everything. . . . Something funny happened because of Bubu. When I was a bit chubby and I'd put on white robes, all my buddies would tell me: "You're Bubu." He was large, too. I was fat but not around the belly, just fat and large. . . . So at school I would wrap my headdress around my face (*atalaththem*), throw my hand in the air (*he raises a hand, closes his fingers except the forefinger and the middle finger, which he sticks out in a lateral "V," and shakes his hand up and down twice*), I always loved this gesture, and I would imitate Bubu. Then there was that rumor that I *was* Bubu. And this one day, . . . I meet that guy who really thought I was Bubu. And he's like, "Ha? When do you drift?" (*Mata al-kheshsha?*) "What?" "You drift, when do you drift?" And I don't understand, I feel like . . . I tell the guy, "The fuck is wrong with you?" And he's like, "You see, I know you're Bubu, don't worry about it." (*We laugh.*) And I'm like, "Yeah, well, very soon, tomorrow we're gonna drift!" And him, "For whose eyes?" (*Li-'uyun min?*) "For your eyes, baby!"

Bubu's motto was inspired by Sun-Tzu: "Keep your friends close and your enemies closer" (*da' asdiga'k grayyebin wa a'da'k agrab*). Once his followers discovered that one of his fans was a plainclothes officer. Bubu let him into his close circle, and swerved the guy's car in front of a police station, license plates on. Soon the fan was arrested, but his quick release confirmed Bubu's suspicion. Instead of expelling him from the group, he neutralized him by associating him to criminal activities: he had him steal cars and helped him hook up with an underage fan. Bubu filmed him raping the boy and kept the video as a guarantee. Confronted with a brutal environment, Bubu ruthlessly handled his own security.

RAKAN – Bubu has a problem: he doesn't trust anybody. And he still has this problem today.... When he was younger, he wouldn't trust anybody either. Even his closest friends, he didn't trust them. He would always ask me, So-and-so, what does he say? And So-and-so? And So-and-so, what is he doing? And So-and-so? He would always ask what everybody was saying or doing.

PASCAL – Out of security reasons?

RAKAN – That's what I thought in the beginning. But in the end, I started thinking it was for psychological reasons. Security is perhaps only a pretext, and it's true in a way, but the whole story grew bigger, it became, as you say, a fixed idea (*wiswas*).... A paranoia (*baranuya*). And he could trust nobody.... Once I heard him by chance, I was gonna get water, I heard him talk to somebody, he had a meeting with other guys to plan things, when he'd go drift, one of them would follow the police, another one would ride with him, another would come with his car so that, if he had an accident, he could ride with him ... And I heard him telling them that there was another guy, a second guy following the police, and another one who was preparing his car ...

Bubu's assistants often organized ghost sessions to lure police patrols away from the show. When Bubu planned a session at 3 PM in the north of Riyadh, his first assistant would drift at 1 pm in Shifa', in the south, and the second would drift at 2 PM on al-Ba'arin, in the east. Bubu would have one or two hours before the police caught up. Joyriders forced the police to adapt to their drifting strategies. South Californian skateboarders had instituted the "fifteen-minute rule" – "it usually takes five minutes for the people to realize we're there, five minutes for them to call the cops, and five minutes for the cops to arrive."[37] Joyriders kept patrols busy by staging mock drifting shows. They carved out periods of free time and swathes of undisturbed urban space. Bubu and other joyriders didn't systematically avoid the police, however, and often turned confrontation with patrols into an integral part of the show.

RAKAN – For instance, when chased by patrols, [Bubu] wouldn't try to dodge them, but he would start skidding around the police car. And his passengers would throw eggs at the cops, at the windshield. Eggs are sticky; they blur the windshield, even if you use the wipers. Or they would hit the police car windows with their palms. And cops were just helpless. I mean, those kids would throw stones at them.

A YouTube video posted in the summer of 2012 and titled "Youths Chasing a Patrol and Running into it" showed a lone trooper approaching a large group of joyriders on a wide suburban road near the city of Ta'if, in the Hejaz highlands above Mecca. Filmed from the top of a massive gravel heap, the police car made its way through a pack of more than fifty cars and stopped right in the middle of it. The author of the video and his friends commented on the scene:

> – Police! Motherfuckers! (*Hukuma . . . mal'un waldein.*)
> – It's only one patrol . . .
> – They'll pinch him, seriously, they'll pinch him!
> – Stay calm, boys, stay calm. . . .
> – It sucks if he gets arrested. Oh look, people are gathering. (*The trooper drives to the middle of the gathering. He steps out of his car and starts talking to the drifters. Drifters and fans crowd around the patrol. A few drive away but most of them surround the policeman.*) Oh boy, I hope they'll flog him (*the policeman*).
> – By God, they're getting into him. (*One of the fans climbs the police patrol and starts dancing on the rooftop. The trooper jumps back in his car; as he drives off, a first car hits its rear bumper.*)
> – Fuck off! (*Wakhkher.*) Well done! (*Kefu.*) They fucked his mother. (*The patrol speeds away. A second car hits the police car, and then accelerates on its tail with two other vehicles; they chase the trooper and the second car hits the patrol again, this time at full speed.*) . . . Well done! Well done! The big guy fucked him in the ass! (*haddabah ra'i al-rub'.*) (*To the second car's driver.*) I love you! I love you! (*Te'jebni.*)[38]

Drifters almost never called the police by their classical name, *shurta*. To them, the police, a police patrol, or a policeman, all bore the same denomination: *hukuma*, pl. *hakayem*, which also means "government" or "state." The police car was a metonym for the state. It *was* the state confronted in its most basic function: speed control and highway surveillance. Comments on the video webpage alternately glorified or demeaned drifters. Some directed homophobic slurs at the youth who shouted, "I love you," and suggested that he deserved a treatment similar to the one the "big guy" was inflicting on the police. Others described drifters as barbarians (*hamaj*), thugs (*dishir*), lowlife (*huthala*), scum (*sarabit*), backward Bedouin, and even Ta'if monkeys (*gurud al-Ta'if*). Racialized and sexual insults were exchanged between Bedouin and sedentary people, opponents and partisans of the state, and troublemakers and bootlickers.

The Ta'if incident was emblematic of a culture of opposition in which police patrols were affronted as concrete manifestations of a state that had made itself distant, and that could only be accessed through intermediaries (*wastat*) and bribes (*rashawi*). Several *kasrat* celebrated the ongoing war between joyriders and the police:

The more patrols there are	*Hakayem akthar*
The more drifting there is	*Hajwala akthar*
Go drift get drunk	*Fahhet weskar*
And forget about the cops	*Wensa al-'askar*
Drifting is my job	*Al-nutal mihnati*
Skidding is my field	*Wa-l-shutaf khibrati*
Cops are my treat	*Wa-l-hakayem lu'bati*
Camry plays	*Al-Kamri tal'ab*
Police puke	*Wa-l-hakayem tat'ab*[39]

Although the king and the princes were untouchable, police officers could not only be touched, but also humiliated in public. Through speed, crashes, collisions, "confusion" and "disorder" (*hamajia, hajwala*), drifters were in reality challenging state power. They antagonized the disciplinary space of the capital, whose wide avenues favored police action and turned pedestrian demonstrations into an easy target. Cars and speed were ways to bring down surveillance and control, and to create "networks of . . . anti-discipline."[40]

Police officers often sought training among the very drifters they were fighting. They tried to learn the figures, techniques, and tactics that allowed drifters to evade repression and were ready to trade sentence reductions for joyriding lessons. Against the backdrop of Riyadh's rigid street grid, swerves and drifts slowly gained ground, even among law enforcement. Face-to-face in the streets, police officers and young drivers mimicked each other. Disorder, unruliness, and extreme speed subverted an urban space where visibility and control played a crucial role. Drifters created random circulations everywhere the police tried to block them, and forced in turn the police to adopt more fluid strategies. The tactics of the drifters were comparable to those created by pedestrian demonstrators. They formed small packs and large swarms to fight repression:

Packs are small in number and constitute . . . "crowd crystals" (affinity groups, cadres, street theatre groups, etc.) that may precipitate crowds, demonstrations and movements. Packs are always in a process of dispersion and deterritorialization, effecting a Brownian variability of direction. The swarm, by contrast, is large in number, possessing the properties of concentration, hierarchy, and the organization of territoriality. These different multiplicities effect different modes of action. The pack does not openly confront dominating power, it is more secretive, utilizing underground tactics, surprise, and the unpredictability of deterritorialized movement. By contrast, the swarm openly confronts dominating power by weight of numbers, by territorializing space. Swarmings can be either predictable or not, sometimes the prelude to, or the expression of, social movements. At other times swarms may articulate spontaneous moments of defiance, anger or elation that decompose almost as soon as they form. These assemblages, the pack and the swarm, may be interrelated or opposed, a prelude to, or transformation from, the other.[41]

When planning a drifting session, drifters and their attendants formed a pack, a small elite using its affinity to carefully and secretly organize dispersed ghost drifting sessions, the main features of which were deception and surprise. Packs of drifters also organized large crowds thanks to cell phones and the Internet, which were deterritorialized ways of communicating with large constituencies.

Once the procession (*mawkeb*) was assembled and the session (*al-kheshsha*) began, drifters and their followers turned into a swarm, a visible multitude whose strength was no longer in its obscurity, but in its numbers, speed, and nerve. Swarms of cars would disperse upon the arrival of police forces, regroup in another place, and disperse again if the police had followed them. While following 'Ajib, on the night of our accident, Rakan and I became atoms in a swarm flocking from drifting spot to drifting spot and, upon hearing the sirens of patrol cars, dispersing in various directions to regroup miles away in another spot. The success of this tactic depended on the number of cars involved in a single session, on their ability to blend in traffic and to close the ranks once the police was out of sight. Joyriders alternated simultaneity (of ghost sessions, through the dispersion of supporters and of the police) and ubiquity (of supporters, through the formation of processions) to turn the city into a terrain of resistance and, in fine, dominate urban spaces.

The police responded to drifters with such methods as the "net technique" (*taqaniya al-shabaka*). Patrol cars encircled a neighborhood where drifters were performing, blocked all possible exit streets, and then tightened the trap until they caught all drivers. The urban space of the capital molded the confrontation between drifters and patrols as much as it was influenced by it. Space was not just a neutral milieu in which mobilization was merely taking place, but also a player in its own right. Urban spaces conferred meaning upon drifting techniques that, in other environments, would have seemed ridiculously dangerous. Initially a small-scale, low-intensity, and leisure-oriented movement, drifting had become in a few decades a nationwide, lethal, and politically charged phenomenon. This spectacular transformation resulted from the confrontation between the police and drifters.

The new neighborhoods of Riyadh, outside of police surveillance, were strongholds where joyriders isolated themselves and enacted their own panoptic vision of the city. As if to put officialdom at a distance, they viewed Riyadh as a playground, renamed its avenues, and adopted nicknames. The confrontation with joyriders underlined the police's inability to lay claims on space *here and now*. The first scene of joyriding I witnessed, on Takhassussi Avenue in January 2002, ended with the crash of a police patrol against a streetlamp and the flight of the drifter. Once tailing a joyrider's car, the police car was clearly maneuvering within enemy territory, a moving, lethal space carved by the speed of the chase and the joyrider's figures.

Joyriding followed the construction of new real estate projects, which joyriders turned into their strongholds. In a way, road delinquency – or the misusage of roads and cars – was mirroring the white-collar delinquency of real estate investors and developers. The police slowly took control of these new spaces, creating new precincts or planting cameras on the streets. Repression could deprive joyriding of its leaders, but a new generation of drifters would eventually rise, engaging in more daring figures and triggering more accidents. As the police conquered new territories, joyriding thus became paradoxically more visible. Little by little, the state was getting somewhere: it encroached on the spaces anarchically created by developers and investors, while drifters were winning only localized and temporary victories. Its extreme speed, its daring figures, and its celebration of mobility against the sedentary practices of the state showed the limits of joyriding. Speed and mobility ultimately pointed to a nowhere.

Drifters were super-consumers and destroyers. They revolted against mainstream normative society and public order, crashed cars, waged war on the police, cultivated a homosocial culture, and were consciously undoing the polished urban spaces princes, planners, investors, and importers had created after the 1973 oil boom. A famous *kasra* tried to make sense of the apparent madness displayed by joyriders and compared them to the pre-Islamic Bedouin knight and poet 'Antara bin Shaddad:

Go fast, burn tires! Cars make you	*Esra' wa fahhet wa-l-mawatir tkhallik*
The 'Antara of your time	*'Antar zamanek*
Once your time betrayed you	*Yom khanek zamanek*
In the streets where your truck skids	*Fi kul share' bih yahfes 'arawik*
Boys applaud you and prove your value	*Wir'an tahtef lek wa tuthbet mkanek*
The cop beats you on the neck	*Wa-l-'askari yom iaster 'alabik*
No wonder he insults and humiliates you	*Ma hi ghariba tsan sabbek wa hanek*
Since you failed in everything noble	*Yomek fashalt bi-kul she' yi'allik*
Nothing betters your position	*Ma 'ad lek she' yi'alli bi-sha'nek*
You left school and roam with riffraff	*Khalleit 'ilmek wa-lteheit b-sa'alik*
You didn't obey your dad	*Wa la ti't waldek*
When he cried because of you	*Yom iabtsi 'ashanek*
Your mum shouted and exhorted you	*Wa-l-walda yomen tsih wa tuwsik*
Deserted, she wants your humiliation	*Ahmeltha wa egfeit tabgha hawanek*
Go, get lost, let the Lord solve your crises	*Ruh engele' rabbi yifrej balawik*
Go fast, burn tires until your ears explode.	*Esra' wa fahhet len tafga' azhanek.*

'Antara bin Shaddad lived in the steppes of Central Arabia in the sixth century CE and wrote one of the seven prized odes of pre-Islamic Arabia (*al-Mu'allaqat*). His hostility to the sedentary Banu Tamim tribe was legendary. Allies of the Al Sa'ud, the Banu Tamim are today well represented in the Saudi high administration, which drifters defy on a daily basis. Nineteenth century European revolutionaries burned state coaches; today's French disenfranchised youth burn cars; young Saudi Bedouin drift and crash them. Deported by princes and developers and marginalized by the administration and the economy, young Bedouin revolt on the roads.

The new Riyadh, "city of the future," was planned on the expulsion of its most rural elements and the invention of a Saudi urban society based on sedentary and religious values. Drifting was the return of the nomadic repressed, a revolt of mobility and noise against the silent immobility of Riyadh's society. Driven by a revolutionary sentiment, *tufush*, drifters showed their value on the roads, and confronted a Saudi state that had turned them into lowlifes. They had politicized the routine action of driving and turned it into a relentless expression of defiance. But their poignant revolt led to their obliteration in words and deeds: they criticized the space of the city, and were also its most visible victims. The city of Riyadh, with its long, deserted highways, its gusts of wind and its sizzling nights, its empty developments and its walled villas, would always win in the end.

Epilogue

I thank the many people in Riyadh who welcomed me into their lives and helped me better understand their city. I particularly thank Sa'b, Dhaifallah, Bjad, Rakan, and their families. The access and support they granted me, their time, and their generosity make it very difficult to pay them back. I hope they consider this book a down payment.

After I left Riyadh for Yemen, and then Egypt and the United States, Sa'b, 'Adil, and Thamer went abroad to pursue their studies. Dhaifallah didn't disappoint the elders: he got married and moved back to the steppe, where he dabbled in the sheep market while working as a civil servant. Bjad and Rakan lead successful careers in Riyadh, as does Fahad. Sheikh 'Abd al-Ilah hopefully makes a lot of money. Thamer's students are in college, and left Islamic activism behind. So much for the intended consequences of a religious upbringing.

Bubu was arrested the day after we interviewed him. The secret police raided the resthouse where he and his friends were hanging out – he was reportedly giving a religious sermon – and they had landed in jail. The news came as a shock. I knew that the secret police were following me, and I feared that I had caused Bubu's arrest. Rakan called Bubu's family and friends and reconstituted the events with them. According to Rakan, our meeting had played no role in Bubu's detention. Bubu was already on the secret police's radar, and his arrest was an effect of the widespread repression through which, since 2001, the Al Sa'ud were trying to emulate George W. Bush's war on terror. Rakan later told me that Bubu had ultimately been released from jail and admitted to a "rehabilitation" program, along with Guantanamo returnees, suspects of terrorism, and former political prisoners.

I saw 'Ajib for the very last time at the Riyadh airport, where he was working as a security guard. This last meeting confirmed that, as Rakan warned me, you couldn't trust drifters: 'Ajib was not as unemployed as he'd always pretended. I got no news from other joyriders.

The end of my stay in Saudi Arabia deserves to be narrated in detail. One morning in January 2007, I got a phone call from the French embassy. The cultural adviser, who had sponsored my research visa to the country, summoned me to his office, where he was waiting for me with a French police chief. "What we're going to tell you won't be pleasant," he said. Someone high up in the French Foreign Office had been tipped off about a case of pedophilia that "was about to explode in [my] face," as he put it. I was to leave the country within twenty-four hours: Saudi Arabia being an "oil country" – the adviser said – the Foreign Office "couldn't protect me." I met the French ambassador the next day. He wanted to "protect his source" and could only tell me that the mysterious informer was a senior diplomat who had been tipped off by an "anonymous phone call" from Riyadh. Shocked by the turn of the conversation, I said that, because I had nothing to be ashamed of, I would stay in Saudi Arabia.

Leaving the embassy, I drove to the King Faisal Research Center, where I was hosted during fieldwork. I told the story to the center's secretary general, Dr. Yahya Ibn Junaid. He informed me a few sleepless nights later that neither the police nor the courts or the religious police had any record under my name. I knew I was innocent, and the Saudi police were not after me. Where did the accusation come from? I stayed in Riyadh for six more uneventful months. In July of the same year, I had a violent realization. I had become so attuned to living in the city that I feared I would wake up one day and realize that I'd spent my whole life in Riyadh. One week after that, I was on a plane to Sanaa, and then Cairo. There I wrote the PhD thesis on the politicization of youth in Saudi Arabia on which this book is partially based.

Fieldwork in Riyadh was conducted from January 2005 to July 2007 and financed on a doctoral scholarship from the Centre Français d'Archéologie et de Sciences Sociales de Sanaa (CEFAS). My four-year research visa to Saudi Arabia was obtained with the help of the Cultural Services of the French Embassy in Riyadh. The King Faisal Center for Research and Islamic Studies graciously granted me an office, an Internet connection, and a landline. Archival work at the Constantinos A. Doxiadis Archives in Athens in June 2009 and additional fieldwork in Riyadh in August and September 2009 were financed by a grant from the French Agence Nationale de la Recherche (ANR). Part of the research was conducted during a postdoctoral fellowship at Princeton University's Institute for the Transregional Study of the Middle East, North Africa, and Central Asia. I began writing in 2010 during a postdoctoral fellowship at the Harvard Academy for International and Area Study, and completed the manuscript in August 2013, at the end of my second year of teaching at New York University Abu Dhabi. I thank these institutions, as well as the Constantinos and Emma Doxiadis Foundation, for their help during the preparation of this book. I also thank joyriding photographer THE BEST aka 6FOSH (*"tufush"*) for allowing me to reproduce three of his photos, including the cover image.

Arguments from the book have been presented in front of several audiences at the University of Leiden, King's College London, the Institut de Recherche sur le Monde Arabe et Méditerranéen (Aix-en-Provence), the King Faisal Center for Research and Islamic Studies (Riyadh), the Centre de Documentation et d'Etudes Juridiques, Economiques et Sociales (Cairo), the Université de Montréal, Princeton University, New York University, The College of New Jersey, Harvard University, the 2010 MESA meeting in San Diego, Bates College, the Université de Lausanne, Bard College, and New York University Abu Dhabi. I thank all those who, by their questions and comments, helped me think about the project in new ways. Thanks also to my students at Princeton, New York University and New York University Abu Dhabi for our exciting conversations about the book's arguments.

I particularly thank Houda Ayoub, without whose generosity I wouldn't have learned Arabic, François Burgat, who pushed me to study the Arabian Peninsula, and Bernard Haykel, who inspired in me the confidence to start writing in English. I thank Nadine Picaudou for being a wonderful doctoral advisor; Madawi Al-Rasheed, Pierre Boilley, and Olivier Roy for sitting on my dissertation committee; Yahya ibn Junaid, Awadh al-Badi, and Ibrahim al-Hadlaq for their hospitality at the King Faisal Center; Yannis Khemiri, Sophie and Carl Poirier, Sophie Pommier, and Alain and Baria Guépratte for their continuous friendship; Giota Pavlidou for her help at the Constantinos A. Doxiadis Archives; and Joyce Slack and Jola and Roger Hardy for their very warm welcome at Princeton (and London).

I thank my mentors at Harvard University, Steve Caton and Roger Owen, as well as Gareth Doherty, Toby C. Jones, Laurence Ralph, Bob Vitalis, Larry Winnie and Malika Zeghal, for their precious comments on the book's first draft. I started writing my book after reading Steve Caton's *Yemen Chronicle*, which I found so inspiring that I began turning it into a comic book. Had I been a better cartoonist, I might not have written *Joyriding in Riyadh*. For chipping in at various stages of the writing process, many thanks to Youssef El-Chazli, Anne Clément, Muriam Davis, Jonathan Franklin, Greg Halaby, Hatim El-Hibri, Arang Keshavarzian, Baptiste Lanaspèze, Rania Salem, Greta Scharnweber, Hélène Thiollet, and Frédéric Vairel. New York University Abu Dhabi has proven a vibrant intellectual community, and I am grateful for my colleagues' support and encouragement. In particular, conversations with Ginny Danielson, Jim Toth, Phil Kennedy, Marc Michael, Sana Odeh, Nathalie Peutz, Kevin Riordan, Jim Savio, and Justin Stearns helped me shape some of the book's arguments.

Cambridge, MA – Abu Dhabi – New York City

Notes

Chapter 1: A Night with 'Ajib

1. I have modified most names to respect the anonymity of my informants.
2. Nazih Mu'ayyid al-'Azm, *Rihla fi Bilad al-'Arabiyya al-Sa'ida* [Journey to Arabia Felix] (Fadi Press 1985), p. 173.
3. Robert Vitalis, *America's Kingdom: Mythmaking on the Saudi Oil Frontier* (Verso 2009), p. 75.
4. Laton McCartney, *Friends in High Places. The Bechtel Story: The Most Secret Corporation and How It Engineered the World* (Ballantine Books 1989), pp. 80–92 and 113–125.
5. Engseng Ho, *The Graves of Tarim: Genealogy and Mobility Across the Indian Ocean* (University of California Press 2006), pp. 256–262.
6. Edward Said, *Orientalism* (Vintage Books 1979), p. 38.
7. See Turki al-Hamad, *Al-Karadib* (Dar al-Saqi 1999); Muhammad al-Muzaini, *Mafariq al-'Atama* [Crossroads of Darkness] (Al-Mu'assasa al-'Arabiyya li-l-Dirasat wa-l-Nashr 2004); Fahd al-'Atiq, *Ka'in Mu'ajjal* [Life on Hold] (Al-Mu'assasa al-'Arabiyya li-l-Dirasat wa-l-Nashr 2004).
8. Henri Lefebvre, *The Production of Space* (Blackwell 1991), pp. 49–50.
9. Lefebvre, *The Production of Space*, p. 51. See Jo Guldi, *Roads to Power: Britain Invents the Infrastructure State* (Harvard University Press 2012).
10. Timothy Mitchell, *Carbon Democracy: Political Power in the Age of Oil* (Verso 2011), pp. 5–6.
11. Ellis Goldberg and Robert Vitalis, "The Arabian Peninsula: Crucible of Globalization," paper presented at the Second Mediterranean Social and Political Research Meeting, European University Institute, Florence, March 21–25, 2001.
12. Lefebvre, *The Production of Space*, pp. 51–55.
13. Mamoun Fandy, *Saudi Arabia and the Politics of Dissent* (St. Martin's Press 1999), p. 49.
14. Paul Virilio, *Speed and Politics* (Semiotexte 2006), p. 39.

15. Jürgen Habermas, *The Structural Transformation of the Public Sphere: An Inquiry into a Category of Bourgeois Society* (MIT Press 1991), pp. xviii, 22–23, 27.

16. Arlette Farge, *Subversive Words: Public Opinion in Eighteenth-Century France* (Polity Press 1994), pp. 1–3, 198.

17. Sean O'Connell, "From Toad of Toad Hall to the 'Death Drivers' of Belfast: An Exploratory History of 'Joyriding'," *British Journal of Criminology*, 56 (2006), pp. 455–457. See also Sean O'Connell, *The Car in British Society: Class, Gender and Motoring, 1896–1939* (Manchester University Press 1998), pp. 77–111.

18. Madawi and Loulouwa Al-Rasheed, "The Politics of Encapsulation: Saudi Policy towards Tribal and Religious Opposition," *Middle Eastern Studies*, 32.1 (1996), pp. 96–119; Fandy, *Saudi Arabia and the Politics of Dissent*; 'Abd Allah al-Ghazhzhami, *Hikaya al-hadatha fi-l-mamlaka al-'arabiyya al-su'udiyya* [The Story of Modernity in Saudi Arabia) (Al-Markaz al-Thaqafi al-'Arabi 2004); Mansoor Jassem Alshamsi, *Islam and Political Reform in Saudi Arabia* (Routledge 2011).

19. Fandy, *Saudi Arabia and the Politics of Dissent*, pp. 1–60; Alshamsi, *Islam and Political Reform in Saudi Arabia*, pp. 78–136.

20. Mike Featherstone, "Automobilities: An Introduction," pp. 15–16 and Jörg Beckmann, "Mobility and Safety," in Mike Featherstone, Nigel Thrift, and John Urry (eds.), *Automobilities* (Sage Publications 2005), pp. 94–95.

21. Lewis Mumford, *The City in History: Its Origins, Its Transformations, and Its Prospects* (Harcourt 1961), pp. 450–452.

22. See Pierre Bourdieu (ed.), *The Weight of the World: Social Suffering in Contemporary Society* (Stanford University Press 1999); Florence Weber and Stéphane Beaud, *Guide de l'enquête de terrain. Produire et analyser des données ethnographiques* (La Découverte 2003).

23. See Pierre Boudieu, *Pascalian Meditations* (Stanford University Press 2000).

24. Said, *Orientalism*, p. 11.

25. Vincent Crapanzano, *Tuhami: Portrait of a Moroccan* (The University of Chicago Press 1980), pp. x–xi.

26. Talal Asad (ed.), *Anthropology & the Colonial Encounter* (Humanity Books 1973), p. 18.

27. Paul Rabinow, *Reflections on Fieldwork in Morocco* (University of California Press 1977), pp. 9–17.

28. Lila Abu-Lughod, "Zones of Theory in the Anthropology of the Arab World," *Annual Review of Anthropology*, 18 (1989), p. 278.

29. Abu-Lughod, "Zones of Theory . . . ," p. 273.

30. See Mouloud Feraoun, *Journal, 1955–1962: Reflections on the French-Algerian War* (Bison Books 2000); Pierre Bourdieu, *Sketch for a Self-Analysis* (Polity 2007), pp. 53–54.

31. Pierre Bourdieu, "Colonialism and Ethnography: Foreword to *Travail et Travailleurs en Algérie* [1963]," *Anthropology Today*, 19.2 (2003), p. 14. See also Pierre Bourdieu, *Esquisses algériennes* (Seuil 2008).

32. Philippe Bourgois, *In Search of Respect: Selling Crack in El Barrio* (Cambridge University Press 1996); Stéphane Beaud and Michel Pialoux,

Retour sur la condition ouvrière. Enquête aux usines Peugeot de Sochaux-Montbéliard (Fayard 1999) and *Violences urbaines, violence sociale. Genèse des nouvelles classes dangereuses* (Fayard 2003); Loïc Wacquant, *Body and Soul: Notebooks of an Apprentice Boxer* (Oxford University Press 2006).

33. Appadurai, "Theory in Anthropology: Center and Periphery," Comparative Studies in Society and History, 28.2 (1986), pp. 356–357.

34. Abu-Lughod, "Zones of Theory...," p. 294.

35. Bourgois, *In Search of Respect*; Beaud and Pialoux, *Violences urbaines, violence sociale*.

36. Both *New York Times* journalist Robert Worth ("Saudis Race All Night, Fueled by Boredom," *New York Times*, March 8, 2009) and Saudi blogger Ahmed Al Omran ("The Broken Frame," March 9, 2009, http://saudijeans. org/2009/03/09/nyt-saudi-youth/) share a moralizing and individualistic interpretation of joyriding, which they equate with private boredom and the lack of entertainment venues. "Bored? Go read a book, rent a movie, go swimming..., but please oh please don't get behind the wheel" (Al Omran, "Blood on Asphalt," December 20, 2007, http://saudijeans.org/2007/12/20/blood-on-asphalt/).

37. Lila Abu-Lughod, "The Romance of Resistance: Tracing Transformations of Power through Bedouin Women," *American Ethnologist*, 17.1 (1990), pp. 41–55.

38. Loïc Wacquant, *Urban Outcasts: A Comparative Sociology of Advanced Marginality* (Polity Press 2008).

39. Bourgois, *In Search of Respect*, p. 11.

40. Quoted by Iain Borden, *Skateboarding, Space and the City: Architecture and the Body* (Berg 2001), p. 173.

41. Asef Bayat, *Life as Politics: How Ordinary People Change the Middle East* (Stanford University Press 2010), pp. 115–158.

42. Quoted by Bourgois, *In Search of Respect*, p. 18.

43. See Paul Bonnenfant, "La capitale saoudienne: Riyadh," in P. Bonnenfant (ed.), *La Péninsule arabique d'aujourd'hui* (CNRS 1982), vol. 1, pp. 655–705; Nelida Fuccaro, *Histories of City and State in the Persian Gulf: Manama since 1800* (Cambridge University Press 2009); Andrew Gardner, *City of Strangers: Gulf Migration and the Indian Community in Bahrain* (Ilr Press 2010); Yasser Elsheshtawy, *Dubai: Behind an Urban Spectacle* (Routledge 2010); Ahmed Kanna, *Dubai: The City as Corporation* (Minnesota University Press 2011).

44. James Holston, *The Modernist City: An Anthropological Critique of Brasília* (The University of Chicago Press 1989), pp. 7–9.

Chapter 2: Repression and Fieldwork

1. Asma al-Sharif, "Detainees Disappear into Black Hole of Saudi Jails," Reuters, August 25, 2011.

2. Al-Hamad, *Al-Karadib* (Dar al-Saqi, 1999).

3. See "Human Rights and Saudi Arabia's Counterterrorism Response: Religious Counseling, Indefinite Detention and Flawed Trials" (Human Rights

Watch 2009); "Saudi Arabia: Repression in the Name of Security" (Amnesty International 2011). Local groups are the Human Rights First Society, created in 2002 (see http://hrfssaudiarabia.org/) and the Saudi Civil and Political Rights Association, created in 2009 (its website was shut down and some of its leaders arrested in 2011, see http://hrfssaudiarabia.org/, Communiqués, March 23 and 25, 2011).

4. "Human Rights in Saudi Arabia: A Deafening Silence" (Human Rights Watch 2001), p. 2.

5. "Saudi Arabia: Assaulting Human Rights in the Name of Counter-Terrorism" (Amnesty International 2009), pp. 23–26.

6. See Nic Robertson, "Jihad Rehab is a Possibility for Post-Gitmo," www.cnn.com, January 27, 2009. Christa Case Bryant, "For Saudi Ex-Jihadis: A Stipend, a Wife, and a New Life," *The Christian Science Monitor*, May 25, 2012. Ellen Knickmeyer, "Saudis Try to Quell Jihadists," *The Wall Street Journal*, May 3, 2013.

7. Thomas Hegghammer, *Jihad in Saudi Arabia: Violence and Pan-Islamism since 1979* (Cambridge University Press 2010), pp. 236–237.

8. Ibid., pp. 74–77.

9. See "Precarious Justice: Arbitrary Detention and Unfair Trials in the Deficient Criminal Justice System of Saudi Arabia" (Human Rights Watch 2008); "Assaulting Human Rights in the Name of Counter-Terrorism" and "Human Rights and Saudi Arabia's Counterterrorism Response."

10. Thomas Hegghammer, *Jihad in Saudi Arabia*, pp. 7 and 195–198.

11. See John Habib, *Ibn Sa'ud's Warriors of Islam: The Ikhwan of Najd and their Role in the Creation of the Saudi Kingdom, 1910–1930* (Brill 1978).

12. See Madawi Al-Rasheed, *A History of Saudi Arabia* (Cambridge University Press 2002), p. 49 sq.

13. See Donald P. Cole, *Nomads of the Nomads: The Al Murrah Bedouin of the Empty Quarter* (Harlan Davidson 1975), pp. 144–158.

14. Cole, *Nomads of the Nomads*, p. 143.

15. See Francois Pouillon, "Un Etat contre les Bedouins, l'Arabie Saoudite" (with Thierry Mauger), *Maghreb-Machreq Monde Arabe*, no. 147, 1995, pp. 132–148.

16. See Bichr Farès, "Muru'a", in *The Encyclopaedia of Islam*, 2nd ed. (Brill 1993) and Claude Gilliot, "Arrogance", in *The Encyclopaedia of Islam*, 3rd ed. (Brill 2007).

17. See Amélie Le Renard, *Femmes et Espaces Publics en Arabie Saoudite* (Dalloz 2011), pp. 87–119 and 230–258.

18. Madawi Al-Rasheed, *Contesting the Saudi State: Islamic Voices from a New Generation* (Cambridge University Press 2007), p. 26.

19. See Askar al-Enazy, *The Creation of Saudi Arabia: Ibn Saud and British Imperial Policy, 1914–1927* (Routledge 2009); Vitalis, *America's Kingdom: Mythmaking on the Saudi Oil Frontier* (Verso 2009).

20. See Guido Steinberg, "The Wahhabi Ulama and the Saudi state, 1745 to the Present," in *Saudi Arabia in the Balance* (New York University Press 2005), pp. 11–34.

21. Al-Rasheed, *Contesting the Saudi State*, p. 67.

22. *Hay'a al-amr bi-l-ma'ruf wa-l-nahi 'an al-munkar*. The committee was created by 'Abd al-'Aziz Al Sa'ud in 1926, to counterbalance the power of the Ikhwan army in the newly conquered province of Hejaz.

23. Field note, Jeddah, April 16, 2005. My emphasis.

24. See Pascal Menoret, "Apprendre à voter? Le cas des élections saoudiennes de 2005," *Genèses*, 77, 2009, pp. 51–74.

25. Al-Rasheed, *Contesting the Saudi State*, p. 75.

26. Ibid., p. 110.

27. Koran, 60:1: "*La tattakhizhu a'duwwi wa-'aduwwkum awliya' tulquna ilayihim bi-l-mawadda*". The concept of *al-wala' wa-l-bara'* (association with Muslims and dissociation from infidels) has been recently developed by several 'ulama. See Al-Rasheed, *Contesting the Saudi State*, p. 107 and Joas Wagemakers, "The Transformation of a Radical Concept: *al-wala' wa-l-bara'* in the Ideology of Abu Muhammad al-Maqdisi", in Roel Meijer (ed.), *Global Salafism*, *op. cit.*, p. 81–102.

28. Pierre Bourdieu, *Algeria 1960* (Cambridge University Press 1979), p. 41.

29. See Quintan Wiktorowicz (ed.), *Islamic Activism: A Social Movement Theory Approach* (Indiana University Press 2004), Introduction, p. 12.

30. Bourdieu, *Pascalian Meditations* (Stanford University Press 2000), p. 241.

31. See a French translation of it in Pascal Menoret, "De la rage à l'enthousiasme: le parcours d'un jeune électeur saoudien", *Chroniques Yéménites*, no. 12, 2005 (http://cy.revues.org/188).

32. See Wiktorowicz (ed.), *The Management of Islamic Activism: Salafis, the Muslim Brotherhood, and State Power in Jordan* (State University of New York Press 2000), pp. 111–144, and Pascal Menoret, "Leaving Islamic Activism Behind: Ambiguous Disengagement in Saudi Arabia", in Joel Beinin and Frederic Vairel (eds.), *Social Movements, Mobilization, and Contestation in the Middle East and North Africa* (Stanford University Press 2011), pp. 43–47.

33. See Menoret, "Leaving Islamic Activism Behind," pp. 43–44.

34. See John D. Kelly, Beatrice Jauregui, Sean T. Mitchell, and Jeremy Walton (eds.), *Anthropology and Global Counterinsurgency* (The University of Chicago Press 2010).

35. See "Leading Saudi Dissident Freed", BBC News, March 25, 2003; Kim Murphy, Asma Alsharif, "Saudi Activist Acquitted of Terrorism Charges," Reuters, February 12, 2012.

36. See William Rugh, "Education in Saudi Arabia: Choices and Constraints," *Middle East Policy*, 9, 2, 2002, pp. 40–55; Michaela Prokop, "Saudi Arabia: The Politics of Education," *International Affairs*, 79, 1, 2003, pp. 77–89; Ahmad al-'Isa, *Islah al-Ta'lim fi-l-Su'udiya bayna Ghyab al-Ru'iya al-Siyasiya wa-Tawajjus al-Thaqafa al-Diniyya wa 'Ajz al-Idara al-Tarbawiyya* [Education Reform in Saudi Arabia: Lack of Political Vision, Cultural Sheepishness, and Powerless Institutions] (Dar al-Saqi 2009).

37. Mamoun Fandy, *Saudi Arabia and the Politics of Dissent* (St. Martin's Press 1999), pp. 50–60, 115–148; Mansoor Jassem Alshamsi, *Islam and Political Reform in Saudi Arabia: The Quest for Political Change* (Routledge 2011), pp. 99–109.

38. Al-Rasheed, *Contesting the Saudi State,* p. 54.
39. Jane Jacobs, *The Death and Life of Great American Cities* (Vintage 1992), p. 35.
40. See Muhammad al-Saif, *Madkhal ila Dirasa al-Mujtama' al-Su'udi* [Introduction to the Study of Saudi Society] (Dar al-Khariji 2003) in particular chap. 4; Sulaiman al-Falih, *Al-Zhubt al-Ijtima'i Mafhumuhu wa Ab'aduhu wa-l-'Awamil al-Muhaddida lahu: Dirasa Maidaniya 'ala-l-Mujtama' al-Su'udi* [Social Control, its Concept, Dimensions and Defining Character: A Fieldwork Study of Saudi Society] (Maktaba al-'Ubaikan 2003).
41. Field note, June 12, 2006.
42. Al-Sharif, "Detainees Disappear."
43. See Steffen Hertog, *Princes, Brokers, and Bureaucrats: Oil and the State in Saudi Arabia* (Cornell University Press 2011), pp. 41–136.
44. Ibid., pp. 5–6 and 21–35.
45. Cole, *Nomads of the Nomads,* pp. 82–104.
46. See Le Renard, *Femmes et Espaces Publics,* pp. 59–72 and 148–154.
47. See, for instance, Muhammad al-Saif, *Al-Zhahira al-Ijramiyya fi Thaqafa wa Bina' al-Mujtama' al-Su'udi, Bayna al-Tasawwur al-Ijtima'i wa Haqa'iq al-Ittijah al-Islami* [Crime and the Structure of Saudi Society: Between Social Imaginations and Islamic Guidance] (Markaz Abhath Mukafaha al-Jarima, 1996); 'Abd al-'Aziz al-Shithri, *Waqt al-Faragh wa Shaghluhu fi Madina al-Riyadh* [Free Time and How to Fill it in Riyadh] (Riyadh Islamic University 2001).
48. Bourdieu, *Pascalian Meditations,* p. 208.
49. Ibid., p. 209.
50. "Akhiran, al-Kitab al-Mamnu': al-Hajwala fi 'Ilm al-'Arbaja" [Finally, the Forbidden Book: Escapism in the Science of Hooliganism], personal archives.
51. Mikhail Bakhtin, *Rabelais and his World* (MIT Press 1968), p. 42.
52. Herman Melville, *Moby Dick,* ch. XLIX.

Chapter 3: City of the Future

1. See Wilferd Madelung, *The Succession to Muhammad: A Story of the Early Caliphate* (Cambridge University Press 1997), pp. 59–68.
2. P-SAU-A 27 (Photographs 31785), photo 15.
3. Al-Muzaini, *Mafariq al-'Atama* (al-Mu'assasa al-'Arabiya li-l-Dirasa wa-l-Nashr 2004), p. 171.
4. Ibid., p. 171.
5. Ibid., p. 172.
6. Rem Koolhaas and Hans Ulrich Obrist, *Project Japan: Metabolism Talks* (Taschen 2009), p. 552.
7. Constantinos A. Doxiadis, *Architecture in Transition* (Oxford University Press 1963), pp. 96–99.
8. Philip Deane, *Constantinos Doxiadis: Master Builder for Free Men* (Oceana 1965), pp. 1–4, 125–28.
9. On the biography of Doxiadis, see Alexandros-Andreas Kyrtsis, *Constantinos A. Doxiadis: Texts, Design Drawings, Settlements* (Doxiadis Foundation 2006), pp. 303–399. Deane, *Constantinos Doxiadis,* pp. 21–58.

10. Quoted by Panayiota Pyla, "Back to the Future: Doxiadis's Plans for Baghdad," *Journal of Planning History*, 7, 3, 2008, pp. 6 and 18.
11. Guian McKee, "Liberal Ends Through Illiberal Means: Race, Urban Renewal and Community in the Eastwick Section of Philadelphia, 1949–1990," *Journal of Urban History*, 27, 5, 2001, p. 552.
12. Quoted by Ahmed Mahsud, "Constantinos A. Doxiadis' Plan for Islamabad: the Making of a 'City of the Future' 1959–1963," PhD thesis, Katholieke Universiteit Leuven, 2008, p. 142.
13. Ibid., p. 141.
14. Nathan Citino, "Suburbia and Modernization: Community Building and America's Post-WWII Encounter with the Arab Middle East," *Arab Studies Journal*, 13–14, 2006, p. 52.
15. Quoted by Panayiota Pyla, "Back to the Future," pp. 13–14.
16. Lefteris Theodosis, "Containing Baghdad: Constantinos Doxiadis's Program for a Developing Nation," *Revista de crítica arquitectónica*, 2008, special issue on *Ciudad del Espejismo: Bagdad, de Wright a Venturi*, p. 168.
17. Anne Harper, "The Idea of Islamabad: Unity, Purity and Civility in Pakistan's Capital City," PhD Thesis, Yale University, 2010, pp. 93–98. On Doxiadis's operations in Karachi, see Steve Inskeep, *Instant City: Life and Death in Karachi* (Penguin 2011), p. 81–112.
18. Doxiadis, *Architecture*, p. 100.
19. Constantinos A. Doxiads, *Ekistics: An introduction to the Science of Human Settlement* (Oxford University Press 1968), p. 365, fig. 365.
20. Ernest Burgess, "The Growth of the City," in Robert Park and Ernest Burgess, *The City* (University of Chicago Press 1967), pp. 50–59.
21. Deane, *Constantinos Doxiadis*, p. 94.
22. Harper, "The Idea of Islamabad," pp. 116–118.
23. Quoted by ibid., p. 66. On high modernism see James Scott, *Seeing like a State: How Certain Schemes to Improve the Human Condition Have Failed* (Yale University Press 1998), pp. 103–146.
24. Harper, "The Idea of Islamabad," pp. 123–124. On informal settlements in Brasilia see James Holston, *The Modernist City: An Anthropological Critique of Brasilia* (University of Chicago Press 1989), pp. 257–288.
25. Matthew Hull, "Paper Travails: Bureaucracy, Graphic Artifacts, and the Built Environment in the Islamabad Metropolitan Area, 1959–1998," PhD Thesis, the University of Chicago, 2003, pp. 65–78. The quotation is p. 77.
26. Albert J. Mayer papers, Harvard Pusey Library, Box 11, File 1: "Discussion with Prince Musa'id, Riyadh 23 June," 1962.
27. Albert J. Mayer papers, Harvard Pusey Library, Box 11, File 1: Telegram sent by Meyer to Jeddah, June 25, 1962.
28. Albert J. Mayer papers, Harvard Pusey Library, Box 11, *Addendum to the Report of the Special US Economic Mission to Saudi Arabia*, sent by Meyer to Fowler Hamilton, director of USAID in Washington, DC, July 9, 1962.
29. Constantinos A. Doxiadis Archives, Archive File 23308, C-SAU-A349, November 25, 1968.
30. *Al-Riyadh, Madina al-Mustaqbal* [Riyadh: City of the Future] (Arab Urban Development Institute 1983).
31. P-SAU-A 5, Photos 31767, No. 31.

32. Constantinos A. Doxiadis Archives, Archive file 23308, C-SAU-A154, February 22, 1968.

33. After the deaths of his brothers Sultan bin 'Abd al-'Aziz (1930–2011) and Nayef bin 'Abd al-'Aziz (1933–2012), Salman bin 'Abd al-'Aziz (born 1935) became crown prince in June 2012. He had been the governor of the Riyadh province for nearly half a century.

34. Constantinos A. Doxiadis Archives, Archive File 23307, R-SAU-A20, October 31, 1968.

35. Taha El-Farra, "The Effects of Detribalizing the Bedouins on the Internal Cohesion of an Emerging State: The Kingdom of Saudi Arabia," PhD Thesis, University of Pittsburgh, 1973, p. 170.

36. See "Summary of Saudi Arabia's Five Year Development Plan," Constantinos A. Doxiadis Archives, Documents on Saudi Arabia, File 210, SAUDI-ARABIA-3D, p. 54.

37. Constantinos A. Doxiadis Archives, Archive File 23308, C-SAU-A228, May 28, 1968; Archive File 23309, C-SAU-RD154, May 4, 1968.

38. Constantinos A. Doxiadis Archives, Archive File 23325, *Final Master Plan*, July 1971, p. 70.

39. Constantinos A. Doxiadis Archives, Archive File 23309, C-SAU-RD285, July 18, 1968.

40. Constantinos A. Doxiadis Archives, Archive File 23309, C-SAU-RD331, October 16, 1968.

41. Abdal-Majeed Daghistani, *Ar-Riyadh: Urban Development and Planning* (Saudi Ministry of Information 1985), p. 102.

42. Constantinos A. Doxiadis Archives, Archive File 23313, C-SAU-A451, April 4, 1969.

43. Fahd bin 'Abd al-'Aziz (1923–2005) became King in 1982; after a stroke incapacitated him in 1995, Crown Prince 'Abd Allah bin 'Abd al-'Aziz (born 1924) became the de facto ruler.

44. Constantinos A. Doxiadis Archives, Archive File 23324, C-SAU-RD851, Town Planning Office report to 'Abd Allah al-Sudayri, March 7, 1970.

45. See Faisal A. Mubarak, "Urban Growth Boundary Policy and Residential Suburbanization: Riyadh, Saudi Arabia," *Habitat International*, Vol. 28, 2004, p. 576.

46. Al-Ghazhzhami, *Hikaya al-Hadatha*, p. 120.

47. See Fahad al-Said, "The Pattern of Structural Transformation of the Saudi Contemporary Neighborhood: The Case of al-Malaz, Riyadh," Communication at the 39th Congress of the International Society of City and Regional Planners, Cairo, 2003.

48. P-SAU-A 27 (Photographs 31785), photo 6.

49. Citino, "Suburbia and Modernization," pp. 46–49.

50. Mubarak, "Urban Growth Boundary Policy," pp. 579–580.

51. El-Farra, "The Effects of Detribalizing," p. 171.

52. Ugo Fabietti, *El Pueblo del Desierto* (Mitre 1983), p. 183–194.

53. Paul Bonnenfant, "L'évolution de la vie bédouine en Arabie centrale. Notes sociologiques," *Revue de l'Occident musulman et de la Méditerranée*, 23, 1977, p. 127.

54. Ibid., p. 154.

55. Fabietti, *El Pueblo*, p. 185. François Pouillon, "Un Etat contre les bédouins, l'Arabie Saoudite," *Monde Arabe Maghreb Machrek*, 147, 1995, pp. 134–138.
56. Constantinos A. Doxiadis Archives, Archive File 23305, *Riyadh: Report on Existing Conditions*, DOX-SAU-A2, p. 96.
57. Constantinos A. Doxiadis Archives, Archive File 23309, C-SAU-RD366, November 19, 1968.
58. Constantinos A. Doxiadis Archives, Archive File 23309, C-SAU-RD371, November 28, 1968.
59. Constantinos A. Doxiadis Archives, Archive File 23312, R-SAU-A22, January 22, 1969.
60. See 'Abd al-Nabi al-'Ikri, *Al-Tanzhimat al-Yasariyya fi-l-Jazira al-'Arabiyya wa-l-Khalij al-'Arabi* [Leftist Organizations in the Arabian Peninsula and the Gulf] (Dar al-Kunuz al-Adabiyya), 2003, pp. 42–57 and 202–228. Alexei Vassiliev, *The History of Saudi Arabia* (Saqi Books 2000), pp. 336–372. Turki al-Hamad, *Adama* (Saqi Books 2003).
61. Albert J. Meyer papers, Harvard Pusey Library, Box 11, *Addendum to the Report of the Special US Economic Mission to Saudi Arabia.*
62. R. Smithers, *The Haradh Project* (Ford Foundation 1966), po. 18–19, quoted by Donald Cole, *Nomads of the Nomads: the Al Murrah Bedouin of the Empty Quarter* (Harlan Davidson 1975), p. 148.
63. Constantinos A. Doxiadis Archives, Documents on Saudi Arabia, File 210, SA-SAUDI ARABIA-6D, "A Report on the Administrative Methods Applied to Urbanized Districts and the Administrative Problems Arising from the Accelerated Urbanization Expansion," March 1963, pp. 6–8.
64. Cole, *Nomads of the Nomads*, pp. 148–150. Also see El-Farra, "The Effects of Detribalizing," pp. 169–208; Mohammed H. Ebrahim, "Problems of Nomad Settlement in the Middle East with Special Reference to Saudi Arabia and the Haradh Project," PhD Thesis, Cornell University, 1981; and Toby C. Jones, *Desert Kingdom: How Oil and Water Forged Modern Saudi Arabia* (Harvard University Press, 2010), p. 74 sq.
65. Janet Abu-Lughod, "Migrant Adjustment to City Life: The Egyptian Case," *The American Journal of Sociology*, 67, 1, 1964, p. 10.
66. See Matruk Al-Faleh, *Al-Mujtama' wa-l-Dawla wa-l-Dimuqratiyya fi-l-Buldan al-'Arabiyya: Dirasa Muqarina li-Ishkaliyya al-Mujtama' al-Madani fi Dhaw' Tarayyuf al-Mudun* [Society, State and Democracy in the Arab Countries: A Comparative Study of the Question of Civil Society in the Light of the Ruralization of Cities] (Markaz dirasat al-wahda 2003).
67. El-Farra, "The Effects of Detribalizing," p. 170.
68. Constantinos A. Doxiadis Archives, Documents on Saudi Arabia, File 210, SA-SAUDI ARABIA-6D, "A Report on the Administrative Methods Applied to Urbanized Districts and the Administrative Problems Arising from the Accelerated Urbanization Expansion," March 1963, pp. 6–8.
69. Bonnenfant, "La capitale saoudienne," p. 669.
70. Constantinos A. Doxiadis Archives, Archive File 23307, R-SAU-A20, October 31, 1968.
71. Constantinos A. Doxiadis Archives, Archive File 23305, DOX-SAU-A2, *Riyadh: Existing Conditions*, p. 178.

72. Constantinos A. Doxiadis Archives, Archive File 23309, C-SAU-RD52, March 10, 1968.
73. Constantinos A. Doxiadis Archives, Archive File 23305, DOX-SAU-A2, *Riyadh: Existing Conditions*, p. 37.
74. Constantinos A. Doxiadis Archives, Archive File 23308, C-SAU-A232, May 31, 1968.
75. Constantinos A. Doxiadis Archives, Archive File 23309, C-SAU-RD13, February 18, 1968.
76. Constantinos A. Doxiadis Archives, Archive File 23305, DOX-SAU-A2, *Riyadh: Existing Conditions*, p. 38.
77. Constantinos A. Doxiadis Archives, Archive File 23305, *Riyadh: Existing Conditions*, p. 187, fig. 48.
78. Ibid., p. 107.
79. Ibid., p. 132.
80. Ibid., p. 287.
81. Constantinos A. Doxiadis Archives, Archive File 23309, C-SAU-RD364, November 19, 1968.
82. Scott, *Seeing Like a State*, p. 57.
83. Constantinos A. Doxiadis Archives, *DA Review*, April 1968, "Interview with the Lord Mayor of Riyadh, sheikh 'Abd al-'Aziz Al Thunayyan," pp. 8–9.
84. Constantinos A. Doxiadis Archives, Archive File 13307, R-SAU-A20, October 31, 1968.
85. P-SAU-A 27, Photographs 33877.
86. Constantinos A. Doxiadis Archives, Archive File 23314, C-SAU-RD594, July 15, 1969.
87. Constantinos A. Doxiadis Archives, Archive File 23312, R-SAU-A22, January 22, 1969.
88. Constantinos A. Doxiadis Archives, Archive File 23314, C-SAU-RD484, April 2, 1969 and Archive File 23313, C-SAU-A457, April 10, 1969.
89. Constantinos A. Doxiadis Archives, Archive File 23314, C-SAU-RD552, June 17, 1969.
90. Laton McCartney, *Friends in High Places: The Bechtel Story, the Most Secret Corporation and How It Engineered the World* (Ballantine 1998), p. 88.
91. Constantinos A. Doxiadis Archives, Archive File 23323, C-SAU-A621, January 16, 1970.
92. Constantinos A. Doxiadis Archives, Archive File 23329, C-SAU-RD1125, January 20, 1971.
93. Constantinos A. Doxiadis Archives, Archive File 23324, C-SAU-RD929, May 30, 1970.
94. Constantinos A. Doxiadis Archives, Archive File 23324, C-SAU-RD788, January 3, 1970.
95. Constantinos A. Doxiadis Archives, Archive File 23314, C-SAU-RD649, November 5, 1969.
96. Constantinos A. Doxiadis Archives, Archive File 23324, C-SAU-RD813, January 27, 1970.

97. Constantinos A. Doxiadis Archives, Archive File 23324, C-SAU-RD880, April 1, 1970.

98. Antahopoulos' letter to DA Athens office, June 13, 1971 (Constantinos A. Doxiadis Archives, Archive File 23329, C-SAU-RD1199).

99. Le Corbusier, *The Radiant City: Elements of a Doctrine of Urbanism to Be Used as the Basis of Our Machine-Age Civilization* (Orion Press 1964), p. 181, quoted by Scott, *Seeing Like a State*, p. 112.

100. Constantinos A. Doxiadis Archives, Archive File 23325, *Final Master Plan*, July 1971, DOX-SAU-A19, p. xiii.

101. Archive Files 23325, *Final Master Plan*, July 1971, DOX-SAU-A19, p. 131, fig. 9.

102. Constantinos A. Doxiadis Archives, archive File 23325, *Final Master Plan*, July 1971, p. 138–139 and 144.

103. Ibid., p. 64–65.

104. Constantinos A. Doxiadis Archives, archive File 23354, C-SAU-A1143, April 17, 1973.

105. Constantinos A. Doxiadis Archives, archive File 23325, *Final Master Plan*, July 1971, p. 66.

106. Constantinos A. Doxiadis Archives, Archive File 23354, C-SAU-A1143, Doxiadis's letter to king Faisal, April 17, 1973.

107. Constantinos A. Doxiadis Archives, Archive File 23324, C-SAU-RD850, March 4, 1970.

108. Constantinos A. Doxiadis Archives, Archive File 23325, *Final Master Plan*, July 1971, p. 59.

109. Ibid., p. 142.

110. Ibid., pp. 139–140.

111. Ibid., p. 284.

112. Ibid., p. 264.

113. Constantinos A. Doxiadis Archives, Archive File 23307, R-SAU-A 20, Oct. 31, 1968, p. 107.

114. Constantinos A. Doxiadis Archives, Archive File 23325, *Final Master Plan*, July 1971, p. 327.

Chapter 4: The Business of Development

1. Abdelrahman Munif, *Cities of Salt*, vol. 2: *The Trench* (Vintage 1993), p. 23.

2. Steffen Hertog, *Princes, Brokers, and Bureaucrats: Oil and the State in Saudi Arabia* (Cornell University Press 2011), pp. 39, 83.

3. Constantinos A. Doxiadis Archives, Archive File 23325, *Final Master Plan*, July 1971, p. 279, 293.

4. Abdal-Majeed Daghistani, *Ar-Riyadh: Urban Development and Planning* (Ministry of Information 1985), p. 161.

5. Paul Bonnenfant, "La capitale saoudienne," in Paul Bonnenfant (ed.), *La Peninsule Arabique d'Aujourd'hui* (Editions du CNRS 1982), vol. 2, pp. 684–685.

6. Al-Ghazhzhami, 'Abd Allah, *Hikaya al-Hadatha fi-l-Mamlaka al-'Arabiyya al-Su'udiyya* [The Story of Modernity in Saudi Arabia] (Al-Markaz al-Thaqafi al-'Arabi 2004), pp. 151–164.

7. Faisal A. Mubarak, "Urban Growth Boundary Policy and Residential Suburbanization: Riyadh, Saudi Arabia," *Habitat International*, 28, 2004, pp. 581–582.

8. Bonnenfant, "La capitale saoudienne," p. 686.

9. Interview with a voter during the 2005 campaign for the municipal election.

10. Hertog, *Princes, Brokers, Bureaucrats*, pp. 85–86.

11. Ibid.

12. See Roni Zirinski, *Ad Hoc Arabism: Advertising, Culture, and Technology in Saudi Arabia* (Peter Lang 2005).

13. Nathan Citino, "Suburbia and Modernization: Community Building and America's Post-World War II Encounter with the Arab Middle East," *Arab Studies Journal*, 13–14, 2006, p. 39.

14. Mubarak, "Urban Growth," pp. 581–582.

15. Daghistani, *Ar-Riyadh*, pp. 163–164. Lucie Haguenauer-Caceres, "Construire à l'étranger : Le rôle de la SCET Coopération en Côte d'Ivoire de 1959 à 1976," *Histoire Urbaine*, 3, 23, 2008, pp. 145–159.

16. David Hogarth, *The Penetration of Arabia* (Cambridge University Press 2011), pp. 79–83 and 244–250.

17. Daghistani, *Ar-Riyadh*, p. 164.

18. Peter Theroux, *Sandstorm: Days and Nights in Arabia* (Norton 1990), p. 198.

19. See Waleed Kassab al-Hemaidi, "The Metamorphosis of the Urban Fabric in an Arab-Muslim City: Riyadh, Saudi Arabia," *Journal of Housing and the Built Environment*, 16, 2001, pp. 190–195.

20. Bonnenfant, "La capitale saoudienne," p. 676.

21. Theroux, *Sandstorm*, p. 137.

22. Bonnenfant, "La capitale saoudienne," p. 688 sq.

23. See http://ahm1.com/vb/showthread.php?t=100418 and http://carlostamim.worldpress.com/2008/01/26/1-19 (last access November 2010). See also "Hara al-Mughtasiba Tuhim fi Bahr min al-Faqr wa-l-'Awz . . . wa Buyutuha la Tuqawim al-Bard" [The 'Violated Quarter' Floats on a Sea of Poverty and Indigence . . . and its Houses Do not Resist the Cold], *Al-Iqtisadiyya*, January 13, 2008.

24. Mubarak, "Urban Growth Boundary Policy," p. 589.

25. Vitalis, *America's Kingdom: Mythmaking on the Saudi Oil Frontier* (Verso 2009), pp. 1–24, 68–74 and 110–115. Jones, *Desert Kingdom*, pp. 92–131.

26. Jones, *Desert Kingdom*, pp. 55 and 84.

27. See Michael Field, *The Merchants: The Big Business Families of Saudi Arabia and the Gulf States* (Overlook 1996).

28. Quoted by Al-Rasheed, *Contesting the Saudi State, op. cit.*, p. 30.

29. See Zain al-'Abidin al-Rikabi, *Mafhum al-Wataniyya: al-Watan al-Mujtaba munzhu Khamsat 'Ashir Biliyun Sana* [The Notion of Nationalism: The Prostrated Nation since Fifteen Billion Years) (Rayna 2005).

30. See, for instance, Thomas Lippman, *Saudi Arabia on the Edge: The Uncertain Future of an American Ally* (Potomac 2012), pp. 1–7 and 177–182.
31. See http://www.khaled-alfaisal.com/vb/showthread.php?t=2422.
32. Al-Ghazhzhami, *Hikaya al-Hadatha*, pp. 151–164.
33. Ibid., pp. 156–157.
34. 'Abd Allah al-Turaigi, *Al-A'mal al-Kamila* [Complete Works] (Markaz Dirasa al-Wahda al-'Arabiyya 1999), p. 107–108.
35. See Khaled al-Rabish, "Ibn Sa'idan: Akthar min Khamsa wa-Sab'un 'Aman fi Khidma al-Suq al-'Aqari" [Bin Sa'idan: More than 75 Years Serving the Real Estate Market], *Al-Riyadh*, May 4, 2010, http://www.alriyadh.com/2010/05/04/article522625.html). See also the website of the bin Sa'idan company: http://www.bin-saedan.com/english/overview.asp.
36. Al-Ghazhzhami, *Hikaya al-Hadatha*, pp. 171–172.
37. Bonnenfant, "La capitale saoudienne," pp. 687–688.
38. Mubarak, "Urban Growth Boundary Policy," p. 584.
39. Quoted by Bonnenfant, "La capitale saoudienne," p. 686.
40. See Hertog, *Princes, Brokers, Bureaucrats*.
41. See "Fill'er Up!," *Aramco World*, 8, 1, January 1957.
42. Ministry of Planning, *Achievements of the Development Plans*, 1984, quoted by Altorki and Cole, *Arabian Oasis*, p. 121. Secil Tuncalp, "The Automobile Market in Saudi Arabia: Implications for Export Marketing Planning," *Marketing Intelligence and Planning*, 11, 1, 1993, pp. 28–36.
43. See Hertog, *Princes, Brokers, Bureaucrats*.
44. "The Success Story of Ghassan al-Sulayman," Riyadh Chamber of Commerce and Industry, March 11, 2007 (field notes). See http://www.youtube.com/watch?v=QDZzxg870go (last access July 14, 2012).
45. See http://www.afford-house.com/.
46. *Atarazzez wa-l-'arab ma 'abbaruni – rahat flusi wa majhudi khasara – laitahum yum an-nata'ij 'ayyanuni – law assawi ash-shayy fi wast al-wizara – wa athruhum ya li-l-asaf ma rashshahuni – la 'adhu majlis wa la haris 'imara.*

Chapter 5: Street Terrorism

1. Many streets of Riyadh are nicknamed after their width (in meters) on the master plan of the capital: *thalathin* (thirty), *arba'in* (forty) and *sittin* (sixty) streets are to be found in various neighborhoods, and residents distinguish between them by adding the name of the neighborhood, Thalathin al-'Ulayya or Sittin al-Malazz for instance.
2. See "Al-Amr bi-l-Ma'ruf: 59% min al-Shabab Yumarisun Sulukiyat Muharrama wa Makruha" [Religious Police: 59% of Youth Engage in Forbidden or Reprehensible Behavior), *Al-Hayat*, December 25, 2012, http://alhayat.com/Details/465622.
3. See "Saudi Police 'Stopped' Fire Rescue," March 15, 2002, http://news.bbc.co.uk/2/hi/middle_east/1874471.stm. See also Alain Gresh, "Saudi Arabia: Breaking the Silence," *Le Monde Diplomatique*, English edition, May 2002.
4. Lefebvre, *The Production of Space, op. cit.*, p. 23.

5. See "Murur al-Riyadh: Saher Khaffadha Wufiyat al-Hawadith ila 20 Hala fi-l-Shahr al-Awwal" [Riyadh Police Department: *Saher* Reduced Road Deaths to 20 during first Month of Operation], *al-Watan*, June 3, 2010, http://www.alwatan.com.sa/Local/News_Detail.aspx?ArticleID=5084& CategoryID=5. See also www.saher.gov.sa.

6. See "Saudi Arabia Clamps Down on Drug Traffickers," *Al-Sharq al-Awsat*, September 5, 2012, http://www.asharq-e.com/news.asp?section=1& id=30947.

7. See Gilles Kepel, *Fitna: Guerre au Coeur de l'Islam*, Paris: Gallimard, 2004 (English translation *The War for Muslim Minds: Islam and the West*, Cambridge: Belknap, 2006).

8. See "Al-Qabdh 'ala Ru'us Fitna at-Tafhit fi-l-'Asima al-Riyadh" [The Leaders of the Joyriding Secession Arrested in Riyadh], *Al-Jazira*, April 11, 2006.

9. See Tawfiq al-Zaydi, "Al-Jarima al-Murakkaba" [The Complex Crime], December 2006. Accessible on http://www.youtube.com/watch? v=nWsnnDoQ2Xo (last access February 21, 2012).

10. See "Tafhit al-Sayara min Hiwaya ila Idman Iantahi bi-l-Shabab al-Khaliji li-l-Mawt" [Joyriding: From a Hobby to an Addiction and to Death for Gulf Youth], alarabiya.net, August 14, 2005, Readers' Comments, http://www .alarabiya.net/articles/2005/08/14/15875.html (last access August 14, 2005).

11. "Al-'arbaja."

12. "T'allim aham Harakat al-Tafhit" [Learn the Main Joyriding Figures], October 7, 2008, http://www.hasamah.com/vb/showthread.php?t=1523 (last access January 8, 2013).

13. Data for the three first months of 1424 H, that is, March–May 2003. Quoted by Sulayman al-Duwayri'at, "Al-Dawafi' ila-Thahira al-Tafhit wa Iqtirah al-Hulul" [Joyriding Motivations and Proposed Solutions], Proceedings of the Second Road Safety National Conference, King 'Abd al-'Aziz City for Science and Technology, 2004, p. 656.

14. Salih al-Rumayh, "Al-'Awamil al-Mu'aththira fi Irtifa' Thahirat al-Tafhit bayna-l-Shabab al-Su'udi wa Turuq al-Wiqaya minha: Dirasa Muqarina li-Waqi' al-Thahira fi Kull min al-Riyadh, Jidda wa-l-Dammam" [The Factors Influencing the Increase of Drifting among Saudi Youth and the Ways to Prevent it: A Compared Study of Riyadh, Jeddah and Dammam], *Majalla al-Buhuth al-Amniyya* (Journal of Security Study), King Fahd Security College, 15, 34, 2006, p. 197.

15. On violence against migrant workers in Saudi Arabia, see *Bad Dreams: Exploitation and Abuse of Migrant Workers in Saudi Arabia* and *As if I Am not Human: Abuses Against Asian Domestic Workers in Saudi Arabia*, Human Rights Watch report, July 2004 and July 2008; on the plight of South Asian migrants, see Andrew Gardner, *City of Strangers: Gulf Migration and the Indian Community in Bahrain* (Ilr Press 2010) and Junaid Rana, *Terrifying Muslims: Race and Labor in the South Asian Diaspora* (Duke University Press 2011).

16. On minors in the judicial system, see *Adults before their Time: Children in Saudi Arabia's Criminal Justice System*, Human Rights Watch report, March 2008.

17. Sulayman ad-Duwayri'at, "Al-Dawafi' ila-Thahira al-Tafhit wa Iqtirah al-Hulul" [Joyriding Motivations and Proposed Solutions], p. 654–655.

18. See Al-Riyadh Development Authority, "Nahwi Tatwir Nizham Naql Amen wa Fa"al fi Madina al-Riyadh" [Toward the Development of a Safe and Efficient Public Transportation System in Riyadh], 2001, pp. 3–11.

19. Roland Barthes, "The New Citroën," in *Mythologies* (Hill and Wang, 1972), p. 88.

20. Mike Featherstone, Nigel Thrift, and John Urry (eds.), *Automobilities* (Sage Publications 2005), p. 4.

21. Borden, *Skateboarding, Space and the City: Architecture and the Body* (Berg 2001), p. 13.

22. See "Tafhit al-Sayara min Hiwaya ila Idman."

23. "Kitab al-Hajwala (min al-Bidaya hatta al-'An)" [The Book of Joyriding, from the Beginning until Now], www.ra7al.com/vb/showthread.php?t=11514 (last access March 14, 2012).

24. See Secil Tuncalp, "The Automobile Market," *Marketing Intelligence and Planning*, 11.1, 1993, pp. 29, 35.

25. Ibid., p. 28.

26. See http://ra7al.net/cgi-sys/suspendedpage.cgi?t=26938&goto=nextoldest, January 23, 2005 (last access November 15, 2006).

27. "Kitab al-Hajwala" [The Book of Joyriding].

28. See "Man huwa al-King? Huwa Badr 'Awadh" [Who Is the King? Badr 'Awadh], November 29, 2010, http://www.vb.eqla3.com/showthread.php?t=758531 (last access January 1, 2013).

29. Muhammad as-Sabir, "Al-Kamriyun wa Malhamat al-Tahawwur wa-l-Tafhit" [The Camryst and the Butchery of Temerity and Drifting], *Al-Jazira*, July 12, 2001. Quoted by Sulayman ad-Duwayri'at, "Al-Dawafi' ila-Thahira al-Tafhit wa Iqtirah al-Hulul" (Joyriding Motivations and Proposed Solutions), p. 656.

30. 'Utaiba is an important tribal confederation whose territories roughly extend from Riyadh to Mecca.

31. See "Ash'ar Hajwala 'ala-l-Kayf" (Drifting Slogans – All You Can Read), http://www.m7shsh.com/vb/6372.html (last accessed January 1, 2013).

32. Urry, "The 'System' of Automobility," in Featherstone, Thrift and Urry (eds.), *Automobilities*, pp. 27–29.

33. See David Harvey, *Rebel Cities: From the Right to the City to the Urban Revolution* (Verso 2012), p. 91.

34. Only 30 percent of Saudis own their homes. See "Kingdom Tackles Home, Loan Demand," *Saudi Gazette*, March 21, 2011, http://www.saudigazette.com.sa/index.cfm?method=home.regcon&contentID=2011032196361 (last access April 18, 2013).

35. "Al-'Arbaja, Nash'atuha wa Numuha" [The Origins and Evolution of Thugs], August 1, 2004, http://www.alqasir.net/forum/showpost.php?p=12947&postcount=1 (last access February 21, 2012).

36. Borden, *Skateboarding*, p. 33.

37. Andrew Gardner, "The Amalgamated City: Petroleum Wealth and Urban Space in Doha, Qatar," paper presented at the conference: *Boom Cities:*

Urban Development in the Arabian Peninsula, organized by Claire Beaugrand, Amelie Le Renard, Pascal Menoret and Roman Stadnicki at NYU Abu Dhabi, December 3, 2012.

38. Mike Davis, *City of Quartz: Excavating the Future in Los Angeles* (Verso 1992), p. 293.

39. Borden, *Skateboarding*, p. 142.

40. Colin McFarlane, *Learning the City: Knowledge and Translocal Assemblage* (Wiley-Blackwell 2011), p. 43.

41. "Tawsif Shawari' al-Hajwala" [Description of Joyriding Streets], March 1, 2007, http://ra7al.net/vb/showthread.php?t=26525&goto=nextoldest (last access May 2007).

42. On the notion of bodily capital and its management, see Loic Wacquant, "Pugs at Work: Bodily Capital and Bodily Labor among Professional Boxers," *Body and Society*, 1, 1, 1995, pp. 65–94, and Loic Wacquant, *Body and Soul: Notebooks of an Apprentice Boxer* (Oxford University Press 2004), p. 127 ff.

43. Borden, *Skateboarding*, p. 38. Borden quotes the skateboarding magazine *Thrasher*, 6, 5, May 1986, p. 35.

44. On female homosocial practices, see Amélie Le Renard, *Femmes et Espaces Publics en Arabie Saoudite* (Dalloz 2011), pp. 199–230.

45. See 'Isam bin Hashim al-Jifri, "Jarima al-Liwat" [The Crime of Sodomy], http://www.saaid.net/ Doat/aljefri/116.htm.

46. See for instance "Amn al-Turuq bi-l-Layth Yaqbudhu 'ala Majhulin bi-Ziy Nisa'i" [Layth Police Force Arrest Cross Dressing Suspects], *Al-Riyadh*, July 15, 2009 (http://www.alriyadh.com/2009/07/15/article444830.html); "Al-Qabdh 'ala Arba'a Ashkhas Mutanakkirin bi-Ziy Nisa'i fi Mutarada Amniya bi-l-Ta'if" [Arrest of Four Suspects Wearing Women's Dress in a Police Chase in Ta'if], *Al-Riyadh*, October 10, 2010 (http://www.alriyadh.com/2010/10/10/article566797.html).

47. See Khaled El-Rouayheb, *Before Homosexuality in the Arab-Islamic World, 1500–1800* (University of Chicago Press 2005). See also Joseph Massad, *Desiring Arabs* (University of Chicago Press 2007) and Wilson C. Jacob, *Working Out Egypt: Effendi Masculinity and Subject Formation in Colonial Modernity, 1870–1940* (Duke University Press 2011).

48. Muhammad Al-Saif, *Al-Zhahira al-Ijramiyya fi Thaqafa wa Bina' al-Mujitama' al-Su'udi bayna al-Tasawwur al-Ijtima'i wa Haqa'iq al-Ittijah al-Islami* [Crime in Saudi Society's Culture and Construction, between Social Imagination and Islamic Guidance] (al-Kitab al-Jame'i 'an al-Mujtama' al-Su'udi), pp. 108–109.

49. Wacquant, *Body and Soul*, pp. 58–59.

50. Madawi Al-Rasheed, *Contesting the Saudi State: Islamic Voices from a New Generation* (Cambridge University Press 2007), pp. 156–163.

51. See 'Atiq al-Biladi, *Al-Adab al-Sha'bi fi-l-Hijaz* [Popular Literature in the Hejaz] (Dar Makka 1982), pp. 52–54.

52. This mobile phone, one of the first Bluetooth devices sold on the Saudi market, owed its nickname to its signature black and white livery and its rounded edges.

53. Pascal Menoret and Nadav Samin, "The Bleak Romance of Tahliya Street," *Middle East Journal of Culture and Communication*, 6 (2013), pp. 213–228.

54. Tim Edensor, "Automobility and National Identity: Representation, Geography and Driving Practice," in Mike Featherstone, Nigel Thrift, and John Urry (eds.), *Automobilities*, p. 104.

55. *Top Gear*, BBC Two, Season 3, Episode 1, 2003.

Chapter 6: Street Politics

1. See "Masra' 4 Shabab Hirqan fi Tasadum Sayara Mufahhat Ma' Ukhra" [Death of 4 Youths Burned after the Collision of a Joyrider's Car with another Car], *Al-Watan*, March 16, 2006; and http://www.lahdah.org/vb/t23082.html, April 3, 2006 (last access January 15, 2013).

2. See "'Uyun la Tanam . . . al-'Aqid al-Muqbil li-l-Jazira: al-Qabdh 'ala Ru'us Fitna al-Tafhit fi-l-'Asima" [Eyes that never Sleep . . . the Colonel al-Muqbil declares to *al-Jazira*: We Arrested the Leaders of the Joyriding Sedition in the Capital], *Al-Jazira*, April 11, 2006.

3. See "Murur al-Riyadh: Qabadhna 'ala al-Mutahawwir fi Mat'am bi-l-'Uraija" [The Riyadh Police Department: We Arrested al-Mutahawwir in a Restaurant in al-'Uraija], *Al-Jazira*, April 16, 2006.

4. Al-Duwayri'at, "Al-Dawafi' ila-Thahira al-Tafhit wa Iqtirah al-Hulul" [Joyriding Motivations and Proposed Solutions], pp. 657–659.

5. See, for instance, *Al-Tafhit wa Qiyada Sughar al-Sinn li-l-Sayara: Dirasa Maydaniyya li-Ba'dh al-Mawqufin bi-Murur al-Riyadh wa Dar al-Mulahazha* [Drifting and Underage Driving: A Field Study Conducted on Inmates at the Traffic Police and Riyadh Reformatory], King Saud University, Department of Social Studies, 1982.

6. Ruling of the governor of the Riyadh's province, no. 267, 01/13/1403 AH (1982 CE). Quoted by al-Rumayh, "Al-'Awamil al-Mu'aththira fi Irtifa' Thahirat al-Tafhit," p. 175.

7. Riyadh Traffic Administration, Traffic Office, Administrative regulation pertaining to the misdemeanor of drifting, 01/22/1403 AH (1982 CE). Quoted by al-Rumayh, "Al-'Awamil," p. 181.

8. 'Abd al-Meguid Sayyid Ahmad Mansur, "Al-Tafhit min Mazhahir al-'Unf 'ind al-Shabab," http://www.bab.com/persons/97/show_particle.cfm?article_id=316 (last accessed March 22, 2012).

9. Ibid., my emphasis.

10. See Hamza al-Fa'r, *Nazhra fi Mushkila al-Shabab was Kaifiyya Mu'alajatiha* [Youth Issues and their Solutions] (Dar al-Andalus al-Khadhra' 1993); Ibrahim al-Juwaiyyir, *Al-Shabab wa Qadhayah al-Mu'asira* [Youth and their Contemporary Issues] (Maktaba al-'Ubaykan 1994); 'Abd al-'Aziz al-Shithri, *Waqt al-Faragh wa Shughluhu fi Madina al-Riyadh* [The Usage of Idleness in Riyadh] (Imam Muhammad bin Saud Islamic University Press 2001).

11. *Al-Tafhit wa Qiyada Sughar al-Sinn li-l-Sayara: Dirasa Maydaniyya li-Ba'dh al-Mawqufin bi-Murur al-Riyadh wa Dar al-Mulahazha* [Drifting and Underage Driving: A Field Study Conducted on Inmates at the Traffic Police and Riyadh Reformatory].

12. Al-Rumayh, "Al-'Awamil," p. 186.
13. See the presentation of the committee on the website of the King 'Abd al-'Aziz City, http://www.kacst.edu.sa/ar/about/stc/Pages/TrafficSafety.aspx (last access January 21, 2013).
14. See Karam Allah 'Abd al-Rahman, "Hawadeth al-Murur: Asbabuha wa Turuq al-Wiqaya minha" [Road Accidents, their Causes and the Way to Prevent them], Riyadh: Institute of Public Administration, 1982; 'Abd Allah al-Nafe' and Khaled al-Saif, "Tahlil al-Khasa'is al-Nafsiyya wa-l-Ijtima'iyya al-Muta'alleqa bi-Suluk Qiyada al-Sayara fi-l-Mamlaka al-'Arabiyya al-Su'udiyya" [Analysis of the Psychological and Social Characteristics of the Driving Behavior in Saudi Arabia], Riyadh: King 'Abd al-'Aziz City for Sciences and Technology, 1986 (quoted by al-Rumayh, "Al-'Awamil").
15. See Muhammad al-Saif, "Al-'Awamil al-Ijtima'iyya al-Murtabita bi-Numut al-Jarima al-Jinsiyya" [The Social Features of Sexual Crime], doctorate thesis, Imam Muhammad bin Sa'ud Islamic University, 1993, and *Al-Zhahira al-Ijramiyya*.
16. Mamoun Fandy, *Saudi Arabia and the Politics of Dissent* (St. Martin's Press 1999).
17. Al-Rasheed, *Contesting the Saudi State: Islamic Voices from a New Generation* (Cambridge University Press 2007), pp. 52–101.
18. See Barbara Metcalf, "Living Hadith in the Tablighi Jema'at," *Journal of Asian Studies*, 52, 3, 1993, pp. 584–608; and "Travelers' Tales in the Tablighi Jema'at," *The Annals of the American Academy of Political and Social Science*, 588, 2003, pp. 136–148. On the Tabligh in Saudi Arabia, see Nasir al-Huzaimi, *Ayyam ma' Juhayman* [Days with Juhayman] (al-Shabaka al-'Arabiyya li-l-Abhath wa-l-Nashr 2011), p. 42ff.
19. Abu Zegem, "The Story of Repented Drifters Abu Zegem and Abu Hasan," DVD published in 2004 and bought in the street in Ta'if in December 2005.
20. See www.dweesh.com and www.almurabbi.com (last access March 18, 2012). See Muhammad al-Duwaish, *Ta'ammulat fi-l-'Amal al-Islami* [Reflections on Islamic Activism] (Kitab al-Muntada 2001).
21. Muhammad al-Duwaish, "Hina Yaghib al-Hiwar" [When Dialogue Vanishes] and "Mu'assassat al-Mujtama' wa-l-Shabab" [Youth and Social Institutions], Jeddah, April 14 and 15, 2005.
22. Al-Duwayri'at, "Al-Dawafi' ila-Thahira al-Tafhit wa Iqtirah al-Hulul," p. 657.
23. Interior Ministry Statistical Yearbook, quoted by al-Duwayri'at, "Al-Dawafi'," p. 657.
24. Interior Ministry Statistical Yearbook, quoted by ibid., p. 656.
25. Interior Ministry Regulation No. 1607, 02/28/1422 AH (2001 CE). Quoted by al-Rumayh, "Al-'Awamil," p. 175n.
26. Ibid., p. 175.
27. Fatwa No. 22036, 07/27/1422 H. (2001 CE).
28. See Muhammad al-Tuwaijri, "Qiyada Sughar al-Sinn wa Ta'thiruha 'ala al-Mukhalafat al-Mururiyya" [Underage Driving and its Influence on Road Infractions], 2004, p. 15.

29. Al-Migrin 2001, quoted by al-Rumayh, "Al-'Awamil."
30. See chapter 5, note 13.
31. Al-Rumayh, "Al-'Awamil," pp. 183–184.
32. Ibid., pp. 208–215 and 224.
33. Ibid., p. 199.
34. Ibid., p. 202.
35. Ibid., pp. 208–215 and 220.
36. Ibid., p. 227.
37. Borden, *Skateboarding...*, p. 48.
38. "Mutarada Shabab li-l-Dawriya wa Sudmuha (Rah Ihtiram Rijal al-Amn)" [Youths Chasing and Running into Patrol (The Police's Honor Is Gone)], YouTube video, August 24, 2012, http://www.youtube.com/watch?v=zOblj_fk5Bk (last access January 19, 2013). See also "Bi-l-Fidio: Mufahhitun bi-l-Ta'if Yutaridun Dawria Amniya wa Yasdumunha" [Video: Ta'if Drifters Chase and Run into Police Patrol], *Sabq*, August 26, 2012, http://sabq.org/aCmfde (last access January 19, 2013).
39. See "Ash'ar Hajwala 'ala-l-Kayf" [Drifting Slogans – All You Can Read].
40. Michel de Certeau, *The Practice of Everyday Life* (University of California Press 1984), p. xv.
41. Paul Routledge, "Critical Geopolitics and Terrains of Resistance," *Political Geography*, 15, 6/7, 1996, p. 521. See also Paul Routledge, "A Spatiality of Resistance: Theory and Practice in Nepal's Revolution of 1990," in Steve Pile and Michael Keith (eds.), *Geographies of Resistance* (Routledge 1997), p. 76.

Bibliography

Archives

Constantinos A. Doxiadis Archives, Benaki Museum, Athens
Albert Julius Mayer Papers, Harvard University Pusey Library, Cambridge, MA

Secondary Sources

Abu-Lughod, Janet. "Migrant Adjustment to City Life: The Egyptian Case." *The American Journal of Sociology*, 67, 1, 1961, 22–32

Abu-Lughod, Janet. *Cairo: 1001 Years of the City Victorious*. Princeton: Princeton University Press, 1971

Al-Biladi, 'Atiq. *Al-Adab al-Sha'bi fi-l-Hijaz* [Popular Literature in the Hejaz]. Mecca: Dar Makka, 1982

Al-Duwayri'at, Sulaiman. "Al-Dawafi' ila-Thahira al-Tafhit wa Iqtirah al-Hulul" [Joyriding Motivations and Proposed Solutions]. Proceedings of the Second Road Safety National Conference. Riyadh: King 'Abd al-'Aziz City for Science and Technology, 2004, p. 652–703

Al-Faleh, Matruk. *Sakaka al-Jawf fi Nihaya al-Qarn al-'Ashrin: Al-Tahdith wa-l-Tanmiya wa Tahawwulat al-Nukhba fi-l-Rif al-'Arabi al-Su'udi* [Sakaka in the Late 20th Century: Modernization, Development, and Elite Change in the Saudi Countryside]. Beirut: Baisan, 2000

Al-Faleh, Matruk. *Al-Mujtama' wa-l-Dimuqratiyya wa-l-Dawla fi-l-Buldan al-'Arabiyya: Dirasa Muqarina li-Ishkaliyya al-Mujtama' al-Madani fi Dhaw' Tarayyuf al-Mudun* [Society, State and Democracy in the Arab Countries: A Comparative Study of the Question of Civil Society in the Light of the Ruralization of Cities]. Beirut: Markaz Dirasa al-Wahda al-'Arabiyya, 2002

Al-Faleh, Matruk. *Hamad al-Wardi (1952–2003): Sira Nidhal wa Qissa Ightiyal Hilm al-Tatwir wa-l-Islah* [Hamad al-Wardi: A Lifetime of Struggle and the Story of the Assassination of the Dream of Development and Reform]. Beirut: n.p., 2008

Al-Ghazhzhami, 'Abd Allah. *Hikaya al-Hadatha fi-l-Mamlaka al-'Arabiyya al-Su'udiyya* [The Story of Modernity in Saudi Arabia]. Beirut: Al-Markaz al-Thaqafi al-'Arabi, 2004

Al-Hamad, Turki. *Al-Karadib*. Beirut: Dar al-Saqi, 1999

Al-Hathloul, Saleh and Narayanan Edadan (eds.). *Urban Development in Saudi Arabia: Challenges and Opportunities*. Riyadh: Dar Al Sahan, 1995

Al-Huzaimi, Nasir. *Ayyam ma' Juhayman: Kuntu ma' "al-Jama'a al-Salafiyya al-Muhtasiba"* [Days with Juhayman: I Belonged to the Salafi Volunteer Group]. Beirut: al-Shabaka al-'Arabiyya li-l-Abhath wa-l-Nashr, 2011

Al-Jibrin, Jibrin. *Al-'Unf al-Usari khilal Marahil al-Haya* [Family Violence during Life's Phases]. Riyadh: Mu'assasa al-Malik Khalid al-Khayriyya, 2005

Al-Juwayyir, Ibrahim. *Ta'akhkhur al-Shabab al-Jame'i fi-l-Zawaj* [The Delayed Marriage of University Students]. Riyadh: 'Ubaikan, 1995

Al-Khalifa, 'Abd Allah. *Al-Muhaddadat al-Ijtima'iyya li-Tawzi' al-Jarima 'ala Ahiya' Madina al-Riyadh* [Social Determinants of Crime Distribution in Riyadh's Neighborhoods]. Riyadh: Wizara al-Dakhiliyya, 1993

Al-Khalifa, 'Abd Allah. *Ab'ad al-Jarima wa Nuzhum al-'Adala al-Jana'iyya fi al-Watan al-'Arabi* [Crime and Penal Justice in the Arab World]. Riyadh: Akadimiya Nayyif al-'Arabiyya li-l-'Ulum al-Amniyya, 2000

Al-Muzaini, Muhammad. *Mafariq al-'Atama* [Crossroads of Darkness]. Beirut: al-Mu'assasa al-'Arabiyya li-l-Dirasa wa-l-Nashr, 2004

Al-Rasheed, Madawi. *A History of Saudi Arabia*. Cambridge: Cambridge University Press, 2002

Al-Rasheed, Madawi. *Contesting the Saudi State: Islamic Voices from a New Generation*. Cambridge: Cambridge University Press, 2007

Al-Rasheed, Madawi and Robert Vitalis (eds.). *Counter-Narratives: History, Contemporary Society, and Politics in Saudi Arabia and Yemen*. New York: Palgrave MacMillan, 2004

Al-Saif, Muhammad. *Al-Zhahira al-Ijramiyya fi Thaqafa wa Bina' al-Mujtama' al-Su'udi bayna al-Tasawwur al-Ijtima'i wa Haqa'iq al-Ittijah al-Islami* [Crime in Saudi Society's Culture and Construction, between Social Imagination and Islamic Guidance]. Riyadh: al-Kitab al-Jame'i 'an al-Mujtama' al-Su'udi, 1996

Al-Salim, Khalid. *Al-Dhubt al-Ijtima'i wa-l-Tamasuk al-Usari* [Social Control and Family Cohesion]. Riyadh: n.p., 2000

Alshamsi, Mansoor Jassem. *Islam and Political Reform in Saudi Arabia: The Quest for Political Change and Reform*. London: Routledge, 2011

Al-Shithri, 'Abd al-'Aziz. *Waqt al-Faragh wa Shaghluhu fi Madina al-Riyadh: Dirasa Maidaniyya* [Free Time and Its Usage in Riyadh: A Fieldwork Study]. Riyadh: Jami'a al-Imam Muhammad bin Su'ud al-Islamiyya, 2001

Altorki, Soraya and Donald P. Cole. *Arabian Oasis City: The Transformation of 'Unayzah*. Austin: University of Texas Press, 1989

Al-Turaigi, 'Abdullah. *Al-A'mal al-Kamila* [Complete Works]. Beirut: Markaz Dirasat al-Wahda al-'Arabiyya, 1999

Al-Wardi, Hamad. *Al-Biruqratiya wa-l-Tamthil al-Biruqrati wa-l-Takafu' fi-l-Mamlaka al-'Arabiyya al-Su'udiyya: Dirasa Tahliliya li-l-Mukhassasat al-Maliya* [Bureaucracy, Bureaucratic Representation and Equality in Saudi

Arabia: an Analysis of Financial Allocations]. Beirut: Markaz Dirasa al-Wahda al-'Arabiyya, 2006

Aminzade, Ronald R., Jack A. Goldstone, Doug McAdam, Elizabeth J. Perry, William H. Sewell, Jr., Sydney Tarrow and Charles Tilly. *Silence and Voice in the Study of Contentious Politics*. Cambridge: Cambridge University Press, 2001

Arebi, Saddeka. *Women and Words in Saudi Arabia: The Politics of Literary Discourse*. New York: Columbia University Press, 1994

Asad, Talal (ed.). *Anthropology and the Colonial Encounter*. Amherst: Humanity Books, 1973

Babayan, Kathryn and Afsaneh Najmabadi (eds.). *Islamicate Sexualities: Translations across Temporal Geographies of Desire*. Cambridge, MA: Harvard Center for Middle Eastern Studies, 2008

Bakhtin, Mikhail. *Rabelais and His World*. Cambridge, MA: MIT Press, 1968

Bayat, Asef. *Street Politics: Poor People's Movements in Iran*. New York: Columbia University Press, 1997

Bayat, Asef. *Life as Politics: How Ordinary People Change the Middle East*. Stanford: Stanford University Press, 2010

Beaud, Stéphane and Florence Weber. *Guide de l'enquête de terrain*. Paris: La Découverte, 2003

Becker, Howard S. *Outsiders: Studies in the Sociology of Deviance*. New York: The Free Press of Glencoe, 1963

Beinin, Joel and Frédéric Vairel (eds.). *Social Movements, Mobilization, and Contestation in the Middle East and North Africa*. Stanford: Stanford University Press, 2011

Bin Sunaitan, Muhammad. *Al-Nukhab al-Su'udiyya: Dirasa fi-l-Tahawwulat wa-l-Ikhfaqat* [The Saudi Elites: A Study of Transformations and Failures]. Beirut: Markaz Dirasa al-Wahda al-'Arabiyya, 2004

Bonnenfant, Paul. "L'évolution de la vie bédouine en Arabie centrale. Notes sociologiques." *Revue de l'Occident musulman et de la Méditerranée*, 23, 1977, 111–178

Bonnenfant, Paul. "Mouvements migratoires en Arabie centrale." *Revue de l'Occident musulman et de la Méditerranée*, 23, 1977, 179–223

Bonnenfant, Paul (ed.). *La péninsule arabique d'aujourd'hui*. Paris : Editions du CNRS, 1982

Borden, Iain. *Skateboarding, Space and the City: Architecture and the Body*. Oxford: Berg, 2001

Borden, Iain. *Drive: Journeys through Film, Cities and Landscape*. London: Reaktion Books, 2013

Borneman, John and Abdellah Hammoudi (eds.). *Being There: The Fieldwork Encounter and the Making of Truth*. Berkeley: The University of California Press, 2009

Bourdieu, Pierre. *Outline of a Theory of Practice*. Cambridge: Cambridge University Press, 1977 [1972]

Bourdieu, Pierre. *Algeria 1960. The Disenchantment of the World. The Sense of Honor. The Kabyle House or the World Reversed*. Cambridge: Cambridge University Press, 1979 [1963, 1972]

Bourdieu, Pierre. *Distinction: A Social Critique of the Judgment of Taste.* Cambridge, MA: Harvard University Press, 1984 [1979]

Bourdieu, Pierre (ed.). *The Weight of the World: Social Suffering in Contemporary Society.* Stanford: Stanford University Press, 1999 [1993]

Bourdieu, Pierre and Abdelmalek Sayad. *Le déracinement: la crise de l'agriculture traditionnelle en Algérie.* Paris: Minuit, 1964

Bourgois, Philippe. *In Search of Respect: Selling Crack in El Barrio.* Cambridge: Cambridge University Press, 1996

Bujra, Abdalla S. *The Politics of Stratification: A Study of Political Change in a South Arabian Town.* Oxford: Clarendon Press, 1971

Caldeira, Teresa P. R. *City of Walls: Crime, Segregation, and Citizenship in São Paulo.* Berkeley: University of California Press, 2000

Caton, Steven. *"Peaks of Yemen I Summon:" Poetry as Cultural Practice in a North Yemeni Tribe.* Berkeley: University of California Press, 1990

Caton, Steven. *Yemen Chronicle: An Anthropology of War and Mediation.* New York: Hill and Wang, 2005

Cefaï, Daniel (ed.). *L'engagement ethnographique.* Paris: Editions de l'Ecole des hautes études en sciences sociales, 2010

Certeau, Michel de. *The Practice of Everyday Life.* Berkeley: University of California Press, 1984

Chaline, Claude and Adib Fares. *The Contemporary Town Planning and Riyadh: An Introduction to the Planning of Human Settlements in Arab and Western Countries.* Riyadh: n.p., n.d.

Chatty, Dawn. *Mobile Pastoralists: Development, Planning and Social Change in Oman.* New York: Columbia University Press, 1996

Chatty, Dawn (ed.). *Nomadic Societies in the Middle East and North Africa: Entering the 21st Century.* Leiden: Brill, 2006

Citino, Nathan. "Suburbia and Modernization: Community Building and America's Post-World War II Encounter with the Arab Middle East." *Arab Studies Journal,* 13–14, 2006, p. 39–64

Cole, Donald Powell. *Nomads of the Nomads: The Al Murrah Bedouin of the Empty Quarter.* Arlington Heights: Harlan Davidson, 1975

Corbett, Claire. *Car Crime.* Cullompton: Willan Publishing, 2003

Crapanzano, Vincent. *Tuhami: Portrait of a Moroccan.* Chicago: The University of Chicago Press, 1980

Daghistani, Abdal-Majeed Ismail. *Ar-Riyadh: Urban Development and Planning.* Riyadh: Ministry of Information, 1985

Davis, Mike. *City of Quartz: Excavating the Future in Los Angeles.* New York: Verso, 1990

Davis, Mike. *Planet of Slums.* New York: Verso, 2006

Deane, Philip. *Constantinos Doxiadis: Master Builder for Free Men.* Dobbs Ferry: Oceana, 1965

Doxiadis, Constantinos A. *Architecture in Transition.* Oxford: Oxford University Press, 1963

Doxiadis, Constantinos A. *Ekistics: An Introduction to the Science of Human Settlement.* New York: Oxford University Press, 1968

Doxiadis, Constantinos A. "Three Letters to an American." *Daedalus*, 101, 4, 1972, 163–183

Duffy, Enda. *The Speed Handbook: Velocity, Pleasure, Modernism*. Durham: Duke University Press, 2009

Dwyer, Kevin. *Moroccan Dialogues: Anthropology in Question*. Baltimore: Johns Hopkins University Press, 1982

Ebrahim, Mohammed Hossein Saleh. "Problems of Nomad Settlement in the Middle East with Special Reference to Saudi Arabia and the Haradh Project." PhD Thesis, Cornell University, 1981

El-Farra, Taha Osman. "The Effects of Detribalizing the Bedouins on the Internal Cohesion of an Emerging State: the Kingdom of Saudi Arabia." PhD Thesis, University of Pittsburgh, 1973

El-Rouhayeb, Khaled. *Before Homosexuality in the Arab-Islamic World, 1500–1800*. Chicago: The University of Chicago Press, 2005

Elsheshtawy, Yasser (ed.). *Planning Middle Eastern Cities: An Urban Kaleidoscope in a Globalizing World*. London: Routledge, 2004

Elsheshtawy, Yasser (ed.). *The Evolving Arab City: Tradition, Modernity and Urban Development*. London: Routledge, 2008

Elsheshtawy, Yasser. *Dubai: Behind an Urban Spectacle*. London: Routledge, 2010

Escobar, Arturo. *Encountering Development: The Making and Unmaking of the Third World*. Princeton: Princeton University Press, 1995

Fabietti, Ugo. *El Pueblo del Desierto. Historia, Economia, Estructura Familiar, Religion, etc., de un Pueblo Nomada*. Barcelona: Editorial Mitre, 1985

Facey, William. *Riyadh: The Old City*. London: Immel, 1992

Fandy, Mamoun. *Saudi Arabia and the Politics of Dissent*. London: St. Martin's Press, 1999

Farge, Arlette. *Fragile Lives: Violence, Power and Solidarity in 18th Century Paris*. Cambridge: Harvard University Press, 1993

Farge, Arlette. *Subversive Words: Public Opinion in 18th Century France*. Cambridge: Polity Press, 1994

Farge, Arlette and Jacques Revel. *The Vanishing Children of Paris: Rumor and Politics before the French Revolution*. Cambridge: Harvard University Press, 1991

Ferguson, James. *The Anti-Politics Machine: "Development," Depoliticization, and Bureaucratic Power in Lesotho*. Cambridge: Cambridge University Press, 1990

Ferguson, James. *Expectations of Modernity: Myths and Meanings of Urban Life on the Zambian Copperbelt*. Berkeley: University of California Press, 1999

Field, Michael. *The Merchants: The Big Business Families of Saudi Arabia and the Gulf States*. Woodstock: Overlook, 1985

Foucault, Michel. *Discipline and Punish: The Birth of the Prison*. New York: Vintage, 1977

Fuccaro, Nelida. *Histories of City and State in the Persian Gulf: Manama since 1800*. Cambridge: Cambridge University Press, 2009

Gardner, Andrew M. *City of Strangers: Gulf Migration and the Indian Community in Bahrain*. Ithaca: Cornell University Press, 2010

Ghannam, Farha. *Remaking the Modern: Space, Relocation, and the Politics of Identity in a Global Cairo*. Berkeley: University of California Press, 2002

Guldi, Jo. *Roads to Power: Britain Invents the Infrastructure State*. Cambridge: Harvard University Press, 2012

Habermas, Jürgen. *The Structural Transformation of the Public Sphere: An Inquiry into a Category of Bourgeois Society*. Cambridge: MIT Press, 1991 [1962]

Haguenauer-Caceres, Lucie. "Construire à l'étranger : Le rôle de la SCET Coopération en Côte d'Ivoire de 1959 à 1976." *Histoire Urbaine*, 3, 23, 2008, pp. 145–159.

Hall, Peter. *Cities of Tomorrow: An Intellectual History of Urban Planning and Design in the Twentieth Century*. Malden, MA: Blackwell, 2002

Hammoudi, Abdellah. *A Season in Mecca: Narrative of a Pilgrimage*. New York: Hill and Wang, 2006

Hanieh, Adam. *Capitalism and Class in the Gulf Arab States*. New York: Palgrave MacMillan, 2011

Harper, Annie. "The Idea of Islamabad." PhD thesis, Yale University, 2010

Harvey, David. *Rebel Cities: From the Right to the City to the Urban Revolution*. London: Verso, 2012

Hayden, Dolores. *Building Suburbia: Green Fields and Urban Growth, 1820–2000*. New York: Vintage Books, 2004

Herrera, Linda and Asef Bayat (eds.). *Being Young and Muslim: New Cultural Politics in the Global South and North*. Oxford: Oxford University Press, 2010

Hertog, Steffen. *Princes, Brokers, and Bureaucrats: Oil and the State in Saudi Arabia*. Ithaca: Cornell University Press, 2011

Hibou, Béatrice. *The Force of Obedience: The Political Economy of Repression in Tunisia*. Cambridge: Polity Press, 2011

Hirschkind, Charles. *The Ethical Soundscape: Cassette Sermons and Islamic Counterpublics*. New York: Columbia University Press, 2006

Ho, Engseng. *The Graves of Tarim: Genealogy and Mobility across the Indian Ocean*. Berkeley: University of California Press, 2006

Hobsbawm, Eric J. *Primitive Rebels: Studies in Archaic Forms of Social Movement in the 19th and 20th Centuries*. New York: Norton, 1965

Hobsbawm, Eric J. *Bandits*. New York: The New Press, 2000

Holston, James. *The Modernist City: An Anthropological Critique of Brasília*. Chicago: The University of Chicago Press, 1989

Jacobs, Jane. *The Death and Life of Great American Cities*. New York: Random House, 1961

Jeffrey, Craig. *Timepass: Youth, Class, and the Politics of Waiting in India*. Stanford: Stanford University Press, 2010

Jones, Toby Craig. *Desert Kingdom: How Oil and Water forged Modern Saudi Arabia*. Cambridge, MA: Harvard University Press, 2010

Kanna, Ahmed. *Dubai: The City as Corporation*. Minneapolis: University of Minnesota Press, 2011

Katakura, Motoko. *Bedouin Village: A Study of a Saudi Arabian People in Transition.* Tokyo: University of Tokyo Press, 1977

Kelly, John D., Beatrice Jauregui, Sean T. Mitchell and Jeremy Walton. *Anthropology and Global Counterinsurgency.* Chicago: The University of Chicago Press, 2010

Khal, 'Abduh. *Tarmi bi-Sharar* [Hell Throws Sparks]. Beirut: Manshurat al-Jamal, 2010

Klinenberg, Eric. *Heat Wave: A Social Autopsy of Disaster in Chicago.* Chicago: The University of Chicago Press, 2002

Kurpershoek, P. Marcel. *Oral Poetry and Narratives from Central Arabia.* Leiden: Brill, 1994–2005, 5 vol.

Kyrtsis, Alexandros-Andreas. *Constantinos A. Doxiadis: Texts, Design Drawings, Settlements.* Athens: Doxiadis Foundation, 2006

Le Corbusier. *The Radiant City: Elements of a Doctrine of Urbanism to be Used as the Basis of Our Machine-Age Civilization.* New York: Orion Press, 1964

Le Corbusier. *The City of To-Morrow and its Planning.* New York: Dover, 1987

Lefebvre, Henri. *The Urban Revolution.* Minneapolis: The University of Minnesota Press, 2003 [1970]

Lefebvre, Henri. *The Production of Space.* Oxford: Blackwell, 1991 [1974]

Lefebvre, Henri. *Critique of Everyday Life.* London: Verso, 1991, 2002, 2005 [1947, 1961, 1981]

Lefebvre, Henri. *State, Space, World.* Minneapolis: University of Minnesota Press, 2009

Le Renard, Amélie. *Femmes et Espaces Publics en Arabie Saoudite.* Paris: Dalloz, 2011

Limbert, Mandana E. *In the Time of Oil: Piety, Memory and Social Life in an Omani Town.* Stanford: Stanford University Press, 2010

Luhr, Eileen. *Witnessing Suburbia: Conservatives and Christian Youth Culture.* Berkeley: University of California Press, 2009

Mahsud, Ahmed Zaib. "Constantinos A. Doxiadis' Plan for Islamabad: The Making of a 'City of the Future' 1959–1963." PhD Thesis, Katholieke Universiteit Leuven, 2008

Massad, Joseph. *Desiring Arabs.* Chicago: The University of Chicago Press, 2007

McCartney, Laton. *Friends in High Places: The Bechtel Story, the Most Secret Corporation and How It Engineered the World.* New York: Ballantines, 1988

McFarlane, Colin. *Learning the City: Knowledge and Translocal Assemblage.* Oxford: Blackwell, 2011

Metcalf, Barbara. "Travelers' Tales in the Tablighi Jama`at." *Annals of the American Academy of Political and Social Scences.* Vol. 588, *Islam: Enduring Myths and Changing Realities* (Special Editor: Aslam Syed), July 2003 issue, pp. 136–148

Metcalf, Barbara. "Traditionalist" Islamic Activism: Deoband, Tablighis, and Talibs." In Craig Calhoun, Paul Price and Ashley Timmer (eds.), *Understanding September 11.* New York: The New Press, 2002, pp. 3–66

Metcalf, Barbara. "Meandering Madrasas: Knowledge and Short term Itinerancy in the Tablighi Jama`at." In Nigel Crook (ed.), *The Transmission of Knowledge in South Asia: Essays on Education, Religion, History, and Politics.* Delhi: Oxford University Press, 1996 pp. 49–61

Mitchell, Timothy. *Colonizing Egypt.* Berkeley: University of California Press, 1988

Mitchell, Timothy. *Rule of Experts: Egypt, Techno-Politics, Modernity.* Berkeley: University of California Press, 2002

Mitchell, Timothy. *Carbon Democracy: Political Power in the Age of Oil.* London: Verso, 2011

Mubarak, Faisal A. "Urban Growth Boundary Policy and Residential Suburbanization: Riyadh, Saudi Arabia." *Habitat International,* 28, 2004, 564–591

Mumford, Lewis. *The City in History: Its Origins, its Transformations, and its Prospects.* San Diego: Harcourt, 1989

Munif, Abdelrahman. *The Trench.* New York: Vintage, 1993

Ouzgane, Lahoucine (ed.). *Islamic Masculinities.* London: Zed Books, 2006

Pine, Adrienne. *Working Hard, Drinking Hard: On Violence and Survival in Honduras.* Berkeley: University of California Press, 2008

Pine, Jason. *The Art of Making Do in Naples.* Minneapolis: University of Minnesota Press, 2012

Piven, Frances Fox and Richard A. Cloward. *Poor People's Movements: Why They Succeed, How They Fail.* New York: Vintage, 1979

Pouillon, Francis. "Un Etat contre les Bédouins, l'Arabie Saoudite. Jalons pour une thèse." *Monde Arabe Maghreb-Machrek,* 147, 1995, pp. 132–148

Prakash, Gyan and Kevin M. Kruse (eds.). *The Spaces of the Modern City: Imaginaries, Politics, and Everyday Life.* Princeton: Princeton University Press, 2008

Pyla, Panayiota. "Back to the Future: Doxiadis's Plans for Baghdad." *Journal of Planning History,* 7, 1, 2008, 3–19

Rabinow, Paul. *Reflections on Fieldwork in Morocco.* Berkeley: University of California Press, 1977

Ramos, Stephen J. *Dubai Amplified: The Engineering of a Port Geography.* Farnham: Ashgate, 2010

Roncayolo, Marcel. *Lectures de Villes: Formes et Temps.* Marseille: Parenthèses, 2002

Said, Edward W. *Orientalism.* New York: Vintage Books, 1979.

Said, Edward W. *Culture and Imperialism.* New York: Vintage Books, 1994.

Sawalha, Aseel. *Reconstructing Beirut: Memory and Space in a Postwar Arab City.* Austin: University of Texas Press, 2010

Scheper-Hughes, Nancy and Philippe Bourgois (eds.). *Violence in War and Peace: An Anthology.* Oxford: Blackwell, 2004

Scott, James C. *Weapons of the Weak: Everyday Forms of Peasant Resistance.* New Haven: Yale University Press, 1985

Scott, James C. *Domination and the Arts of Resistance: Hidden Transcripts.* New Haven: Yale University Press, 1990

Scott, James C. *Seing like a State: How Certain Schemes to Improve the Human Condition Have Failed.* New Haven: Yale University Press, 1998

Scott, James C. *The Art of Not Being Governed: An Anarchist History of Upland Southeast Asia.* New Haven: Yale University Press, 2009

Sewell, William H., Jr. *Structure and Mobility: The Men and Women of Marseille, 1820–1870.* Cambridge: Cambridge University Press, 1985

Shamekh, Ahmed A. "Spatial Patterns of Bedouin Settlement in Al-Qasim Region, Saudi Arabia." PhD Thesis, University of Kentucky, 1975

Singerman, Diane. *Avenues of Participation: Family, Politics, and Networks in Urban Quarters of Cairo.* Princeton: Princeton University Press, 1995

Singerman, Diane and Paul Amar (eds.). *Cairo Cosmopolitan: Politics, Culture, and Urban Space in the New Globalized Middle East.* Cairo: The American University in Cairo Press, 2006

Singerman, Diane (ed.). *Cairo Contested: Governance, Urban Space, and Global Modernity.* Cairo: The American University in Cairo Press, 2009

Taussig, Michael. *Law in a Lawless Land: Diary of a Limpieza in Colombia.* Chicago: The University of Chicago Press, 2003

Theroux, Peter. *Sandstorm: Days and Nights in Arabia.* New York: Norton, 1990

Thompon, E. P. *The Making of the English Working Class.* London: Victor Gollancz, 1963

Tienda, Marta and William Julius Wilson (eds.). *Youth in Cities: A Cross-National Perspective.* Cambridge: Cambridge University Press, 2002

Tilly, Charles and Sidney Tarrow. *Contentious Politics.* Boulder: Paradigm, 2007

Tuncalp, Secil. "The Automobile Market in Saudi Arabia: Implications for Export Marketing Planning." *Marketing Intelligence and Planning*, 11, 1, 1993, pp. 28–36

Vassiliev, Alexei. *The History of Saudi Arabia.* London: Saqi Books, 2000

Virilio, Paul. *Speed and Politics: An Essay on Dromology.* Los Angeles: Semiotext(e), 2006 [1977]

Vitalis, Robert. *America's Kingdom: Mythmaking on the Saudi Oil Frontier.* London: Verso, 2009

Wacquant, Loïc. *Body and Soul: Notebooks of an Apprentice Boxer.* Oxford: Oxford University Press, 2004

Wacquant, Loïc. *Urban Outcasts: A Comparative Sociology of Advanced Marginality.* Cambridge: Polity Press, 2008

Weber, Florence. *Le travail à-côté. Etude d'ethnographie ouvrière.* Paris: INRA-EHESS, 1989

Wedeen, Lisa. *Ambiguities of Domination: Politics, Rhetoric, and Symbols in Contemporary Syria.* Chicago: University of Chicago Press, 1999

Wedeen, Lisa. *Peripheral Visions: Publics, Power, and Performance in Yemen.* Chicago: University of Chicago Press, 2008

Whyte, William Foote. *Street Corner Society: The Social Structure of an Italian Slum.* Chicago: The University of Chicago Press, 1943

Photo Credits

Photos 1.1, 2.1, 2.2, 4.1, 4.2, 5.1, 5.2, 5.4, 5.5, 6.1, and 6.4 have been taken by the author. Photos 1.2 and 5.3, as well as the cover image, are reproduced with the permission of THE BEST. Photos 3.1, 3.2, 3.3, 3.4, 3.5, 3.6, and 3.7 are reproduced with the permission of the Constantinos and Emma Doxiadis Foundation, Athens.

Index

Other Books in the Series